THE CHICAGO GUIDE FOR
FREELANCE EDITORS

**Chicago Guides
to Writing, Editing,
and Publishing**

A complete list of series titles is available on the University of Chicago Press website.

The Chicago Guide for Freelance Editors

HOW TO TAKE CARE OF YOUR BUSINESS, YOUR CLIENTS, AND YOURSELF FROM START-UP TO SUSTAINABILITY

Erin Brenner

THE UNIVERSITY OF CHICAGO PRESS / CHICAGO AND LONDON

The University of Chicago Press, Chicago 60637
The University of Chicago Press, Ltd., London
Published 2024
Printed in the United States of America

33 32 31 30 29 28 27 26 25 24   1 2 3 4 5

ISBN-13: 978-0-226-81851-1 (cloth)
ISBN-13: 978-0-226-83306-4 (paper)
ISBN-13: 978-0-226-83305-7 (ebook)
DOI: https://doi.org/10.7208/chicago/9780226833057.001.0001

Library of Congress Cataloging-in-Publication Data

Names: Brenner, Erin, author.
Title: The Chicago guide for freelance editors : how to take care of
    your business, your clients, and yourself from start-up to sustain-
    ability / Erin Brenner.
Other titles: Chicago guides to writing, editing, and publishing.
Description: Chicago ; London : The University of Chicago Press,
    2024. | Series: Chicago guides to writing, editing, and publishing |
    Includes bibliographical references and index.
Identifiers: LCCN 2023054063 | ISBN 9780226818511 (cloth) |
    ISBN 9780226833064 (paperback) | ISBN 9780226833057 (ebook)
Subjects: LCSH: Editing—Vocational guidance. | Self-employed—
    Handbooks, manuals, etc. | Business—Handbooks, manuals, etc. |
    BISAC: LANGUAGE ARTS & DISCIPLINES / Editing & Proofreading |
    LANGUAGE ARTS & DISCIPLINES / Writing / General
Classification: LCC PN162 .B666 2024 | DDC 808.02/7023—dc23/
    eng/20231229
LC record available at https://lccn.loc.gov/2023054063

♾ This paper meets the requirements of ANSI/NISO Z39.48-1992
(Permanence of Paper).

Contents

Making the Decision to Freelance

To freelance or not to freelance?

That's a question many people, both new editors and those thinking of switching careers, ask themselves.

As an employee, you're responsible only for your own tasks. There are other employees who run the business, create processes and rules, and so on. But when you're a freelancer, it's all you. You are the CEO, sales and marketing, editorial, IT, HR—everything. You also take all the risk. An employer guarantees you a salary as long as you work for them, even when the work is slow or the profits are nonexistent. As a freelancer, if you're not working, you're not earning.

Yet freelancing can be so rewarding. You decide who the clients are and negotiate costs and deadlines. You determine how the work should be done. You choose your own equipment and time off. You control your career, being accountable only to yourself and your clients. You might take a financial hit when work is slow, but you take all the profit when the work flows in.

Why I Decided to Freelance

In 2005, I found myself stuck in a box. I'd been working full-time as a copyeditor for the ClickZ website for five years, most of that time at home, taking care of our two preschoolers while my husband, Bill, worked an office job. Up to that point, I had appreciated the situation. I had started at ClickZ when I was pregnant with our first child, survived two rounds of layoffs, and had a second child. I now had the flexibility to meet the needs of two young children. My boss was incredibly supportive. As long as I met my deadlines, I could blend motherhood with my job in the way that worked best for me.

Yet by 2005, I was bored with my work. I had found my rhythm long ago, and the website had become a mature publication with set processes. It was now part of a larger organization with more opportunities, but none of them were right for me. So I started doing what an earlier generation called "moonlighting": taking on a few editing projects here and there to earn extra money and keep my interest in editing alive. ClickZ published articles on digital marketing, and I had had a good education from some of the top practitioners on how to market myself in this new medium. I had a fair idea of what I wanted to edit and for whom. As a web editor in the early days of web publishing, I had some valuable skills and knew how to work in the corresponding content management systems.

After a little research, I joined Mediabistro to try to connect with suitable clients. I named my business Right Touch Editing (RTE) and then created a basic web page on Mediabistro to promote my new freelance business. I kept a close eye on its job board, as well as on a couple of others. I soon found a client and then a few more. I really enjoyed the variety.

Meanwhile, ClickZ was sold a couple of times, each time creating the stress of a new job without an increase in pay or a chance to do something new. Even when ownership was stable, upper management changed frequently, always promising to reinvent the website and give me new opportunities. Those things never happened. I continued to do the same job, year in and year out, without hope of growth or challenge. And then came the year we had to switch health insurance plans three times—once with just twenty-four hours' notice. That was when I decided I was done working for someone else. Boredom I could put up with, but this level of stress and lack of control over my life? No way.

I got serious about RTE. I dug deep into marketing myself and finding more clients. Bill and I saved money so I could afford to earn less while building my business. It was a lot of work, but I really wanted it and Bill supported me. When my in-laws said they'd invest in my business, I knew it was time to jump. I quit ClickZ in October 2009 and never looked back. That's not to say that I didn't struggle and didn't sometimes wonder whether I should go back to a full-time job. But then something would happen—a payment would hit my bank account, a prospective client would offer an interesting project, or some other benefit of freelancing would make itself known. I would remember what running my own business meant to me, and I'd recommit myself to the path I'd chosen.

Finding Your Own Motivation

What motivates someone to strike out on their own depends on the individual. You might be a work-at-home parent or a family caregiver, as I was. You might freelance so you can work remotely and set your own schedule, in one place or while traveling the world. Or you might freelance to supplement a job that doesn't offer you full-time work. Perhaps you live someplace where there aren't any editing jobs and you don't want to move. Maybe you have a disability that makes working a traditional nine-to-five job difficult or impossible.

When we take risks, such as depending only on ourselves for our income, understanding our motivations is important. Our motivations are what we think about on the hard days. They keep us pushing forward—or, if we realize they no longer apply, help us decide to change course. And they're what we use to define success. Because while making a living is part of freelancing success, so is being able to do a job you love. Or being able to take care of your aging parents. Or being able to work on your own schedule, while sitting at your dining room table or exploring a different culture on the other side of the world. Or living where you want and still doing a job you love. Or just working in an environment that meets your physical and mental needs.

Freelancing is about making your own path for your own reasons. It doesn't mean doing it alone, though; there's a whole community of editors ("edibuddies") waiting to support you. It does mean being responsible for defining and creating your own success. It means bushwacking a path through a forest of opportunities and decisions, allowing yourself to take a side path if the mood strikes you, to stay at a midway point as long as you want, even forever, or to climb as high as you can to find fantastic views at the top.

What Does It Take to Be a Freelancer?

The freelance life is full of risk and uncertainty, administrative tasks, and decision-making. That's not for everyone, and there's nothing wrong with that. We each have our own strengths and weaknesses and are happiest when our work fits with who we really are. The key is to know who you are.

The most successful freelancers are self-starters—people who can motivate themselves on days when success seems out of reach. Other traits that are helpful include the following:

+ *Discipline.* You need to be willing to work when you don't want to but the project is due. Many editors already have this trait.
+ *Risk tolerance.* Risk is a part of every business. If you prefer security over independence, you might struggle a lot with freelancing.
+ *A business mindset.* Your profits are your income. You need to be able to think strategically and make choices that benefit your business in the long term.
+ *Drive.* It's helpful to be comfortable with putting a lot of time into the business side of things and with sticking with something when it's difficult.
+ *Failure tolerance.* Running a business is a discovery process. There are no guarantees and no surefire blueprint. You need to be comfortable with failing and trying again.

+ *Willingness to learn.* No one knows it all. You want to be able to identify gaps in your knowledge and work to fill them in.

There's no perfect set of traits, and many of the above can be cultivated as you go along. At your core, though, you need to be able to rely on yourself and be willing to seek out support when you need it.

You also need to determine how you will support yourself financially while you're building your business. While not everyone will be able to solve this financial dilemma, there are many options to try. You might save money ahead of time or borrow money to see you through, as I was able to. You might also cut costs, sometimes drastically, such as by moving someplace cheaper, getting a roommate, selling your car, or even all three. You could continue to work your full-time job for several years while starting your freelance business, taking a slower path to your goal. A financial adviser can give you more specific advice, if you're unsure.

You also want to think about health insurance and other benefits traditionally provided by an employer. Where will you get health insurance from, and how can you fit that into your budget? How will you set aside money for retirement? Do you need to purchase your own life or disability insurance? You may not be able to replace everything all at once, so prioritize your replacement list and set goals for tackling them.

And if you try freelancing but it just doesn't work for you, it's OK to go back to an employee position. Better to be honest about what's not working than to get into debt that you can't get out of.

Will AI End Human Editing?

As this book went to press, generative AI tools like OpenAI's ChatGPT and the race by other tech companies to put out similar products were raising the question of what effect AI tools would have on the editing community. Some people wondered whether they might replace human editing entirely. I can't predict what the eventual outcome of generative AI will be. No one can. What I can predict is that as long as it makes someone money, it's not going away. It will also improve over time. Market pressures will make sure of that. Whether it becomes a better editor and how much editing it takes over from humans is anyone's guess. At this moment, chatbots are only as good as their training database and their user. To get quality out of one, you need precise prompts and the ability to evaluate its results. It's a bit like working with a brand-new editor: they know a lot about editing, but they're still developing their editorial judgment and they sometimes struggle to juggle all tasks involved in editing.

That leaves us with the job of educating our prospective clients on how these tools can help them and where the limitations are. Unlike human editors, AI can't intuit and it doesn't think laterally. It doesn't think at all. It predicts the likely next word based on the query and its training database. And there are limits to both those things.

Some people will see AI as a way to eliminate editors, whether because it is cheaper or saves them time or they just don't value the skills of a human editor. Take note: These are not our clients. They never were. These are the folks who rely solely on spelling and grammar checkers—and we know the pitfalls of those tools. People who hire editors value how editing can improve the quality of their final product. They understand that editing matters, improving the text in a way that benefits both reader and writer. We are often educating prospective clients and the world at large on these points. AI is just another part of that discussion.

Editors will need to stay curious about generative AI, though. We need to know how it can be used, testing out tools as advances are made. We need to understand how generative AI affects our clients and how we can best support them. We need to decide on AI-related policies for our businesses and how to communicate them to our clients.

For now, those deeper discussions are beyond the scope of this book. I have mentioned AI tools where relevant throughout the book—however, with the caveat here that they are evolving quickly and may be outdated by the time you read this.

What This Book Will and Won't Do for You

If you've decided to freelance or are seriously considering it, this book will guide you through creating your unique freelance business, helping you envision your goals and create a map to those goals. You can change that map at any time. It's your business, after all. This book contains lessons I've learned along the way, as well as wisdom from other editors and business owners. Because each of us has a unique set of experiences with common themes, hearing from more voices can help you make decisions that are best for your individual situation.

This book won't teach you how to edit, however. The assumption is that you know how to do at least one level of editing, such as copyediting, and have at least some experience working as an editor. If you're new to editing, though, you don't need to put this book down. You'll find plenty of editor training options in the Resources section. Just be sure to do your training before launching your business.

Here, you'll learn about concepts like branding and goals and how to apply them to your new business. You'll learn about details like priority grids and why you should track your time, even when you're not paid hourly. Most important, you'll learn the basics of starting an editing business. The book is full of things I wished I'd known when I was starting out, like how to negotiate fees and how to set SMART goals.

Each freelance business is unique to the freelancer. Your business might resemble someone else's, but it will never be an exact replica, any more than you are an exact replica of someone else. Because of that, you won't find a lot of rigid rules. Instead, you'll find suggestions and guidance to make your own decisions.

This book won't teach you everything, of course. No book could. But it will get you started, and the Resources section will lead you to more sources. Note, too, that this book is not meant to be legal advice. I'm not a lawyer; when in doubt, always consult with the right professional.

How This Book Is Organized

Planning a business can be a chicken-and-egg problem: How can you know what services you'll provide if you don't first know how much you can earn with them? How do you know how much to charge until you know what value the service will have to the client? You've got to start somewhere, but you can revise as you go, just as you would in an editing project.

I've chosen to start this book with advice on defining your passion because that's what will motivate you in the lean times. We'll look first at why you want to freelance and what kind of services you want to offer. What do you want from your freelance career? From there, we'll look at your personal budget and fees, where you may discover that the clients you want to work for don't pay the fees you need to charge. That's OK. You can revise your services and clients, working with your budget and fees, until you find a balance you can live with. Maybe that's taking on some boring but higher-paying work so you can also do the more exciting but lower-paying work. Maybe you start by offering copyediting but find that you're best at line editing, so you switch your offerings. You can adapt as you go.

Next you'll learn to define your business structure and processes, including marketing and selling, organizing your work time, creating a workspace, coming up with goals, handling difficult clients, and continuing your training. If you're a more experienced editor or have done some freelancing already, go ahead and start elsewhere in the book. Pick a topic you want to know more about and start there.

One chapter I hope you won't skip is the last one. I close the book with a discussion of how critical it is to take care of yourself. One thing I've learned since my ClickZ days, sometimes painfully, is to treat myself better. Rest isn't something you earn; it's something you need regularly and frequently, much as you need food and exercise. No matter where you are in your freelancing career, no matter what your business needs, take care of yourself first. It will make running your business easier.

I wrote my advice as generally as I could so that, no matter where you live and work, you can follow it. However, my advice and information on country-specific issues such as business structures reflect a US perspective. Where practical, I've included brief information on options in other countries. It's by no means all-inclusive. Use what's here, including the Resources section, to do research for your specific situation. I also discuss tools and resources that are current as of the writing of this book. These are all subject to change over time, particularly technology. Keep in mind the purpose behind them, and you'll be able to identify the latest tools and resources to fit your needs.

I hope this book will help you create your just-right business, one that meets your definition of success, and I hope you get there with less stress and pain than my own journey gave me. But even if it is sometimes painful, I hope you get there.

Grab your compass, and let's create your perfect business map together.

Setting Up Your Business

CHAPTER ONE

Defining the Scope of Your Business

You've decided to freelance, but where do you start? There are so many decisions to make and an entire structure to build that it's easy to feel overwhelmed. The goal of this book is to help you create a business, step-by-step, that fits you.

We start with the end: What are your goals with this business? Where do you want to end up? Once you know where you want to go, you can create a map to get you there and determine the tools and skills you'll need along the way. That's what the rest of this book will help you do.

Defining Your Purpose

The main reason to start a business, of course, is to earn money. We'll talk about budgets in the next chapter. First, though, I want you to think about what will make you happy in your work. What are you passionate about? Running your own business is a *lot* of work. If you're going to take that on, you want to be well grounded in your purpose. There will be hard days ahead, and you'll need something to keep you going. There are reasons to quit, but something getting a little harder shouldn't be one of them.

Start by identifying what motivates you as an editor. Why did you want to edit in the first place, and why do you want to make it your business now? Some editors are passionate about words or reading. Others want to help authors improve their writing skills or create something. Your motivation may change over time, too. That's OK. The point is to know what it is that motivates you at the moment.

I started in editing because I was an English major, and editing fit my skill set. I loved to read, and I was good at grammar and usage. These things are still true, but these days I edit because I like to help my **clients** finish a project and achieve their goals. (You'll find definitions of the bolded terms in the Glossary at the back of the book.) I like being part of a team that creates something worthwhile. The fact that my role is to help apply order to the text just makes the work all that more satisfying.

But what if the things you want to edit won't cover all your bills? You might not be able to afford to take a job editing for nonprofits that work toward social justice, for example, but as a freelancer you can balance your passion work with projects that offer better **fees**. You can build a combination of clients that will let you express that passion.

Take the time to journal about your purpose for both editing and freelancing. Your purpose will not only become a touchstone for you, but it will also help you make more appropriate decisions for your business. Knowing your purpose will help motivate you during challenging times and indicate when it might be time to redefine your business or change your work status.

Defining Your Services

With experience, editors generally realize that there are no set definitions for different types of editing. Even the names differ, depending on which source you follow. *The Chicago Manual of Style* lays out its definitions for those working in trade book publishing. Some professional editing organizations, such as Editors Canada and the Bay Area Editors' Forum, offer their own definitions. And many clients ask for "proofreading" or a generic "edit" without understanding what those terms mean. Which names and definitions you use are less important than clearly communicating to your clients what you actually do.

WHAT KIND OF EDITING WILL YOU DO?

The following are my definitions for different types of text editing. They're based on my years of experience in the field and in my

niche, or specialty, where publishing is a less rigorous process, as well as on some general agreement within our trade. Your names or definitions might be different. That's fine. These are meant to get you thinking about what you want to do.

Developmental editing. I picture the different types of editing as different views of the forest—the **manuscript**—before you. For developmental editing, imagine standing on top of a mountain and viewing trees below you. From here, you get a view of the whole forest: groups of trees and the paths winding through them. As a developmental editor, you are helping an author see their work from this view in order to develop their ideas and structure and organize the manuscript.

Your client might come to you with an outline or even just an idea for some piece of writing they have in mind. They have a vague idea about what they want the finished piece to be, but they need help viewing their ideas as a whole or conceptualizing where the paths through the forest should be. Clients might want help writing a book, an article, a website, or something else. I've helped indie authors develop books from their blog posts, edited articles to be shopped to major business publications, and created a series of **marketing** emails to send to clients. This type of developmental editing is particularly helpful for **professionals who write**—people who don't write for a living but have a writing project or must write as a small part of their job. They often need some additional guidance on fleshing out that initial idea.

With this type of developmental editing, you will advise the client on what should be included in the manuscript and the structure it should take. You'll also consider what auxiliary items might be helpful. Are more headers needed? How about images or appendixes? You'll look, too, at the intended audience and advise on an appropriate writing style for them.

When working on a completed manuscript, some developmental editors write extensive notes (a.k.a. **cover letters** or **transmittal notes**), guiding the writer on how to revise the manuscript. In creative works, for example, you may suggest a new character or plot line for the author to create. Other developmental editors will actively revise the manuscript, moving or deleting material and writing a few sentences, especially transitions, as well as making suggestions for changes. This is more common in nonfiction when the manuscript relies less on the author's imagination. How you approach developmental editing will depend on your work style and the type of clients you work for. Talk with your clients about what will work best for them and for you.

Stylistic editing. Also known as **line editing**, content editing, or substantive editing, stylistic editing has a slightly lower view: you're getting a sense of pattern in the forest's canopy. The chief concern is how paragraphs are structured and flow from one to the other. You'll also edit for sentence structure, meaning and logic, readability, and writing style. While you can offer this as a stand-alone service, stylistic editing is more frequently done with developmental editing or copyediting, either in a separate editing pass or in the same pass.

Copyediting. One of the most well-known types of editing, copyediting has a view about midway down to the forest floor, looking at the health of the trees, items like grammar, spelling, punctuation, and similar sentence-level considerations. It's often further broken down into light, medium, and heavy edits:

+ In a **light copyedit**, you will correct errors in language mechanics (punctuation, spelling, capitalization, hyphenation, numerals, etc.), grammar, and usage. You'll also check any cross-references (e.g., chapter and section titles against the table of contents) and the organization of lists (e.g., proper alphabetizing). You'll query unclear terms and facts.
+ In a **medium copyedit**, you'll perform a light copyedit, plus edit for word choice, transitions, and writing style, such as awkward constructions, overuse of passive voice, and inappropriate tone. You'll edit or query issues of sensitive language, such as ableism, racism, and sexism (the website Conscious Style Guide is an excellent resource for this). You'll also query writing issues, like wordiness, ambiguity, factual inaccuracies, logic

DEFINING THE SCOPE OF YOUR BUSINESS   17

problems, and content organization problems at the paragraph level.

+ In a **heavy copyedit**, you'll perform a medium copyedit, except that instead of querying writing issues, you'll correct them. You may also add headers or change heading levels to improve the manuscript's organization and you may write brief explanatory information, such as the definition of a term.

Although heavy copyediting includes writing, as a copyeditor you won't add or delete the author's ideas. Instead, you'll support those ideas, and the manuscript as a whole, with your writing and editing. (For more details on what's included in a copyedit, see *The Copyeditor's Handbook* by Amy Einsohn and Marilyn Schwartz.)

You can modify the levels of copyediting to best suit your clients. At RTE, we most often perform a medium copyedit, correcting for items like sensitive language and word choice. You can also pair stylistic editing with copyediting, especially for clients outside of the publishing industry.

Proofreading. If you work with clients who are unfamiliar with publishing, you may find that most will ask for proofreading without really knowing what it is. Proofreading sits on the forest floor. You're looking up at the trees, trimming back low-hanging branches, and down at the ground, removing rocks and fallen branches from the path. This is the last chance to catch any errors or infelicities before the manuscript is published. Proofreaders ensure not only that the text is correct but that design elements are the right color and size and are in the correct place.

There are two main types of proofreading. **Comparison proofreading** compares **dead copy** against **live copy**. You ensure that the new version matches the last approved version of the manuscript and that all noted changes have been made. In **editorial proofreading**, you'll do a **cold read**, reviewing the latest version of the manuscript for errors without comparing it to an earlier version. In both types of proofreading, you'll correct for spelling, grammar, punctuation, and style while also checking design elements, like footers, and URLs. For digital publications, you'll click links and buttons, ensuring that they work, they go where they're supposed to, and the page they go to works.

It's not unusual for clients to be unfamiliar with the different levels of editing and what editing really costs. Closely define your services on your website and in client communications so that they understand what they're purchasing. When you offer a combined service, such as a stylistic edit and a copyedit, be sure to define both to help justify the fee you're charging. You might find it advantageous to list each service separately with an option to combine two edits for a special price—something higher than your single-service fee but less than the total of two service fees. This way, you're paid appropriately for the amount of work, but the client can easily see the financial advantage of your hybrid option.

WHAT WILL YOU EDIT?

If you've been working as an editor already, it's natural to want to do the same kind of editing for similar clients as a freelancer. But maybe you're ready for something new. If so, this is the moment to dream about it. What other opportunities would excite you? After all, as editor Adrienne Montgomerie says, "If it has words, it can be edited." What kind of words do you want to edit? Many new editors start as generalists ("I'll edit anything!"), but it's hard to stand out from the crowd when you're a generalist. Specializing helps you define who your clients are and focus your marketing efforts. You can add as many specialties, or niches, as you want, but you'll likely need to market them separately. When you're getting started, choose a niche to focus your marketing on while taking on whatever work you're capable of doing.

The first big choice is between poetry, fiction, and nonfiction. Will you specialize in a specific type of poetry? What level of editing would you offer poets? Will you edit novels, stories, or both? Realism or genre? Which genres? You can get as specialized as you want here: cowboy romances, cottage mysteries, sword and sorcery fantasies, social realism, psychological realism—whatever fits your subject expertise, skills, and interests.

Nonfiction is an even bigger category. Do you want to work on academic and reference texts? Memoirs? How about journalism, instructional texts, or business writing? These broad categories can be narrowed down even further, such as marketing and promotional copy, scientific papers, humanities journal articles, news articles, self-help books, and so much more.

As you try to narrow down what you'll edit, consider the medium. Books, articles, and short stories are among the most popular, but how about website and email copy? Would you be interested in editing online courses or mobile apps? How about product packaging and instruction manuals? Financial reports or grants?

As you consider these categories, ask yourself the following:

+ What kind of copy interests me? What will keep me editing day after day?
+ Do I need special skills to edit this copy? Medical copy, for example, often requires a certain level of medical knowledge.
+ How much work is there for this kind of copy? Is it easy to find?
+ Do I know people in a specific industry or subject who can help me get started?
+ What's the pay like for the copy that interests me? Can I make a living editing it, or will I need to add another niche?

Sometimes we make choices based on where our lives have taken us. I have a master's degree in literature, so you would think I'd specialize in fiction editing, but I don't. My first job after college was proofreading nonprofit direct mail. My next jobs were copyediting industry market reports and then articles about digital marketing. When I moved on to freelancing, I had a network of marketing professionals and some deep knowledge about the then-new digital marketing. I leveraged those into a new business and have been on that path ever since. That's not to say you can't move away from where you've been. It's harder if you don't have the network or subject knowledge, but if you put the time into gaining both, you can make it work. I like editing business copy, and doing so has not only allowed me to earn more (corporations tend to pay better than trade publishers), but it has also let me enjoy reading fiction without feeling like I'm working.

WHO WILL YOUR CLIENTS BE?

Just as we often think of books first when we think of editing, we often picture working for book publishers, especially the biggest ones in both trade and academic circles. However, there are also **book packagers**: companies that produce a book for the publisher, handling editing, design, approvals, and other production tasks that will take the manuscript to a finished product. You can also work for smaller specialty book publishers. The Appalachian Mountain Club, for example, publishes its own books and maps and hires freelance editors. Are there any publishers who specialize in your interests or hobbies?

You might also consider periodicals. Magazines, journals, websites, and newspapers all need editors, and their regular schedules can build predictability into your work. In the academic world, you can edit student theses and dissertations (though you're limited to copyediting and proofreading), which could lead to also editing for professors as you build your reputation within a department or college. Even business publishing offers many different opportunities. Think about those investment prospectuses you receive in the mail. Someone had to edit them. And every company with a website could use a copyeditor or proofreader at least once in a while.

Here are some other client types you can seek out:

+ Indie authors of both fiction and nonfiction
+ Authors seeking a literary agent
+ Nonprofits
+ Governments and NGOs

+ Agencies, including ad, content, and editing agencies
+ Bidding platforms, such as Fiverr or Reedsy

Scanning job sites, such as those listed in Resources, can provide ideas about possible clients. You could also work with a business coach to help you determine your strengths and passions and identify potential clients. Remember: If it has words, it can be edited.

A WORD ABOUT AGENCIES AND BIDDING PLATFORMS

Agencies and bidding platforms have become an important part of the landscape for freelance editors in recent years, an indirect way to get projects. Does taking work from them mean you're not really running a business? Not at all! It's true that working with an intermediary means having less control, but you're also letting these organizations do the work of finding and managing the clients. It can be a good way to get work on your desk and build your reputation, especially when you're starting out. You can keep building your business while working for an intermediary, marketing to your desired client base. The intermediary is simply one of your clients.

But not all agencies and bidding platforms are equal, and there are downsides to working for them, depending on your reasons for freelancing in the first place. When you work for an agency, they will assign you work from their clients, and you'll bill the agency. That's going to limit the type of editing you do to what the agency focuses on. This may not be a bad thing if you work with agencies in your desired niche. An editing agency that specializes in science fiction and fantasy stories could help you build your fiction-editing business, while an ad agency could help you develop expertise in editing marketing and sales copy.

Working with an agency can also provide you with that rarity in freelancing: feedback. I expanded RTE into an agency a few years ago, and it's my policy to review an editor's work before handing it to the client. I give my editors feedback on what they've done well and what could be improved. This helps my business produce better editing, but it also helps my contractors gain valuable experience they can apply to all their future work. Some agencies may even offer training or resources to help you grow. As well, agencies can give you a small community of editors to network with and lean on, even on outside projects. Pikko's House, run by Crystal Watanabe, uses Slack to create a community for its contractors. Watanabe encourages her team to ask each other questions, share ideas, or just blow off steam.

Bidding platforms work a little differently than agencies. Although the platform is doing a lot of the marketing work for you, its main benefit is as an online space to connect freelancers and clients, similar to what Uber and Lyft offer to drivers and riders. Each platform may differ slightly, but the result is generally the same. Some platforms, like Fiverr, allow anyone to create a profile and post or answer requests. No one from the platform works directly with the client, so no one is filtering out poor project requests. As a result, you may have to sift through a lot of inappropriate requests to find work. Too, whenever you're bidding on a project, you're competing with others for the same work. In this situation, clients tend to go with the lowest bidder. That can make charging a livable fee difficult.

On the other hand, author-services firm Reedsy doesn't let just anyone on its freelancer roster. You must demonstrate having done a specific number of projects with one or more of the major publishing houses. And even if you have the right experience, Reedsy may still turn you down. Some editors have done well with this platform, getting enough work to fill a portion of their time, while others have struggled to find worthwhile projects.

With both organization types, you will be earning a portion of the fee the client is charged. This is only fair, since the agency or bidding site has done the work to find and set up the client and will be at fault if the client is unhappy with your editing. Fees and percentages vary greatly from organization to organization. When you're considering working with one, be sure the fee you receive meets your needs and that you benefit from working with the organization, such as not having to deal with any problem clients.

As with any other type of client, agencies and bidding sites have to be a good fit to work well. When you're starting out, they can be a good way to get projects flowing in while you build the rest of your business. Later on, they can be good for filling gaps. But you will trade control for convenience, and you want to be sure you're making a good trade. Before signing on with any agency, research the following:

+   The type of work the agency offers
+   The average pay rate
+   How often they pay and how they pay you
+   The agency's reputation

Once you've signed on, give the agency a month or two to see if it's a good fit. Ask yourself:

+   Am I able to make the rate I'm looking for within a few projects?
+   Are the projects what I expected?
+   Is the agency supportive?

If after a few projects you don't think the relationship is working, remove yourself from the agency's list and move on.

WHAT OTHER SERVICES CAN YOU OFFER?

Offering services related to editing can help grow your business by giving current clients more ways to hire you and drawing in clients who might not need editing. What other skills do you have that your preferred clients would benefit from? What other tasks do you enjoy doing? Here are some other ideas to get you thinking:

+   Writer coaching
+   Copy writing

+ Ghostwriting
+ Search engine optimization (SEO)
+ Serving as managing editor
+ Production management
+ Indexing
+ Social media management
+ Fact-checking
+ Graphic art
+ Print book designing (interior and/or cover)
+ Ebook designing and uploading
+ Book marketing
+ Editor or writer training

As you build your client base, listen carefully to your clients. What other jobs do they need done? What causes them pain in their publishing process? These are opportunities for you to be more helpful—and increase your earnings. For example, several years ago I copyedited and proofread a digital magazine for one of my clients. After the first few issues, I realized the editorial director was really struggling to manage the production process in addition to all his other duties. Because I was already tracking the stories from copyediting through proofreading for myself, I offered to take on production management for the whole team. My client was thrilled to have the help without having to hire someone new, and I was thrilled to earn a fee for something I was mostly doing already. Watch for these opportunities in your own work.

THERE ARE TOO MANY DECISIONS!

If all of this leaves your head spinning, you're not alone. When I taught copyediting for the University of California, San Diego (UCSD), many of my students were overwhelmed with the choices. Which client types would work out for them? What kind of writing would be the most interesting or fun to edit? What would be the most financially advantageous? Which would be easiest to break into?

There's no right answer. By thinking in categories like those outlined above, you might find that a pattern emerges. For example, if you're an avid hiker, you might start by editing hiking content for major book publishers and packagers and specialty publishing houses. You might add hiking magazines and organizations devoted to hiking as you expand your network. Your niche is subject related: it's all about hiking.

Like me, you might desire variety. I started working on marketing copy, later branching out into self-published business books. Over the years, I've added government and nonprofit reports. I've worked on local history, tech books and articles, websites, and training tools. I've done all levels of editing, often combining levels or customizing them to fit the project. I've also done rewriting, content writing, and copy writing. The mix of subjects, media, and tasks has kept me energized about my business.

To get started, pick a niche that excites you. If the first niche you pick doesn't work, try something else. If you want to add a niche, do it. Let your business grow with your interests. Most importantly, let go of the idea that you're going to be perfect from the start. Building a business, remember, is a discovery process. We take a wrong trail sometimes. We trip over roots. We get caught in rainstorms. We make mistakes or events work against us. The key to success isn't perfection at the start but making adjustments as we go along. That doesn't make you an impostor or unsuited to the work or a failure. It makes you human. Embrace that.

Making a Professional Assessment of Yourself

If you've been working as an editor already, you likely have a good idea of your skills and any gaps you need to fill. If you're new to editing or branching out into a new type of editing or content, though, you need to be brutally honest with yourself about your skills. You'll be relying on these skills to earn your living.

Seek out information on the type of editing you're looking to do. Editors Canada's *Professional Editorial Standards* is an excellent place to start. It gives detailed descriptions of the knowledge and skills needed for the types of editing the organization offers certification in. Also check out the syllabi for editing courses and the tables of contents of editing training books. Take online copyediting and proofreading tests, attend a workshop, or enroll in a class. When I was teaching copyediting at UCSD, I had several students who had worked informally as copyeditors. They had enrolled in the certificate program because they wanted to find out what they didn't know and improve their skills. (Note that a *certificate* is proof of learning, while *certification* is proof of skill and knowledge. Many university programs offer a certificate in editor training; Editors Canada offers certification.)

Do you really need training, though? There's a popular idea that if you're good at spotting typos, you can be a copyeditor, for example. Spotting typos shows an eye for details, and that's a great start. But so much more goes into copyediting, and there can be hundreds of edits needed for even a 20,000-word document. Finding the one error left after several rounds of editing and proofreading is one thing; finding hundreds or thousands is another. Even deciding what an error is and isn't takes editorial judgment honed by training and experience. Typo-spotting may indicate that you have a capacity for and an interest in editing, but editing is about more than finding the lone remaining error. The same holds true for other types of editing.

If you have no previous experience as an editor, you need training, period.

How to Develop Your Own Training

As a freelancer, you're responsible for all your training, both initially and later on. There's no standard curriculum for teaching editing, so you have a lot of options. But this also means that not all editor training is created equally. Some training programs will be better than others. Start by thinking about how you learn best.

COURSES AND CERTIFICATES

Some people learn best by sitting in a classroom or taking an online class, with an instructor who will hold them responsible for getting the work done and who can answer questions. If you want to get into copyediting, you'll find a lot of courses and certificates online. Several US universities offer editing certificates in non-degree programs, including UCSD, University of Chicago (through its Professional Education program), and Emerson College. In Canada, Toronto Metropolitan University and Queen's University both have noted programs, and in the UK you can check out the College of Media and Publishing.

There are only a few developmental editing courses out there, such as the one offered by the University of Chicago. There are even fewer stylistic editing courses, such as the one offered by Canada's Simon Fraser University. You'll have more choices with proofreading, with the Chartered Institute of Editing and Proofreading (CIEP) offering a three-part course, Simon Fraser offering a semester-long course, and several smaller organizations and individuals offering everything from webinars to multi-lesson courses.

CONFERENCES AND WORKSHOPS

Professional editing organizations and other training organizations offer workshops, courses, and conferences on various editing topics, filling the gaps left by higher education. The Editorial Freelancers Association (EFA) excels at this. It offers live and recorded webinars, as well as asynchronous and real-time multi-lesson courses.

Conferences can be a little tougher to depend on for initial training, as programs change year to year and won't always cover the topics you need. However, they're great places to learn about trends in editing, such as editing for conscious language. Plus you can get to know other editors and start building your professional network.

When looking at training organizations, check out what's covered. Some teach only the minimum of what you need to know. Good choices include the UK's Publishing Training Centre and the Writer's Digest University. You can also look to fellow editors for training, as many have started offering their own courses independently. For example, you could take a course on editing memoirs, making books more inclusive, or improving your branding and marketing. You can find many more offerings in my Database of Training for Editors, by Editors on Google Drive (see Resources for URL).

SELF-DIRECTED LEARNING

But maybe you're better at directing your own learning. There are several books available that can enhance your understanding of the editing profession. *What Editors Do: The Art, Craft, and Business of Book Editing* is a high-level view of what's involved in book editing, written by experts in the field. *Developmental Editing* by Scott Norton offers a great introduction to this type of editing, and Amy Einsohn's *The Copyeditor's Handbook* and the companion workbook are fantastic for learning all about copyediting. *McGraw-Hill's Proofreading Handbook* by Laura Anderson is one of a few good options for proofreading.

Especially for copyediting and proofreading, you'll want a working knowledge of at least one style guide based on the subject area you'll edit in. Purchase a copy and study it. Also study grammar and usage guides to build your language knowledge. Take care with usage guides, however. Apart from *Merriam-Webster's Dictionary of English Usage*, which describes usage, usage guides tend to be prescriptive, with advice that will help you write or edit in a specific writing style. *Garner's Modern English Usage* is considered a heavyweight among usage guides, but following its advice closely creates a rigid, formal writing style. If that's not what your clients are looking for, take *Garner's* with a grain of salt.

With all these training options, there's something for every learner and every budget. New programs launch fairly frequently, and program updates happen all the time. Take a look around for options that will work best for you.

Key Takeaways

+   Identify why you want to edit and why you want to run your own business. This will help guide business decisions and keep you motivated on the hard days.
+   Define your services. Briefly describe the type of editing you will do in a way clients will understand.
+   List the media and the topics you will edit.
+   Define the types of clients you want to work for.
+   List other services you might offer.
+   Make an assessment of your professional skills. What are your strengths? What weakness should you shore up?
+   Develop your training program to bring your skills up to a professional level. Choose from structured programs, buffet style, or self-directed study.

CHAPTER TWO

Setting Your Rates

Money is always a delicate topic. On the one side, at least in the United States, our society strongly resists talking about how much we earn. On the other, discussing how we earn money can lead to discussing how we spend that money, and we fear being judged on our spending. Our finances are among the most personal information about us. Yet when talking about starting a business, we must talk about this thorny subject.

Any time I'm giving a talk about freelancing, I'm inevitably asked, "How much should I charge?" This is a difficult question to answer. There are no set rates in editing, and there are no set editing methods that would allow us to compare services and rates. Add to that our individual financial situations, and how could anyone helpfully advise you on the right fee? I'm increasingly thinking that "How much should I charge?" is the wrong question. A better question is "How do I set my rates?" This allows you to learn methods for setting rates that you can apply to your unique situation. Rather than give you a magic number, in this chapter I'll teach you to look at both sides of the pricing equation: yours and your client's.

Let's start with you.

How Much Do You Need to Earn?

While a typical aim for a business is often to provide you with enough money to meet your budget, you might have different needs or goals. You could build a business that supplements other income streams, such as part-time teaching or running short-term-stay rentals. And if you want to earn *more* than your current budget needs, perhaps for a home renovation or more free time, you can build a business to do that, too.

If you've never built a budget before, now is the time. You need to know when you're not bringing in enough money to pay your bills, and the only way to know that is to know how much money you need and how much you have coming in. I like to start with my monthly budget, because the numbers are less intimidating. Make a list of all your weekly and monthly expenses. In addition to bills, such as utilities and rent or mortgage, include expenses like groceries and gas for your car. Don't forget less-frequent items, such as a quarterly water bill; occasional items like clothing or gifts; and annual bills, such as life insurance. You can total less-frequent expenses up and divide them by twelve so that you're putting a little aside each month for them. If possible, add a line item for savings or even retirement. I like to estimate on the high side to give myself a buffer, but your goal is to come up with at least a somewhat accurate annual budget that you can refine over time.

Personal finance apps like You Need a Budget can help you set a budget and track spending. You can also do this with a simple Excel spreadsheet, though that can be more work and is more prone to error. Bill and I ran our household budget for years in Excel using a few simple formulas. We switched to an app because it pulls in account information from our bank and credit cards, and it was easier for us to share budgeting duties with a cloud-based app. Choose what makes sense to how you approach money. You'll find a few more tools in the Resources section.

You'll feed your personal budget with your business, but it won't be every dollar you bring in, just your **net income after taxes**. (This presumes you're running a sole proprietorship. We'll talk about other business structures in chapter 3.) The amount of money you receive from clients is your business's **revenue**. Its **gross profit**, or **gross income**, is the amount of money you bring in minus **production costs**. Production costs include items like raw materials (as an editor, you have none), labor (as a freelancer, you have no employees and therefore no labor costs), general overhead (e.g., office rent and utilities), and marketing costs. If you're working from home, already own your computer, and only do marketing that doesn't cost you anything, your revenue and gross profit are likely the same amount.

However, you will have **business expenses**, also referred to as **deductions**. Software for doing the editing, such as Microsoft Office, and running your business, like Zoho Invoice, are business expenses. So are resources like *The Chicago Manual of Style* and *The AP Stylebook*. Productivity tools such as PerfectIt; daily planners; and office supplies like sticky notes, pens, and printer ink are also business expenses. Even the fees you pay to send or receive funds through a service like PayPal or Wise can qualify as business expenses. For those living in the United States, check out the Small Business and Self-Employed Tax Center of the IRS website for more information. No matter where you live, talk to a tax accountant about your financial situation and tax obligation.

Your revenue minus production costs and deductions gives you your **net income**. This is the amount used to calculate your **income taxes**. When you're an employee, your employer calculates how much income tax you owe the government with help from a form you fill out about your **filing status**. Your employer also sends your taxes directly to the government. As a freelancer, you will be responsible for making your own calculations and sending in payments. For US citizens operating **sole proprietorships** (see chapter 3), this means the **federal income tax** and **self-employment tax** (SET). When you're an employee, federal income tax is applied to your Medicare and Social Security benefits (FICA); your employer also pays a tax to contribute to your FICA. Now you will pay what your employer formerly did—that's your SET. You may also need to pay state or municipal income tax. Check with your accountant or go to irs.gov and your state's and municipality's websites to find out how much money you should be setting aside for taxes.

Let's say in 2021, you lived in New York City, earned $50,000 for the year, and filed as a single individual. At that time, you would have paid federal, state, and city income tax and SET, as outlined in table 1. All of that comes out of the fee you earn from clients.

Now you can see how those business deductions can lower your tax bill. If you're wise (and I hope you are), you'll set aside money for taxes first thing. Some freelancers find it helpful to put tax money into a separate bank account so they don't accidentally spend it.

TABLE 1. Freelancer Income Tax Example

TAX	RATE	AMOUNT
Federal income tax	22%	$11,000
SET	15.3%	$7,650
State income tax	5.97%	$2,985
City income tax	$858 + 3.819% of the excess over $25,000	$2,768
TOTAL		$24,403

Note: Example is for a freelance editor earning $50,000 in 2021, living in New York City, and filing as single.

The same principle holds for readers outside of the United States. You'll want to investigate what your national and local tax responsibilities are. Be aware of related taxes, such as VAT, and note that living outside of your home country may not release you from home country taxes.

Talk with a qualified tax accountant to help you determine your obligations. It's worth paying a professional even for just a couple hours to get the best advice for your business. Start right, and you'll more easily prevent huge problems later. If you don't realize that your city collects income tax until you've been in business for a few years, you could end up owing thousands in back taxes and fines.

Taxes aside, the rest is yours, right? Well . . .

You'll next need to consider expenses your employer once paid for as employee benefits, such as health insurance, retirement savings, disability insurance, and paid time off. Freelancers must cover all these costs themselves. Some items, like disability insurance, may be tax deductible. You also bear the costs of looking for work, billing clients, upgrading your skills, and owning and maintaining office equipment. This makes it imperative that you charge enough in your billable time to cover all this, as well as the non-billable time you'll be working, such as time spent invoicing clients and marketing your business.

You'll need to track all of this, of course. You could do this in your personal finance app or in spreadsheets. I started tracking my business finances in Excel because I was familiar with spreadsheets and, frankly, I didn't have a lot of business to track in my first few years. (All of my business-based spreadsheets are available for free from my website; see Resources for the URL.) When my business started to grow and I needed more features, I first switched to invoicing software and then to bookkeeping software. Consider your financial skills and how you think, as well as cost and desired features. As long as you track your business, you can do what works best for you.

Think Like a Business

Once you have financial goals for your business, you can next consider what you have to offer in exchange for the fee you'll eventually set. Remember, though, you won't be editing forty hours a week. You'll spend some of your time working *on* your business—marketing it, improving your skills, turning client leads into paying clients, and taking care of business administration—all work that's not billable to a client.

Plus, it's unlikely that you can edit eight to ten hours a day and maintain a high quality of editing. Most editors I've talked with agree that four to five hours of editing a day is about what they can do, and that's certainly the case for me. True, there are times when you have to push through and do more editing in a day or week than you know is good for your focus, but that will be balanced with times when you can't focus on editing at all.

That leaves you earning your income in 20–25 hours of editing time a week. You can increase that by editing six or seven days a week, rather than the traditional five, but take care. We all need downtime, and most of us need a couple days a week when we're not working at all. Although editing isn't usually hard on a healthy body, it is hard on the mind. You need to take care of yourself so that you can take care of your business.

What can you offer that will let you earn a fee to do all that?

WHAT YOU BRING TO THE PROJECT

Start by considering the experience and knowledge you bring to the work. Newer freelancers, especially those newer to editing, tend to downplay their experience and knowledge. Editing is a valuable service that not everyone can do. You need an aptitude for language, a solid base of knowledge about the type of editing you do, strong editing skills, sharp editorial judgment, and a base of knowledge around the topic you edit. Because editing is a craft and takes time to learn, the skills of a new editor aren't equal to those of an editor with ten or twenty years of experience. But a newer editor's skills are greater than those of someone with no training at all—even if they've been writing for decades. You need to charge what you're worth.

Another way to look at this is the value you bring to the project: the client isn't paying for the hours you spend on a project but the years of experience you use in those hours. They are paying for your whole brain. What will the client gain from your editing? Your first response might be "perfectly polished prose," but that's a myth. No writing is perfect. Besides, there's a world full of bad writing out there that does the job for readers. Editors cherish polished prose, but few others do. Instead, think about your client's goal. What will better-quality writing lead to? Let's say you've been asked to edit a romance novel that a first-time author will shop around to literary agents. You've been editing romances for a long time and helped many authors get agents because they had a better manuscript to shop around. The risk the author is taking with you is less than with an editor who has never edited a romance. You should be paid for the reduced risk and increased chance of landing an agent.

Sometimes, though, we have to dig a little to understand our client's goals. Clients who come looking for an editor understand that they need editing, but they might not clearly understand why. Ask about their goals for the project. What's the purpose of it? Why are they writing it? What result are they hoping for? Talking to clients about their goals will not only help you determine how editing can help them reach their goals but will signal to your clients that you care about the results. People appreciate when someone understands their problems. You'll tell them early on that your focus isn't on pointing out their mistakes but on helping them succeed.

You can consider all of these factors when deciding how much you want to earn. Now let's look at the client's side of the equation.

CLIENT- AND PROJECT-RELATED LIMITATIONS

The client has their own budget to consider, and the fee they're willing to pay will depend on many factors, such as the market they work in, their understanding of the value of editing, and the particulars of the project itself. Some markets pay better than others. For example, trade and academic publishers tend to have lower fees, and some haven't raised their rates for copyediting and proofreading in decades. Corporations tend to have bigger budgets and are willing to pay for editing. Government agencies' budgets can vary wildly.

You want a good sense of what your desired clients are willing to pay for editing. Research the areas you want to work in. What do other editors generally earn? What does it take to earn that fee? Manuscripts from publishing houses tend to be cleaner because they've received more editing, so the work is likely to take less time. Corporate work might include more than just editing or might have a tight timeline. Even when you're working in an industry that tends to pay better, you can still find clients that can't, or won't, pay as well. Your negotiating skills may get you what you want, but if not, you may just need to walk away.

When working with indie authors, you'll come across a much broader range of ability to pay. Some, such as researchers and company owners, may have access to grants or departmental budgets that can help cover your fee. Others may be paying out of their own pockets. It's critical to educate your potential clients on what a reasonable budget is for editing and for any other part of the publishing process they may have to pay for. If you work with indie fiction authors, for example, you'll want to ensure that they understand all the services they'll need to pay for and how editing is a part of the publishing process.

And, of course, all clients will be affected by the current economy and state of the world. Events such as the COVID-19 pandemic and the global inflation that followed slowed or stopped a lot of work and financially damaged a lot of industries. Even when the economy seems to be more stable, disruptions may lurk around the corner.

Think, too, about the complexity of the project and the amount of time it'll take. The more complex a project is, the more work you have to do and, thus, the higher the fee. Let's say you agree to edit a 200,000-word medical text. Such a big manuscript will be far more complex than several shorter manuscripts that total 200,000 words. You'll have a lot more details to keep consistent, and the content is likely to be complex. Will you receive the entire manuscript at once? If so, you may be working solely on this project for months. That means you won't be able to take on any other work. If you have to turn work away in the meantime, will that work come back later? Alternatively, if you're receiving sections at a time, you'll likely need to include time to reacquaint yourself with some of the details of the project. Both situations mean charging a fee that takes these difficulties into account.

All of these factors can give you a sense of how much the client is willing to pay. From there, you can start to balance your needs against the client's to settle on a fee.

USING SOMEONE ELSE'S FEES

Still, it helps to have a starting point. Some professional editing organizations recommend fees for different editing services. Check out the professional editing organization in your region or your client's region. EFA is well known for its rate chart, and many US freelance editors refer to it to set their own fees. Editors in the UK or working with UK clients can check out CIEP's rate chart, as well as the Freelance Fees Guide from the National Union of Journalists. The Institute of Professional Editors (IPEd) in Australia and Editors Canada also offer rate charts, although the latter's chart is for members only.

Don't follow these fees blindly. Know how the organization arrived at its recommendation first. How closely do you fit the criteria used? How closely matched is your desired client to the criteria? For example, EFA's suggested fees are based on a survey of EFA members, which skews to book editors. If you're not a book editor, those fees might not represent what your client is willing to pay. As well, only a small portion of the membership actually answers the survey. Are there other book editors earning more than that fee? Less? That will change the recommended average.

Use these recommendations as a starting point, adding to it consideration for your needs, the value you offer, and your client's needs and willingness to pay. Then start testing your fee.

SHOULD YOU OFFER A DISCOUNT?

Q. This is kind of a copyedit, but I don't have to edit footnotes. What should I charge?

A. Charge your copyediting fee.

Q. This is a developmental edit, but it's a second pass. What should I charge?

A. Charge your developmental editing fee.

Q. This is mostly a proofread, but . . .

A. (Say it with me:) Charge your proofreading fee.

Why do we freelance editors want to discount a project because it's not exactly one thing or another? No two projects are the same, and many projects don't align perfectly with the type of editing that's being asked for. Instead, we must adjust our work methods to do the job. We may actually need longer to do the edit because we can't use all of our usual efficiency tools. Why does that mean a discount?

I'll say it again: Editors provide a valuable service. Just because the project doesn't fit into predetermined boxes—yours or the client's—doesn't mean it's worth less than a project that does. Instead of reaching for a discount, we need to determine the service the project mostly or best fits, and then charge that fee.

WHEN TO CHARGE A PREMIUM FEE

If the project requires a lot of upsets to your usual process, increasing the time and effort needed to complete it, consider charging a premium fee instead. For example, a client insists that you work in something other than your usual programs. Microsoft Word has been the de facto word-processing software for decades now (though that may change as Gen Z comes up), and editing has adapted to working in this behemoth. If you're asked to use a word-processing software you're not as familiar with or a completely different program that will require you to adapt your process, the project could take significantly longer. You may even have to learn new software. In such a case, you should charge a higher fee because the project will require more work. If you're charging by the hour, this could simply mean you'll charge for more hours; but consider whether a higher hourly fee is warranted as well.

How can you sell that increase to a client? They don't care how much work a project is. They only care that it gets done, accurately, on time and on budget. Here's where you can position your problem as your client's benefit. Some editors will refuse to edit in anything but Word; that's their choice. If you'll work in another software program, you'll have a competitive advantage. You are offering something the client can't get from just any editor. That makes you more valuable to them. And you should be paid accordingly for that value.

Rate Structures

You know how much you need to earn, how many hours you can devote to paying work, and what else you need to consider to set your fee. Now you need a fee structure. Editors have several options:

+ Hourly rate
+ Unit rate
+ Project rate
+ Package rate

Each structure has its merits and detractions. Let's review them.

HOURLY RATE

This may be the least common fee structure, despite the fact that both EFA and CIEP give minimum rates in this structure. Charging by the hour means tracking your time, which is not everyone's favorite thing. I'm a data nerd and my earliest jobs had me punching a clock, even my first proofreading job. I've never lost the habit of tracking my time.

When you charge by the hour, you know exactly what you're selling your time for and almost everyone understands hourly rates, thanks to how most employees are paid. As well, the rates aren't usually scary and are easy to compare. You're also guaranteed to be paid for all the time you put in up to any cap you and the client have agreed to. On the downside, you *do* have to track all your time, and that can mean remembering to start and stop a timer. You'll also need to decide how closely you're going to track your time. Will you track to the minute or on the quarter or even half hour? If you take a five-minute bio break, should you stop your timer? If you're thinking about how to restructure chapter 2 while folding laundry, does that count as work time?

As may be obvious by now, the answer is "it depends." It depends on the kind of work you do, the type of clients you have, and your own habits. When I started freelancing, clients I charged by the hour, I billed to the minute. If I took a bio break, I stopped the clock. If I thought about a project while doing chores, I tracked that time, estimating as closely as I could. Even for a data nerd, that's a lot of effort. I've since switched to billing on the quarter hour. It's made tracking and billing easier. I was even able to set my time tracker up to round my tracked time to the nearest quarter hour, so I don't have to do the math on invoices.

Another downside is that you aren't immediately financially rewarded for being a fast or efficient editor. Instead, you're rewarded by being able to do more projects in a set number of hours. Most of us, though, would like to be paid more *per project* for being efficient and, as a result, have to work less. The workaround here is to raise your hourly rate to reward you for your efficiency.

So why do I charge so many clients by the hour? Because that's what they want. My corporate clients tend to prefer hourly fees, and I'm happy to provide them with that, as long as the hourly fee rewards me for the value I bring to the job.

This fee structure is also good if you're a slower editor, especially for newer editors who haven't yet built up speed or efficiencies. An hourly fee ensures you're getting paid for all the time you put in.

UNIT RATE

Many editors charge by the word, by the page, or by a set number of words (e.g., 1,000 words). These structures all work about the same; the difference is the math you do to get to the total cost. With a per-unit fee, the price point is small and nonthreatening to the client, and, unlike the hourly fee, you can calculate the total cost as soon as you know the project's total word count. That allows both you and the client to know exactly how much you'll charge. Total word count is from the unedited manuscript; you'll read every word, so you should be paid for every word. A per-unit fee rewards you for working more efficiently. If you're a fast editor or you increase your editing speed by using macros and other efficiency tools, you aren't punished financially for finishing in less time.

What if the client adds words during the project? You and they will know exactly how much extra those words will cost. If they remove words during the project and you haven't edited them, you'll both know how much less you'll charge. If you've edited them already, you get paid for them. You've done the work, after all.

When you're dealing with a page fee, you and the client need a shared definition of a page. A manuscript page is generally defined as 250 words. Any editing stage before proofreading deals with manuscript pages. To get an accurate page count, just divide the total number of words by 250. You may need to educate some of your clients on this. Many clients will say that the project is "ten pages." What they generally mean is that there are ten pages in the file. However, the number of words that fit on a page depends on page size, margins, font size, and other variables. Never take the client's word for it; always calculate the page count from the submitted manuscript's word count. And if the client wants to define a page as something other than 250 words? Adjust your per-page fee accordingly.

Once a page is laid out, the number of words on a page will vary greatly. Be sure to review the manuscript to get an idea of how dense with text the pages are and set an appropriate per-page fee. The only time I charged by the page was on a proofreading job for which the client wanted a per-page rate. I was just starting out and hadn't thought about the fact that a laid-out page was not the same as a manuscript page and happily accepted the fee they were offering. Once I saw the project, I realized my mistake. I lost a lot of money on that project, and I never forgot it.

You don't have to limit yourself to words or pages, either. For one client, I edit articles that are written according to a strict, standard outline, and all articles are about the same length. Because these articles are so similar, I charge a per-article fee. I still track word count and time spent on each article, which tells me whether I'm making my desired hourly fee. Some articles will take a lot longer to edit, but those are balanced out by articles that take a lot less time. As long as I'm happy with the average, I know the fee is appropriate.

One thing you'll need to clarify with a per-unit fee is how many editing passes are included in it. Most often, the fee covers *one* round of editing. If the client wants a second round, they'll pay a second, perhaps slightly reduced, fee.

One downside of a per-unit fee is when the work is much harder than estimated, so that it takes more time to complete. It's important to set a fee that takes into account your editing speed and the complexity of the project in order to be paid for all the time you spend on the project. That means not only reviewing the entire document but doing a sample edit for yourself and writing into your contract what happens if the project turns out to be more work than originally anticipated. Be sure to track your time and word count for the project as well, so that you can feed that data into future estimates. Over time, you'll create more accurate estimates as a result.

PROJECT RATE

A project fee is a single, all-inclusive fee, as defined in your contract. You and your client know exactly what the project will cost and what's included in that price. This can make budgeting for a big project easier, especially for indie authors. Any of the above fee structures can be made into a project fee.

The project fee also rewards you for working efficiently—as long as your estimates are fairly accurate. Accurate estimates of the amount of work and the time it will take come from thorough reviews of the project manuscript and your experience. Don't settle for seeing a couple pages of the manuscript. Knowingly or not, the client could send you the best pages and your estimate will be too low. Insist on seeing the entire manuscript and spend the time reviewing it. Especially for book-length materials, you don't need to read the whole thing, but do review every section and watch for items that you know slow down the editing.

Even if you don't offer the client a sample edit, choose what seems to be the section most in need of work and do a sample edit for yourself. That will give you a baseline to work from. You also need to know yourself well: how fast you work, what types of issues will slow you down, how much time you'll need to research or fact-check, and so on. Reviewing data from previous similar projects will help you create more accurate estimates. You can also give yourself a little wiggle room in the fee, estimating 5–10 percent higher to cover longer or rougher manuscripts.

You *will* make mistakes in estimates. Be willing to renegotiate if your estimates are far off. And if your estimating skills are not yet strong, consider quoting an estimated total that can change later.

Because you're charging only one fee, you need to define what goes into it. How many rounds of editing are included? Are meetings included? If so, how many and how much time? What about other, non-editing tasks? Be clear about what the fee covers and what it doesn't. (We'll talk about the details when we talk about contracts.) For example, let's say you'll do a stylistic edit on a 90,000-word nonfiction manuscript. The project will include one full round of edits and one round of cleanup edits after the client has reviewed your full edit and answered your queries. You usually charge $0.05 per word for stylistic editing, which covers the work for both rounds, since with the second round you're only reviewing the client's changes and any responses to your queries. The project fee would be $4,500.

However, the client wants to include a review meeting between editing rounds. For those, you usually charge $65 an hour, so you add that to the project fee for a new total of $4,565. Maybe this is a repeat client who is booking the project three months in advance and paying a 25 percent deposit, which gives them a 5 percent discount. Now the project total is $4,336.75. You list each item on your invoice, with a fee of $1,084.19 due at the time of booking and the balance due according to a schedule you set for the project.

Although your project fee will be based on your hourly or per-unit fee, you'll need to create a fee for each project, which can be time consuming. Consider how you might standardize that fee. If you mostly work with indie authors on book manuscripts of a similar length and level of editing, you might come up with a standard project fee you can apply. You'll still want to review the entire manuscript to ensure that it fits your definition of a standard project. You may even find that you're tweaking your standard project fee each time to account for something in the project, but that's OK. Your project fee, then, is a shortcut to getting to the right custom fee for the project.

PACKAGE RATE

A package of services can be a great way to encourage clients to buy more services from you for a "preferred" (read: slightly discounted) price. While you'll make a little less money on a package than you would if the client purchased the services separately, you'll increase the work you bring in because the package encourages them to buy more than they were originally planning. And if you set your service prices slightly higher than you would want them, the discount you offer on the package won't be a discount for you at all—selling individual services will be a little bonus!

To make packages work, you have to offer services that fit together, such as a developmental edit and copyedit or a copyedit and proofread. You also have to take on work that can use more than one service on a project. Artful Editor, run by Naomi Kim Eagleson, works with self-publishing book authors, offering several levels of editing, as well as other services. If you decide you want your manuscript to be the best it can be, you can purchase the Everything Editing Package, which includes both developmental and line editing.

In addition to offering a more attractive price, a package can reduce the number of decisions clients have to make. Be wary of creating too many packages, however. Too many options can be confusing and actually increase the number of decisions the client has to make, becoming a roadblock rather than a high-speed lane. Start by creating just one or two packages to see how **prospects** respond. If a package doesn't sell—or doesn't encourage the sale of another, less expensive package—discontinue it. As with project fees, you'll need to become good at estimating to make a package fee work. Again, track your data and create limits that will help you adjust the package fee if the project turns out to be more work than you originally anticipated.

You can offer whichever structure makes the most sense to you and your clients. Offer multiple options if that works best for you. The best reason to offer any fee structure is because that's what the client wants. Making it easy to decide to work with you helps you win more clients, and charging the client in the way they want to be charged makes it easier to work with you. Whichever structure you choose, answer the following:

+ Does the fee cover tasks other than editing? If not, how will you charge for those other tasks?
+ Is there a cap on the number of hours you work or number of words included in the project?
+ What editing tasks are explicitly part of your fee?

These details must be worked out before you start the project, and we'll cover them when we talk about contracts. For now, know that these are items to consider when setting your fees.

Finally, I'd encourage you to do one thing. No matter how you charge your clients, always track your editing speed. That means tracking your hours and the number of words for each project. No matter how you price your work, you are selling your time. As we'll see later on, you need to know how much you're selling your hours for to help measure the health of your business.

CHARGING FOR OTHER TASKS AND EXPENSES

Be sure to bill for all the time you spend on a project, including meetings and other communications. When billing by the hour, track all the time you spend on the project and bill accordingly. When billing a project or per-unit fee, estimate all your billable time the fee will cover before agreeing to an amount. Items like commuting costs from your main office, photocopying, and postage are expenses that should be reimbursed by the client. Expected expenses should be agreed to ahead of time; if you run into further expenses during the project, get client approval before spending the money.

Rush fees can also be part of the fee. What constitutes a rush depends on your typical turnaround times and what you need to put aside to meet this deadline. Let's say you typically copyedit all the articles for an academic journal over the course of four weeks, editing articles in batches as they arrive. This time, however, the client needs all of the articles edited in two weeks. To meet this deadline, you'll need to rearrange your other editing projects and maybe work a weekend or two, giving up your free time. As a business owner, you should be compensated for this, and charging a 20 to 50 percent rush fee, on top of your regular fee, would be appropriate.

You'll need to work out the details ahead of time with your client, of course, and you might find that the project isn't as much of a rush as originally thought. The beauty of rush fees is they can help the client better assess whether the work is actually a rush, send the message that you are a professional with professional boundaries, and when it is a rush, compensate you for your efforts.

Negotiate the Editing Work, Not Its Value

Some clients want the impossible. They want the whole trilogy—good, fast, and cheap. In reality, one that some prospects refuse to accept, you can have only two of those. "Good" editing requires time and expertise. We all want the best quality we can get, but

editing every word takes time. Even when you can edit faster, getting the skills and knowledge to make it possible wasn't quick or
free to obtain. If I'm offering a prospect high quality, they're getting the value of my experience, which took years to collect and
refine. An editor doesn't use only lessons learned in their first year
of working. We don't use part of our brains. We bring our whole
selves, all of our experience and all of our knowledge, to every
project. There's no way not to.

Equally, the prospect is going to benefit from better copy. The
difference between mediocre and excellent copy might depend
on the purpose of the copy. What value will the copy bring the
prospect, both immediately and over time? If it's one of dozens of
reports or articles, middle of the road might be just fine. But if it's
a narrative that will help the prospect get that promotion—which
will increase their income and advance their career for years to
come—middle of the road might get them passed over.

"Fast," too, comes at a cost. Everyone wants their projects completed as quickly as possible. But fast doesn't mean doing the same
work in less time. It means working longer hours, turning down
other clients, or rescheduling work to make space in your calendar
to do it all. If I have to work late nights or weekends, giving up
rest and personal time while maintaining quality, to finish a job,
that costs something, too. No one can work without rest without
serious consequences.

That brings us to "cheap." As buyers, we want the best price
we can get. The less we have to pay, the better. The flip side is we
all have bills to pay. Freelancing is a Tetris board of projects you
have to fit together to fill budget lines before the projects crash
around you. Sometimes, though, we do have to compete on price.
Before we do, we should educate the prospect on our value and
then simply state our price—without qualifications, hedging,
or excuses. "For this work, I would charge you $X,XXX." You'd
be surprised how often clients accept the first fee offered when
they understand what they're getting for it and when it's offered
with confidence. And if the prospect does hesitate or state that

the price is too high? Then you can consider negotiating points.

Consider whether negotiating is worth the effort, though. Too many discounted projects won't get you to your financial goals, and time spent negotiating is time you're not spending on actually earning your fee. Ask yourself why you want this client or project. What value does it bring you?

+ It means steady work in the long run.
+ It will teach you something you can then charge other clients to do.
+ It will connect you with a lot of potential clients.
+ The rent is due.

Knowing your reason for wanting to work for the client will help you determine how best to negotiate. And while paying the rent is important, you don't want to build a career on it because you'll always be scrabbling to make your budget. In general, it's better to negotiate on scope rather than price.

It's like choosing options on a new car. You may not be able to afford parking assist, auto-closing doors, and massaging seats, but a backup camera and heated seats may fit your budget. Every option has a cost related to it, and Tetrising them together takes time and effort and often not a little frustration. But putting together a combination that fulfills your needs will increase your satisfaction with your car.

What two options can you help your prospect choose? Fast and good will be the most expensive, but they'll get the best project in the shortest time. Good and cheap will take the most time, but they'll get the best project on budget. Fast and cheap will have the lowest quality but meet their deadline. Perhaps you can do the project for a reduced fee if you don't edit the time-consuming bibliography and citations. Or maybe you can limit the edit to one round rather than the two you usually offer. Consider what tasks you typically perform that you could skip, saving considerable time without sacrificing a lot of quality.

For one client, I reduce the hourly fee slightly to fit her budget, but I also increase the turnaround time. The initial fee would have covered rush jobs and allowed for a same-day turnaround time, which is often a demand for this type of client. For a slightly reduced fee, the client can still have our services, just not as immediately. That allows us to prioritize the workload, making the reduced fee worthwhile.

CAN YOU AFFORD TO WORK FOR THAT FEE?

Sometimes, though, price is the only thing the client will negotiate on. Consider whether you can afford to take the project for the reduced fee. Will doing so mean you can't take on a better-paying project? Or is nothing on the horizon and the wolf is at the door? Will you be locked into this fee for the foreseeable future? Is there anything else the client can offer you, such as free access to software you otherwise would have to purchase, to balance out the loss? Before you negotiate your fee downward, think a little creatively. Consider whether you can reduce your workload for the proffered fee or gain something in addition to offset the loss. And if you can't justify the lower fee? Just say no.

Renegotiating the Fee

There will be times when it's appropriate to renegotiate a fee, especially if the project scope changes. A project might require more work or take more time to edit than you originally estimated, even after you've reviewed the manuscript. When that happens, stop editing and talk with your client. Your contract should have an option to renegotiate the fee, but even if it doesn't, it's better to talk with the client rather than lose money on a project. If you don't speak up, you'll be accepting the situation as is.

Just as with any business, your fees should go up over time. Employees typically receive raises on an annual basis, and your clients shouldn't be surprised that freelancers also raise their rates. However, the client has no reason to offer you an increase.

You will almost always have to initiate the conversation. Determine what your new fee will be. How much you should raise your fees is almost as hard to answer as how much you should charge. Think in percentages of your existing fee. Will a 5 percent fee cover increased costs? Have you greatly improved your service and feel comfortable increasing your fees by 10 percent? Most often, you can simply tell clients that your fee will be increasing on a certain date. You can soften the blow by allowing them to book work to be done after the increase at the old fee if they book before the fee increases. If you're working for corporate clients, keep in mind that the following year's budget is usually set in the fourth quarter. Talking to your client *before* they set the annual budget will help get that increase approved by budget owners.

When the client controls the fee, you'll need to frame the increase as a request. Back up your request with data about current rates and the value you have brought to the work and how it has increased over time. The client may or may not accept your fee increase. If not, determine whether you can afford to keep working for this client. If you can't, you may wish to look for a replacement client before breaking off with the current one.

Key Takeaways

+ Instead of asking "How much should I charge?" ask "How do I set my rates?"
+ If you don't have one already, set up a personal budget and determine how much you need to earn from your new business. Be sure to take taxes and business expenses into account.
+ Your fee needs to be high enough to meet your budget based on the number of hours you intend to edit.
+ Clients are not paying just for your labor. They're paying for your skills, knowledge, and experience.
+ Editing creates value in a manuscript based not only on the improvements made but also on the manuscript's purpose.
+ Some clients are more able to pay your fees than others. Some

are more willing to pay than others. You may need to work with more than one type of client to meet your income goal.

+ Several editing organizations share recommended editing fees. You can use these as a starting point, but always keep your unique situation in mind.
+ Some projects are more complex than others. Charge accordingly.
+ You can charge by the hour, word, page, or project. Use whichever fee structure works best for you. It's OK to charge different clients by different structures.
+ Discount the scope of the project, not your fees.
+ It's better to turn down exceptionally low-paying work and spend your time winning better-paying clients.
+ Sometimes a project doesn't go as planned and the agreed-upon fee no longer covers all the work. Alert your client and come to an agreement about the work and the fee.

Setting Up Shop

Freelance editing doesn't require some of the trappings that reassure us we're running a legitimate business. We don't require a separate office space for clients to visit. We don't need a phone number dedicated to the business. We won't have employees, and since we sell a service, we don't have raw materials or finished products to manage and house somewhere.

But freelance editing *is* a business, and you *do* need to take a few steps to set up your business before taking on your first official client. In this chapter, we'll look at the types of businesses you can create and some important legal forms to prepare in advance. We'll also dive deeply into invoicing, look at some options for how to get paid, and tackle another common freelancer question, "Should I carry insurance?"

Business Structures

If you're working in the United States, you have a few options for business structures. The sole proprietorship is the easiest to open and the cheapest to create and run. But while LLCs and S corps require a bit of work to set up, they offer you more protection as a business owner. Let's review them.

SOLE PROPRIETORSHIPS

Because you can work under your social security number (SSN) with a sole proprietorship, you don't need to fill out any forms to start your business. As noted already, as a sole proprietor, you'll pay the same federal, state, and city income taxes that employees do, plus the applicable self-employment tax (SET). You could wait until April 15 of the following year, when personal tax returns are due, to send in your tax money, but paying your taxes quarterly ensures the government gets its share. You'll also be able to take business deductions, including for your home office. You can deduct those quarterly or annually. Talk to a tax accountant for advice on your personal situation.

There are a few downsides to sole proprietorship. The first is that you'll be giving your SSN to clients you earn more than $600 from, and that may include indie authors. You can protect your personal information by getting a federal **employer identification number (EIN)**. The application, available through irs.gov, can be completed online. Having an EIN is also one of a couple simple steps to getting a business bank account and, sometimes, a business credit card. Having a separate bank account for your business can help keep your finances organized, and if your clients pay by direct deposit or wire, you're giving them access only to your business account. Too, business accounts tend to offer other features you may utilize as a business, such as the ability to wire a payment, a line of credit for business expenses, and more detailed reports.

Another difficulty can be proving your income for personal loans. This will depend on your income stream and the lender you work with, especially if your business is prone to the feast-or-famine cycle. I've been fortunate to not have had a problem getting a loan I needed with just my income, but several editors I know have been turned down for loans they could easily afford. If you anticipate needing a loan in the near future and don't have a cosigner, you may wish to choose a different business structure.

Finally, as a sole proprietor, you can be personally sued by clients. Especially in the United States, which has a litigious culture, this is something to consider. To combat this, you should vet clients carefully before taking them on. Are they who they say they are? Do they have a history of suing people? Do they seem trustworthy, both online and in your interactions with them? (We'll talk about spotting red flags later in the book.) Next, be sure your estimates are as accurate as possible to avoid potential money conflicts, and use a solid contract that protects you from some of the most common client issues, such as a client surprised by the number of changes in their manuscript. Finally, you can carry insurance for genuine problems (more on that below).

A sole proprietorship is a good choice if you're not sure you'll stick with freelancing or you prefer a simpler structure and have ways to mitigate the downsides.

LIMITED LIABILITY COMPANIES

Halfway between a sole proprietorship and a corporation is a **limited liability company (LLC),** a popular choice among freelancers who want some separation between their personal assets and their business but don't want all the requirements of a corporation. An LLC is a separate entity from you personally, with its own EIN. If a client wants to sue you and you're an LLC, they will actually sue your LLC, effectively putting a firewall in front of your personal assets.

Because you are creating a taxable business structure, there are forms and procedures to follow to create an LLC. They vary from state to state, as do the costs for creating your new business. Often, there is an annual filing fee for your LLC. Check with your state for fees and processes.

The other big difference is that as the LLC owner, you draw a salary from your **gross earnings**, that is, the total income you've earned over a period of time. You'll still pay personal income taxes, as well as SET, based on the salary you pay yourself. Technically, the company pays half of your FICA, but because the company is you, it amounts to the same thing. However, the LLC also pays taxes on its **net profit** (**gross receipts** less deductions and salary). Note that LLC taxes have a different payment schedule than personal taxes.

Because an LLC is a separate entity, you can choose to have the LLC pay you, the individual, rent instead of taking a home office deduction. This relieves you of tracking everything that goes into a home office deduction, though you'll have to pay personal income tax on that rent. You can also pay yourself profit sharing, which is taxed at a lower rate than income. Again, talk to a tax accountant about your specific situation so that you stay in the government's good graces.

S CORPORATIONS

Some freelancers choose to fully incorporate their businesses. While there are several corporation structures, the **S corporation (S corp)** is the most common and appropriate for individual freelancers. Like the LLC, the S corp is a separate entity with its own EIN. Here, too, there are forms and procedures, with associated annual costs. The laws regarding S corps are stricter, so you'll need to become familiar with them and stay on top of your administrative tasks. A business lawyer or tax accountant can help you with that.

With an S corp, you will also have a **board of directors** and **shareholders**. Like an LLC, you'll pay personal income taxes on what you earn from your business, but you'll also pay taxes on any profits you pay your shareholders—that is, yourself. Here, too, the processes and fees will vary by state, so it's wise to see what your state requires before deciding on this structure.

The Small Business Administration (SBA) is an excellent resource for more information about US business structures, and services like LegalZoom and Rocket Lawyer can help you complete the necessary paperwork. A business lawyer or a tax accountant can also offer advice on the best structure for your individual situation. Just as it's wise for our clients to hire professional editors to get the best advice for their manuscript, as business owners we benefit greatly from seeking professional advice for matters outside of our expertise.

BUSINESS STRUCTURES OUTSIDE OF THE US

Each country has its own options and laws regarding business structures. Table 2 briefly outlines the options in a sampling of countries. It presumes you're starting a business in your home country. Expats should consult the government of the country they wish to start a business in, as well as a tax accountant who's well versed in international businesses.

TABLE 2. Available Business Structures in Some Other Countries

LOCATION	BUSINESS STRUCTURES	WHERE TO LEARN MORE
United Kingdom	sole trader, partnership, limited company, limited partnership	gov.uk/browse/business
Canada	sole proprietorship, partnership, corporation, cooperative	canada.ca/en/services/business/start.html
Australia	sole trader, company	business.gov.au/guide/starting
New Zealand	sole trader, partnership, limited liability	ird.govt.nz/situations/i-am-starting-a-new-business

Opportunities Beyond Solopreneurship

This book assumes that you will be the only person in your business. This is true for most freelancers, and it's a great way to make a living. But as you start to expand your business, other options may interest you.

BECOMING AN EDITORIAL AGENCY

Maybe you're that go-getter editor who loves running a business. You've topped out on your ability to earn money because you've booked all your available editing hours and can't raise your rates any higher. You're tired of turning away clients who come to you, and you're not interested in creating products to sell. Turning your one-person shop into an agency allows you to keep saying yes and earn more while providing work for your fellow editors. This was the path I started down in 2018. For a few years prior to that, I had co-owned Copyediting.com, and after we sold that business, I missed managing and coaching other editors. And if I'm honest, I never liked turning a client away just because I was busy. Creating a team of editors solved both of those issues.

Expanding your business takes a lot of work, just like launching a solo business. Here, you really need to love the business aspect, because you'll be responsible for a lot more of it, spending less time editing. You need to be comfortable with increased risk, too, because you'll be guaranteeing your contractors' work. And unless you plan on hiring support staff immediately, you want to be good at project management and training. Someone needs to ensure project deadlines are met and contractors' work is up to snuff. Reviewing your contractors' work and helping them improve their skills are a necessary investment in your agency.

Specializing is key. You'll spend a lot of time marketing, so you want to get the most out of it. You'll also be charging higher fees to cover your business costs and make a profit, so you'll want to offer clients something for that fee. Subject expertise and quick turnaround times are good choices. You can also offer complementary services, becoming a one-stop shop. Consider what your clients might need help with, such as writing, project management, design, or marketing strategy. Maybe you'll help an author with their book from developmental edit through to proofreading. Since you're not doing all the actual work, what you offer no longer depends solely on your skill set. All of this is a shift not just in tasks but in mindset. *Virtual Freedom* by Chris Ducker is invaluable for helping you make that shift. As a business owner, you're used to doing it all, but as you expand, you won't be able to. What do you outsource?

Clearly, you're outsourcing some, if not all, of the actual work, but that doesn't mean you should do everything else. As the business owner, you need to focus on the strategy for your business. Ducker advises creating three lists of tasks you usually do: those you don't like doing (such as checking email), those you can't do (developing websites), and those you shouldn't do because they're low-level tasks that take away from the high-level tasks only you can do (updating your Facebook page).

One of the more common examples of agency specialties is working with self-publishing authors. Pikko's House, run by Crystal Watanabe, is all about helping self-publishing novelists go from manuscript to published book, offering beta reading, manuscript critiquing, and several levels of editing while specializing in science fiction and fantasy. Dragonfly Editorial, owned by Samantha Enslen, offers writing, editing, design, and training to its clients, specializing in such complex topics as technology, science, and engineering. If you expand into an agency, consider how you'd like to specialize and who your target audience would be.

FORMING A PARTNERSHIP

For those who want to expand their businesses but don't want to be anyone's boss, forming a partnership with other editors is a good option. In this relationship, all the editors have an equal stake. With partners, you can take on bigger, better-paying projects that you work on together. You can also improve your marketing because you can widen or deepen your marketing reach and share the tasks and costs. Depending on your particular arrangement, you may also have someone to help with your workload when you get sick or otherwise can't complete a job.

The costs of a partnership vary, depending on how much the partners join efforts and how many clients you take on. You could decide to form a **limited liability partnership (LLP)**, which works similarly to an LLC, or you could work as an informal partnership. You and your partners decide how much of your earnings on jobs that come from the partnership go into a shared business account. You could share marketing expenses, such as business cards and a website; technology, like a shared invoicing or accounting system; or group training. Search for the right balance between how much money to invest in the partnership and how much each partner earns on projects. West Coast Editorial Associates is an editorial partnership based in British Columbia, Canada. The partnership dates to 1992, and membership has slowly changed over the years. The partners determine together when a new member should be brought in and what role that person should fill. Each partner contributes a small percentage of project fees to fund the partnership needs.

Like agencies, partnerships attract bigger, better-paying clients because they are easily identified as companies. Companies like to do business with other companies: there's an assurance that the work will be done because it doesn't depend on just one person. Payment can be easier, too; while accounting departments are organized to pay other companies, not all are set up to pay an independent contractor.

Our businesses are as individual as we are, and we can create even more ways to collaborate to increase our earning potential, share the burdens of business, and learn from each other. Maybe you want to create a group to brainstorm and share training. Perhaps you want a business relationship that allows everyone involved to share the costs of business tools and administrative help. It's not a matter of what type of business your government labels it; it's a matter of identifying where you want to go and choosing traveling companions with similar destinations.

Contracts and Other Legal Documents

If you've chosen to become a sole proprietorship, use your SSN, and maintain just a personal bank account, you might not feel like a legitimate business yet. You *are* a business, but if you're getting a case of **impostor syndrome**, this section should cure you quickly. For better or worse, legal forms can highlight the risks in running your own business, if only because they exist to protect you from those risks. Let's go over some basic forms you might need.

THE PROJECT CONTRACT

At its simplest, the **project contract** ensures that the project is properly defined, hopefully eliminating any nasty surprises later. It details items such as who's involved and what they're responsible for. Creating a contract for each job ensures not only that you've defined the job but that you and the client have agreed on what the job is. Especially with the lack of understanding about editing and the different levels of editing, writing down somewhere what level of editing you'll perform and what that means in practical terms can help set client expectations. A contract can also help protect you from situations like the client not paying you or the client wanting to sue you for not delivering them an award-winning manuscript.

What should go into your contract will vary based on the project and your location, but the basics include the following:

+ Contract's effective date
+ Parties involved
+ Project description
+ Milestone dates and final deadline
+ Each party's responsibilities
+ Financial details
+ Terms and conditions
+ Signatures and dates

Create a template for your business that includes the necessary terms and conditions for your jurisdiction and situation and adjust it as needed for each project. Spending the time upfront to create a usable document for your business will help you quickly put together specific contracts for projects as they come in.

There are a lot of templates online, but the quality can vary. Be sure that the template you start from is accurate and will be binding. At the time of writing, LegalZoom, Rocket Lawyer, and PandaDoc all offer business contract templates for a variety of locations; although not perfect documents, the templates are generally considered a good starting point. **Customer relationship management (CRM) services** like Dubsado, 17hats, and Honey-

Book also offer templates. Wherever you get your template, do your homework on what your location requires (or disallows) in a contract. You could also hire a business lawyer to draw up a template for you.

Some editors will use an email chain instead of a formal contract. It's a bigger risk than a thoughtfully worded contract, but a chain of emails can act as a contract if all the required details are present. Again, a template with well-thought-out wording can help you create a defensible contract. Karin Cather and Dick Margulis's *The Paper It's Written On* goes through the basics of what goes into a contract for editing and outlines some of the risks your contract is trying to mitigate. Business mentoring network SCORE is also a great resource for understanding contracts. And it never hurts to consult with a lawyer.

WHEN THE CLIENT HANDS YOU A CONTRACT

Sometimes your client, especially a large company, will have its own contract for you to sign. It's often a template the legal department has created, designed to protect the company and cover all likely vendors. Make sure the contract covers your needs, too. Be comfortable with all the details it outlines before you sign. If the contract is really troubling, don't sign it without legal counsel. And if that legal counsel costs more than the money you'll make on the project, consider whether you should just decline the project instead.

OTHER LEGAL DOCUMENTS YOU MIGHT WANT

Besides the project contract, you might also be asked to sign a **nondisclosure agreement (NDA)** or a **noncompete agreement (NCA)**. The NDA, or confidentiality agreement, states that one or both parties will not share information learned from the other, such as a company's trade secrets. Self-publishing authors sometimes hesitate to give their entire manuscript to an editor for a pre-contract review. Offering to sign an NDA can put them at ease. It reassures them that you are not going to steal their manuscript and publish it yourself. It costs the honest editor nothing to ease the potential client's mind.

The NCA protects the client from the vendor (that's you) luring away the client's customers or from the vendor working for the client's competition. You might run into this if you work for an agency. The agency wants reassurance that you won't steal its clients, at least for a stated period. It protects the agency's business model.

As with the project contract, these agreements can help both parties understand the limits of the business relationship and protect both parties' interests. And just as with a project contract, you should sign only if you're comfortable with all the terms. If not, you can choose to negotiate or walk away. Again, you can work with a lawyer or legal service to draw up templates for your business. Having these forms ready to go helps demonstrate to prospects that you are a legitimate business—and it saves you from making mistakes when you have to scramble to pull a form together before losing a prospect.

Invoicing Fundamentals

Although not a legal document, the **invoice** is another critical document for your business. It's the form that tells your client how much to pay you, when to pay you, and how to do so. Plus it's an opportunity to promote your business. You know I'm going to tell you to create a template, right? Unless a client dictates what file type your invoices should be in, Microsoft Word is your best bet. You're already familiar with the software, and you can create a simple template in just a few minutes. (You can also download a template from my site; see Resources.) Taking the extra step of saving the invoice as a PDF file before sending it to the client discourages anyone from making changes to it. Simply do a "save as" and choose "PDF."

INVOICE BASICS

Your invoice should have the following information:

+ *Your name and contact details.* Include your name, company
  name, mailing address, email address, and phone number. If
  someone has an issue with your invoice, you want them to be
  able to reach you easily.
+ *Your client's business details.* Add your contact's name, mailing
  address, email address, and phone number. You can create
  a template for each client or store this information in text
  expander software for easy pasting. (See chapter 11 for more on
  text expanders.)
+ *The term* invoice *or* bill. If you collect tax as well, you may need
  to use the term *tax invoice* instead. Check with your accountant
  to see which term is best for your business.
+ *Date of the invoice.*
+ *Invoice number.* Don't skip this step. When an invoice or a
  payment goes astray, an invoice number will make tracking it
  down easier.
+ *Description of work.* Include a brief description of the work
  performed, fee structure, and the total amount due for the
  work.
+ *Total amount.* Make sure this number is easy to find and read.
  If you charge tax, list the amount before tax, the tax, and the
  full total. If the client is getting a discount, that would go in this
  section as well.
+ *Payment details.* Explain how the client should pay you, how
  long they have to pay you, and what your late-payment policy is.

Also include any details the client has requested. Purchase
order numbers are common when working for companies. Agencies may want you to include codes or abbreviations of their clients, so they know who to bill. Within reason, include whatever
makes it easier for the client to pay you. If you've given the client your SSN or EIN previously, it's not necessary to add it to the

invoice. In fact, I'd discourage it. Invoices aren't secured documents and might be seen by anyone.

INVOICE EXTRAS

Build in a space for notes to the client. These might vary from project to project or be a standard statement you want the client to know. For example, I use this note to remind clients that no edit is perfect:

> Every effort is made to reduce errors, improve the writing as described above, and not introduce errors. However, perfection is impossible for several reasons. Chief among them is what defines an "error." Editing is both subjective and objective. What one person defines as an error, another defines as a style choice.
>
> Therefore, Right Touch Editing makes no guarantees to an error-free edit. Nor is Right Touch Editing responsible for changes made to a file after it is returned to the client.

You might include the standard definitions of editing that you follow. Or if you're committed to upholding an organization's professional standards, such as those outlined by CIEP, you could include a statement about that. Not only does this give clients important reminders, but it shares a part of your business's brand: the standards you commit to.

Other aspects of your brand can, and should, be included on your invoice. If you have a logo and **tagline**, include them. If you have brand fonts and colors, use them. It's common to put a little thank-you statement on invoices, but you can take it a step further with something like: "Thank you for your business! If you love what we do, please pass our name along to a friend or colleague."

Let a little of your personality shine through here. On her invoices, editor Sherri Hildebrandt includes: "If you like my work, tell others. If you don't, tell me!" I love that Hildebrandt encourages clients to let her know if they're dissatisfied. Editor Adrienne Montgomerie shows her business's personality while reminding clients about payment due dates. Her invoices say:

"Overdue invoices will be reissued in an envelope of glitter."

SENDING AND TRACKING YOUR INVOICES

As part of setting up a new client, be sure you've received all the details for how to invoice, including who to send it to, when, and how. Do your part to receive timely payments by following the directions you've been given. Once you've sent your invoice, log it somewhere, and track who paid you and when. Spreadsheets aren't a bad way for a freelancer to run their business. As you'll see throughout this book, there's a lot of business software aimed at freelancers and small businesses, but costs—and complexity— add up quickly. While a freelancing business might benefit from specialized business software, sometimes Excel works just fine, thank you very much. The important part is to be able to quickly know who hasn't paid you so you can follow up.

In addition to the spreadsheet templates you can download from my website (see Resources), there are two inexpensive spreadsheet packages just for editors that might suit you, available as of this writing. The first is The Editor's Affairs (TEA) from What I Mean to Say, owned by Maya Berger. TEA includes spreadsheets for tracking income, expenses, projects, and professional development. From that, you'll be able to see summaries of your monthly income, expense categories, and client details. Berger will even customize the spreadsheets for you. The second is Editors' Tracking Programs from Beacon Point, owned by Katie Chambers. The Business Finance Tracker will help you calculate gross and net income, taxes, expenses, and mileage. (See Resources for URLs to TEA and Editors' Tracking Programs.)

SHOULD YOU USE INVOICING SOFTWARE?

Using a Word template to create invoices, email to send them, and a spreadsheet to track them is as inexpensive an invoicing system as you can get. But it's also fairly manual and can be time consuming if you bill a lot of clients. I started this way, but as my business grew, invoices were taking me longer and longer. I needed to create several invoices a month, and I had to gather details for each one. Switching to invoicing software saved me time that I could instead use on paid work.

There are many services to choose from. CRMs usually include invoicing and may include time tracking. Or you could go with an accounting service. QuickBooks is a popular accounting service that helps you track a lot of your business's financial data. Some editors find it too advanced for them, however. You may find options like FreshBooks, Zoho Invoice, and Wave Invoicing more your speed. Features and prices can vary greatly, even within a service. To find the best fit, think about what you need the software to do for you and how many clients you'll keep in the system.

When I outgrew Word and Excel, I switched to FreshBooks. It had a timer that fed into projects, saving me a big step every month with all my hourly clients. It also had several service levels so that as I increased the number of clients, I just had to up the service level. Eventually, though, I outgrew that and moved to Zoho Invoice, which allowed me to have more active clients for a lower fee. These days, I'm using Zoho Books, which helps me track all of my business's finances while still giving me a timer, something QuickBooks does not.

WHEN SHOULD YOU INVOICE?

Your clients, especially companies, may dictate when you invoice. The more established the company, the more likely the accounting department will have a system for receiving and paying invoices. To receive timely payments, follow that system.

When you set the terms, however, you have several options, including the following:

+ *Invoicing for the total at the end of the project.* This works for well-established clients you have a good relationship with.
+ *Invoicing for a deposit now and the balance later.* For new clients, especially individuals, protect yourself from nonpayment by breaking up the total into several payments.

+ *Invoicing monthly.* This works well for clients who send you
  several projects a month or a long-term project (think six
  months of ongoing work). It also works well for clients with
  larger accounting departments, as they usually have a schedule
  of when they make payments.

Keep in mind: the bigger the risk that you won't get paid for
your work, the more protections you need to put in place. Some
editors ask for a nonrefundable deposit just to get on their calendar. As well, when you're working on bigger projects over a longer
period, the less money you'll have flowing in from other clients.
Breaking the total fee into payments keeps you solvent. Whatever
terms you decide on should be spelled out in your contract.

Accepting Payments: So Many Options!

Clients don't all like to pay the same way, so it's to your benefit
to have several payment options. Table 3 has a quick overview of
some of the more common payment options. Corporate clients
will have systems for paying; work with them to get everything
set up correctly so you can receive payment. Individual authors
and smaller companies might be more comfortable paying via a
payment gateway like PayPal so they can use a credit card.

Services like QuickBooks and FreshBooks integrate with
several payment gateways, which can streamline the process
of getting paid and tracking payments. Services like Canada's
Interac e-Transfers and POPmoney (for person to person) can
also work.

I prefer payment gateways when direct deposit isn't an option.
Payment is immediate and easy to send, receive, and track, and
clients can choose to use a credit card. But because payment gateways are providing a service, they charge businesses receiving the
money a fee. How else can the business continue to offer the service? The good news is that those fees are likely tax deductible for
your business. And often there's no fee for your client. That's a

baseline for good customer service. A fee to make a payment for a service does not encourage working with you. Successful freelancers clear obstacles for clients rather than create them.

TABLE 3. Popular Payment Options for Clients

PAYMENT TYPE	FEE YOU PAY	COMMENTS
Check	$0	Still very common in the US, with banks offering mobile depositing. Less common in other areas and not accepted at all in New Zealand.
Direct deposit	$0	Usually offered by companies when you work for them on an ongoing basis.
Wire transfer	varies	Can be costly but can also help a client pay you in your desired currency. Banks tend to charge a flat fee for accepting a wire transfer, while payment gateway Wise charges a percentage.
PayPal	percentage of total collected + fixed fee per transaction	Fees vary depending on the country and payment method. Payments made by QR code, for example, are less expensive than those paid by invoice.
Square, Stripe, Wave, Venmo	percentage of total collected + fixed fee per transaction	Alternatives to PayPal. Many invoicing services connect with one or more of these options, as well as PayPal. Note that Venmo is owned by PayPal.

You can work with as many payment options, including checks, direct deposit, and other methods, as you want. Each payment option needs managing, though. I've found the more I offer, the harder it is to reconcile all my accounts. I want options I can manage with minimal help from an accountant.

Late Payment: What to Do

There's no easy way to deal with late-paying clients. Each situation is going to be different based on the client and the reason they're not paying you. No matter what kind of client you have, if a client misses a payment deadline, after a few days, politely follow up.

For example:

> *Dear [Client],*
> Your payment of $X,XXX was due on [date] and is now past due.
> Your invoice is attached for your convenience. Prompt payment is
> appreciated.

A polite inquiry keeps the client from becoming defensive; often the problem is simple human error that the client is willing to fix quickly. Avoid accusing them and don't apologize for requesting the money you earned, but keep in mind that life happens. Maybe your emails are going to spam, or your contact is out of the office and forgot to set up an away message. Remain professional in all your communications. Give them the information they need in each message, so that when one finally reaches them, they can tackle the problem immediately.

As far as possible, try to work with your client. During the COVID-19 pandemic, many people and companies struggled financially. More than one editor I spoke with discovered late payments and missed deadlines were because the client had had COVID. Being able to talk to the client allowed these editors to work out solutions that benefited both parties.

When sending to an accounting department or service, you can ask your main client contact to look into the problem for you. This has worked well for me with my corporate clients, as my contact has a vested interested in seeing that I get paid. If you send your invoices to your main contact and you've heard nothing from them, you could try contacting their supervisor. Again, avoid placing any blame at this point. Just let the supervisor know you can't reach your contact and you have an outstanding invoice. Could they help you?

If this is a client you regularly work for and you feel they are not trying to resolve the payment issue, do not do any more work for them until they are caught up on payments. Do not let them get deeper into debt with you. A promise of a payment that's months late is not going to pay your rent. You are a business, and you have provided a service on agreement of payment. If the client breaks that agreement, you are not obligated to continue working for them. As a solo freelancer, you are the only one who can stand up for your business. Remain professional, but be firm. If the client is just ducking you, you can try making your requests more directly and more urgent. Don't threaten anything you won't follow through on, though. Like kids, clients have an annoying habit of calling your bluff.

Consider sending the bill to collections. If the invoice is big enough, it might be worth the cost. Warn the client. Just saying that if they don't pay in XX days, you'll send to collections might be enough to get them to pay the bill. For example:

> *Dear [Client],*
>
> Invoice #275 for $2,365 is now eight weeks past due. I have sent several reminder emails and left one voice mail for you without a response. If I do not hear from you in three days, I will send this bill to a collections agency.
>
> Please respond immediately to this message with a date of when I can expect payment to avoid your bill being turned over to the collections agency.

You can also seek legal counsel. If the company declares bankruptcy, what are your rights?

If it's a small fee and repeated requests don't work, you may need to let it go. We've all been ripped off at least once. It's never comfortable, but it happens sometimes. As always, become familiar with the laws in your area to see what they can do for you and how they might limit your actions. New York State, for example, has the Freelance Isn't Free Act, which imposes penalties on those who refuse to pay freelancers they've hired.

The Insurance Question

"Do I need insurance?" Some client contracts will state that the vendor needs to carry insurance and may even specify the amount of coverage you should carry. We'll look at two types of insurance your clients might be looking for and whether you really should have them or not.

GENERAL LIABILITY INSURANCE

As the name suggests, **general liability insurance** covers a range of losses a business might face, including physical injury, property damage, and medical bills. If you're renting office space or have clients visiting your home office, you might want general liability insurance to cover expenses due to, say, frozen pipes bursting in your rented office or a client falling while visiting you. If, like most freelance editors, you're working from home and clients never visit you, your homeowner's or renter's insurance can be extended to cover your office equipment.

General liability insurance can also cover claims of libel, slander, misleading advertising, and copyright infringement. How at risk you are for such accusations will depend on your specific editing business and how you advertise it. Editors don't generally create copy, but we do advertise our services. You'll need to gauge your individual risk and talk to an insurance agent about whether this coverage is necessary for you.

Client contracts that include an insurance clause are often meant for *all* of a client's vendors, especially those with a higher risk for accidents (think construction, in which heavy machinery is used) or libel or slander (think writers creating copy for the client). If that isn't you and you've decided you don't need liability insurance for your business, let your client know it isn't appropriate for your situation.

PROFESSIONAL LIABILITY INSURANCE

Also called **errors and omissions (E&O) insurance**, **professional liability insurance** covers you when a client claims you were negligent in your work—in other words, that you omitted something or made an error in the text. E&O insurance might make sense for a writer, who creates the text for the client and therefore might make a mistake the client would otherwise be liable for, such as leaving out an important safety statement in a product owner's manual. But editors do not create copy; we only work with what we're given. Nor are we the last person to touch the copy. Even a proofreader, who is traditionally the last editor to touch the copy, hands off corrections for someone else to make. We have no control over whether that person makes the corrections. We have no way to guarantee that someone else won't change the copy once it's back with the client.

Additionally, editing is subjective. No two editors will edit the same copy the exact same way. You won't even edit the same copy the exact same way twice. That's because most of the changes we're making aren't based on hard-and-fast rules. Changing *beyond twelve months from now* to *beyond the next twelve months* is a decision for rhythm and clarity, not correctness. Both are grammatical; both say the same thing. Neither is superior to the other. It's a matter of rhythm and style.

But let's say you accidentally delete the *not* in *Do not take this medication with food*. That's certainly a meaning change that would have serious consequences. However, we have no power to force a client to make changes. All corrections are suggestions. Clients review them and have the authority to accept them or not. That can be reassuring for the nervous author who isn't keen on having their copy changed, but it also means the client bears the responsibility for those decisions.

Clients who ask you to carry E&O insurance often don't understand how the publishing process works and the editor's place in it. They want to protect themselves from claims against their copy, and rightly so, but editors carrying E&O insurance won't help them. That's not to say that editors shouldn't be held responsible for doing a poor job. If I've missed or introduced a lot of errors, done a different edit than the client expected, or otherwise provided an edit the client is unhappy with, the client is right to complain to me. They'd be right to ask for the work to be redone or to have their money refunded. But it's the client who decides to publish poorly edited materials, not the editor.

There's no requirement I'm aware of, at least in the United

States, that says freelance editors have to carry insurance (but I'm not a lawyer). You can decide to carry either of these types of insurance if you think the risk of costly claims is worth protecting against. That's a personal decision. To date, I have chosen not to carry either. If you decide not to carry insurance and a client contract has a clause about it, educate your client on why it's inappropriate for this situation. Explain how editing works and the control they have over the copy. You can cross out the unnecessary clause and initial it, and then sign the contract as amended. Alternatively, as one of my clients does, the client can supply you with an insurance waiver form to sign, which will state that you waive the client's request to carry insurance.

Key Takeaways

+ Choose a business structure that best fits your needs. You can always decide later to change the structure.
+ Becoming an editorial agency or forming a partnership can help you expand your business beyond the work you can do on your own.
+ The project contract outlines all the details of your relationship with the client, providing guidelines and some legal protections.
+ Some clients have their own contracts. Review them carefully before signing.
+ Nondisclosure agreements prevent you from talking about the client's work publicly.
+ Noncompete agreements state that you won't pilfer any of your client's clients.
+ Invoices spell out all the details of payments and provide an opportunity to brand your company.
+ There are many ways to accept payment. Choose the options that work best for you and your clients.
+ If the client is late paying, professionally address the situation immediately.

+ General liability insurance covers your business from many types of claims, including property damage and libel.
+ Professional liability insurance covers your business from claims of errors and omissions.

Being Uniquely You (Branding!)

Your brand represents you and your company. It tells people who you and your company are and helps them remember you.

Before someone can hire you, they have to become aware of you and know enough about you to want to hire you. That's basic, right? Your brand helps tell prospective clients whether you're someone they could work with. It might communicate the genres or subjects you edit in, how you approach editing, or something about you professionally. When someone first learns about your business, they may not be ready to purchase editing services. You want them to remember you when they're ready. Or maybe they don't need an editor but know someone who would. You want them to tell someone else about you at the right moment. Having a unique, memorable brand, combined with frequent reminders of your brand (which we'll tackle in chapter 6), will help do that.

Branding also communicates something about your business values, which helps build trust. We tend to avoid working with people we don't trust. Imagine being an author who has spent months or years on their manuscript, maybe not yet having shown it to anyone else. Would you want to hand it over to someone who won't respect that work? Brands build trust by communicating values and giving prospects something for nothing—something the brand didn't have to give, such as a timely piece of advice or a moment's entertainment.

Your brand is a story of other people's problems and how you solve them. People engage with stories and emotionally connect to them. You want to tell a story of your business that people will respond positively to and trust.

Discover Your Brand Story

Your brand story must address not only who you are and what you do but also who the client is and what their needs are. Clients want to know how working with you will benefit them. They ask, sometimes only subconsciously, "What's in it for me?" They don't care about your business except in terms of how it helps them. This is a basic human response. You won't try to change it; you'll try to work with it. Freelance editors have a particular challenge in selling their services: unless they target traditional publishers, their clients may have only a vague understanding of editing. Your brand story, then, has to educate them on what editing is and how it solves their problem.

Your client's problem, however, is *not* flawed writing. (I know that breaks your heart. Fixing those flaws is an editor's passion.) Your client's problem is that, in its current state, their writing can't meet its goal. Editing is the *solution*, or part of it, to this problem, and we need to frame it that way for our clients. All writing has a goal. It might be to entertain readers, such as with poetry or novels. It could be to inform readers, as with articles and news stories. The goal could be to educate readers, as with textbooks, or encourage readers to buy a product or service, as with marketing and sales copy.

Whatever the goal, when a manuscript is published without having been edited, it will have mistakes. Readers may notice some of those mistakes, especially basic grammar. This draws their attention to the writing and away from the intended message. Readers may not be able to identify problems of logic and clarity, but they will struggle to understand the text, which will cause them to misunderstand or abandon the text. Either way, the text will fail to reach its goal. You and I know why these things are a problem, but your client may not. To win the project, then, you often need to educate your client on the value of editing in terms of how it helps them reach their goal.

That's one reason it's so important to identify who your clients are—so you can identify their goals and talk with them about those goals, showing your understanding. When you identify those goals in your brand story, the reader can see that you understand them, which starts to build the trust it will take to hire you.

Because your story needs to be memorable, it also has to be simple. Branding guru Kate Manasian notes that if you throw a handful of sugar cubes to someone, they won't be able to catch all of them, but if you throw one, they can catch it. That's what you want to do in your brand story: find that one sugar cube about your brand that your audience can catch. As your audience spends more time with your brand, they'll get deeper into your brand story. That is, they'll learn more about the different services your company offers and how they could benefit from those services. In the beginning, RTE's simple story was that I offered organizations customizable editing on short projects with a quick deadline. With my expansion into an agency, the simple story has shifted somewhat: we offer organizations scalable, specialized editing teams.

Below, we'll look at how to find that story and define your business brand. When you're ready to start work on your own brand, keep these points in mind:

+ *Let go of all constraints when you brainstorm.* Talk to colleagues or friends. Be creative! The only way to get to that simple story is to embrace any complexity or vagueness first.
+ *Look for patterns, relationships, and links within the complexity.* Find the story within the brainstorming.
+ *Order those patterns, relationships, and links.* Put the most important item up top, the less important ones below, stacking them like a pyramid. You're looking for the top of the pyramid, that one sugar cube you can throw.
+ *Create a context for that simple story.* Find a stable center that the changeable elements can move around—a theme with lots of chapters or a bright thread that runs through all your marketing.

+ *Think about your client's experience.* What story does it tell?
  The closer you get to the client experience, the richer the stories
  are. They're more relevant and filled with more emotion.

DEFINE WHO YOU ARE

Let's start with you and the business you're defining. Answer the
following questions. (I've used RTE for example answers.)

+ What levels of editing do you do?
  Developmental editing, stylistic editing, copyediting,
  proofreading.
+ Will you offer other services? If so, what?
  Fact-checking, project management, copywriting, training for
  professionals who write.
+ What subjects, genres, or industries do you work in?
  Business, education, government, local history.
+ What types of media do you work in?
  Articles and blog posts, reports, marketing materials, training
  materials, newsletters, websites, etc.
+ What qualities define your professional work style? Are you a
  fast editor? A nitpicky editor?
  High-quality editing, team approach, supportive.
+ What qualities define your experience? While being a new
  editor might not be a selling point, if you're a science editor, for
  example, having deep experience in science would inform your
  editing.
  Experienced editors, editor trainer, deep experience in business
  and marketing topics.
+ What's your approach to language? Are you a prescriptivist or
  descriptivist? Do you prefer working in a formal register? Do
  you like to play with language?
  We understand that language is a living, changing thing and
  that it bends to meet the needs of the message. We also respect
  how words can affect people, focusing on conscious language
  within our editing.

+ What else defines the kind of editor you are and what you have to offer?
Flexibility. We work with you to define the right editing level, the correct approach to the manuscript, and the best team makeup, and we offer several pricing options.

Your answers may change as your business develops and you evolve as an editor. That's OK. You can always answer the questions again and update or redefine your brand. When I launched my business, my answers and the simple story they created were different. Then, I focused almost solely on marketing copy. My description went like this:

> I'm a seasoned copyeditor, with years of experience in marketing-related copy. I have done both down-and-dirty, we-publish-in-five-minutes copyediting and nitpicky, make-it-perfect copyediting. I've spent the last decade editing in an online environment; the web is my preferred medium. Being a copyeditor means being at least something of a prescriptivist, but I tend to practice more descriptivism than many other copyeditors I know.

Because you are your brand, another part of your branding can include something memorable about you as an individual. Maybe you're someone who likes to dye your hair an unusual color, as medical and STEM editor Heather Saunders does. Heather is known for her orange hair and she wears it well. It's so much a part of her personality that orange is one of her brand colors at Just the Write Type. It's a great, fun way to be remembered. Is there something you're passionate about that you can share in your branding? Maybe it's brightly colored scarves or bow ties. Maybe you're a tea aficionado or you geek out over fountain pens. Building a little of your personality into your brand can help you stand out.

DEFINE WHO YOUR CLIENTS ARE

Now let's look at your business from the client side. Again, I'll offer my answers for one client type as a model.

+ Is your ideal client a person or an organization? If an organization, what type and how big is it?
  A small to midsize business or department (often communications or marketing) within a larger company.
+ What industry does your client work or write in?
  Can vary. Current industries include enterprise software, nonprofit, education, and PR.
+ What is your client's niche or specialty?
  Can vary. Current niches include marketing and client education.
+ What media does your client publish in?
  Online media, including articles/blogs, newsletters, and reports.
+ What problem is your client trying to solve with their manuscript?
  Presenting themselves as content experts.
+ What wakes your client up at 3 a.m.?
  With all the obstacles we've already faced with the project, we're behind. How are we going to publish on time?
+ What are some other defining features of your client? Consider their role, environment, and specific challenges.
  This client is a project or department lead charged with managing a publishing process as part of a project. They don't have a large staff and need to outsource some of the publishing tasks. They may not be sure how to manage the publishing process.

Did you notice that some of my answers weren't precise? The industries this client type works in can vary because what unifies the clients is that they're doing communications or marketing. Even so, we work within a small list of industries that reflects the subjects we edit in. Run through these questions for each client type you're looking for. You might even name each client type to help you keep them separate in your head.

DEFINE YOUR UNIQUE SELLING PROPOSITION

The last set of questions you'll answer will help you define your **unique selling proposition (USP)**. Your USP is that thing about your business that makes it unique—and uniquely qualified to solve your client's problem. In addition to the business having a goal for the project, your main contact for the client has their own business goal. A journal's managing editor wants to publish on time and on budget. A scientist writing an article for that journal wants the journal to accept their article. But the client and your contact face obstacles to reaching their goals. It might be too many errors getting printed, keeping the schedule on track, or following the publication's style guide precisely.

What do you do that helps your clients overcome their obstacles and reach their goals? It could be having expertise in your client's topic or genre. It could mean diligently meeting your editing deadlines. Or it could mean being an expert in applying the publication's style guide. Obviously, you're not the only editor who has that expertise or meets deadlines or anything else. But your USP is something you are good at that will help solve your client's problem. Highlighting it in your brand story helps the prospect identify you as the solution to their problem.

+ What is an aspect of your client's problem that you are particularly skilled or positioned to solve?
  Small to midsize businesses want to do more marketing but don't have the staff or expertise to do it well. Right Touch Editing provides a team to help them reach their goals.
+ What about you do you want to resonate with clients?
  RTE has editors ready to edit whenever copy is (finally!) ready for editing, helping you meet your deadlines.
+ What do you want to come to mind when your ideal client thinks of you?
  Available. Partners. Experts.
+ What attributes do you have that create and identify you?
  Flexible teams, strong communication skills, expert editors.

Now try to state how you uniquely help your clients reach their goals:

> *Right Touch Editing creates a team of subject-expert editors ideally suited to your project, available when your copy is.*

Introduce Your Story with Your Business Name

Your business name is a likely first point of contact with your business. Like your personal name, your business name is what people will remember. And like a book title, your business name can reflect what the business is: its services, its clients, even its voice. With an editing business, especially the one-person shops most freelance editors run, the name should reflect something about the editor or their editing. And like with your personal name, your business name will seem to fit the business as the business develops and people come to know it. The name will build an image in their minds based on your branding and marketing, your work, and your interactions with people.

In the beginning, though, your business name will bring to mind only whatever the name and any accompanying art and text suggest, which leaves you with a problem many new parents face: How do you choose a name that you like and that the new entity will grow into? Fortunately, you've already started to define your business and your clients. Though those things will develop over time, you can use them to help you choose a business name that works now.

Business names fall into four basic categories:

+ Eponymous
+ Fun
+ Descriptive
+ Emotional

YOU ARE YOUR BUSINESS

Eponymous business names are a good choice if you already have
a reputation or if you will be the only one who works in your company. This is a common choice among freelance editors. You can
use just your name (Louise Harnby), add a description to it (Dick
Margulis Creative Services), or play with it a little (eDitmore Editorial Services).

While it's easy to name the company after yourself, if you don't
have a reputation already, you will have to work harder in other
areas to educate your prospective clients on who you are as an
editor and what your business offers. You can build that identity,
though. Just look at Dell, McDonald's, and Walt Disney—all were
named after their founders and have developed separate identi-
ties from them.

WHEN AN APPLE ISN'T JUST AN APPLE

A second option is to choose a name that doesn't closely relate to
your business. Maybe it describes where you live, such as Northern Editorial (based in northern Scotland). It could refer to items
that bring writing and editing to mind, such as Quills and Queries
Editing. Or maybe it's just an image you like, such as Dragonfly
Editorial. I see fewer fun names for editing businesses in my network; perhaps it's because editors focus so much on clarity that we
build it into our business names. Fun names will also demand that
you put more work into your brand so that you can build recogni-
tion. But it can be done. It worked for Apple, didn't it?

WHAT MAKES YOU SPECIAL?

You can also come up with a name that describes something particular about your company or service. I started with a list of qualities
and words related to my business and winnowed them down until
I arrived at Right Touch Editing. I was envisioning how I would
customize the edit to meet the client's requirements. I wanted
clients to understand that I wouldn't edit for my preferences but
theirs. As well, I began by specializing in marketing and business

copy, which often comes with a labyrinth of guidelines, making the name even more apt. PenUltimate Editorial Services takes a similar approach to Right Touch Editing: the name reminds the client that *they* have the last word on their writing, not the editor. (It's also a play on the words *ultimate pen*, which I like.)

Some names tell clients right away what type of editing the business specializes in. Tweed Academic Editing focuses on academic editing, while Romance Refined specializes in romance novels. Choosing a descriptive name does a little of the branding work for you. The downside is if you change your business so that the description is no longer accurate, you may have more work to do to rebrand or may even want to rename your company. You could go with something closely related, the way Dunkin' Donuts became Dunkin'; keep a related idea, the way Match.com became Tinder; or do something completely different, such as Confinity becoming PayPal.

TWO TIPS ON CHOOSING YOUR BUSINESS NAME

A memorable business name helps keep your business on the tip of every potential client's tongue. As you start to put all of your research and ideas into a USP and a name, you'll have a lot of ideas. However, here are two warnings before you make a final decision:

+ Don't use someone else's trademark or brand as part of your name and brand. You might get away with using another business's key term or image, but elements have a cumulative effect. The more you co-opt, the more likely you're infringing on another's brand.
+ Even if a name isn't trademarked, don't use the same name or something too similar to someone else's. Potential clients could be easily confused and inadvertently hire the other business instead of you. Plus, the other business could take offense and make business difficult for you.

Your business name will be the anchor of your business, and

it's not easy to change names later while retaining the reputation you've built. Choosing a business name based on how you're defining your business can help you identify something that will help tell your simple story.

Make Your Story Visual

To help tell your brand story, you'll need visual elements, including a logo, fonts, a color palette, and imagery. Elements like these boost your business name, tagline, and any other text you use to tell your brand story. Individual pieces, especially your logo, can remind people about your business. Use your logo wherever you can: invoices, website, business cards, and giveaway items. Using specific fonts and colors can make anything you create look like it's part of your business. If you create a presentation deck using your fonts and colors and images that fit your imagery style, anyone who sees the deck will know it comes from you.

Think about some of the world's major brands: Amazon. Coca-Cola. Nike. Apple. Did you see their logos in your mind when you read their names? Coca-Cola is so serious about its branding that the original glass Coke bottle was designed to be recognizable even when it had been smashed into several pieces. You want this power for your company, too.

But do you need to pay someone else to create your **brand identity** for you? Maybe. If you lack strong design skills, as I do, paying someone to create a brand identity for you can be worthwhile. It should be a specific identifier of your brand and can be as simple as a logo, with suggestions for fonts and an image style that would pair well with your logo. Services such as 99designs and Fiverr are good sources of limited, inexpensive design help. Or you could work with a designer to also put together a small library of images and icons that fit your brand and even design your website.

If you're lucky enough to possess good design skills, you can do this work on your own, with a few free or inexpensive tools. Canva is excellent for creating logos, as well as materials for putting that logo on, such as your business cards. Pay for the subscription, and you'll have access to its image library as well. Adobe Spark and Adobe Illustrator are also good tools.

Remember that images found online are not free for the taking. The rights belong to the photographer. Services like Getty Images sell rights to use stock photography. Royalty-free images are relatively inexpensive and with some searching, you can find images that aren't popularly used by others, helping you create a unique identity.

Grab Your Website Domain Name

Your website is your online office: it's how people find your business online and learn more about it. While having a LinkedIn account or listings in directories can be helpful, your website is where you can really put your brand to work. People will look for you online, and having your own website gives you a place where you control your message.

The best choice for a domain name is your business name. It is memorable and extends your business branding (think how many places you'll list your web address!). Take a look at your new business name. When it's displayed as one word, is it very long? Can it be read as a different phrase, one that you might not want associated with your business? If so, you may want to use an obvious short version of your business name instead.

If your business name isn't available as a domain name, you have options. SEO expert Neil Patel recommends getting creative with your business name, such as by

+ Adding a verb to it: hireyourbusinessname.com
+ Abbreviating it: ybn.com
+ Adding an adjective to it: awesomeyourbusinessname.com
+ Adding your country to it: yourbusinessnameusa.com[1]

You can also choose a different domain extension (a.k.a. top-level domain, or TLD). While .com is still the most common, especially in the United States, .net is also popular for businesses. If you're outside of the United States, your country's extension is a good option as well. There are actually a lot of TLDs, but these are among the most trusted and most used.

Purchase your domain name from a trusted source. I say "purchase" because that's how we talk about obtaining domain names, but it's important to understand that you don't actually own URLs—you rent them, paying an annual fee to the provider. If you stop paying, your URL can be rented to someone else and you'll lose your online office. GoDaddy, Network Solutions, and Bluehost are among the most well-known domain registrars and website hosts.

Don't Forget an Email Address

Email is one of your main contact points with clients and prospects. You want your email address to be as professional as the rest of your business. Get at least one email address with your domain name (@yourbusinessname.com). Your personal name is a good choice for a user name (yourname@), because people will assume that's your email address. You can use your domain host's email software to access your email or have your email forwarded to an email client like Outlook, Mac Mail, or Gmail.

What's wrong with using that free email address you set up years ago? Whether it's fair or not, people will judge you based on your email address. An informal user name, like obsessive-teadrinker, could have people wondering whether they'll reach you. It's getting harder to get just your name as your user name in many of the free email programs, but even if you get something that looks at least somewhat legitimate, such as ebrenner rather than erinbrenner, you will be judged for your domain choice as well. You might not lose too many professionalism points with Gmail or Mac Mail, but AOL or Yahoo! could give clients pause. Show your professionalism with an email address that matches your website domain.

When you set up your email, be sure to create an email signature. A strong email signature contains not only your basic information but also branding. Use your fonts, colors, and logo, and create live links to your website. A prospective client will want to research you; providing them the research helps you put your best foot forward.

Yes, You Need a Headshot

While I know some folks are camera shy, you will want a professional headshot for your website and social media. Prospects want to know that they're working with a legitimate company, and a headshot shows them a real person is behind the business. Indie authors especially like to see headshots, since they're making a significant personal investment in your service. It's reassuring to see who they're dealing with.

Your headshot should show you as your best professional self. Dress professionally and be well groomed. Most professional headshots are head and shoulders against a neutral background. You should be clear and well lit. A professional photographer can help set up a composition that will display your brand and a little of your personality without becoming too casual.

If you have a strong reason for not using a headshot (e.g., your personal safety), think creatively about how to represent yourself. Could you create a Bitmoji or caricature that represents your professional self while hiding identifying traits? If you find it necessary to skip a personal image completely, use your logo or an icon that matches your brand in spots where you'd normally put a headshot. Don't leave the profile image holder empty. That will make your profile look half done or spammy.

Social Media Accounts

You'll want to promote your business using social media. Whether you create social media accounts separate from your personal ones depends on how you use social media. If you don't want clients to see what you post on your personal accounts, create new ones for your business using handles that match your business name if you can.

If you can't, try a creative handle that incorporates your name or brand clearly. On X (formerly Twitter), Liz Dexter is @Lyzzy-Bee_Libro, which blends her name with her business name, LibroEditing, while Adrienne Montgomerie, who runs her business under her own name, is @scieditor because one of her specialties is editing science textbooks.

You'll want to be on social media platforms where your prospective clients are talking about topics related to your work *and* where you're comfortable socializing. Your clients might talk about writing on LinkedIn, for instance, but if you don't like LinkedIn, you'll be miserable trying to use it. Explore where else your clients talk about writing and go there instead. You don't have to be on every site. In fact, it's better to focus on just one or two, especially in the beginning. The website Social Media Examiner is a great resource for understanding the different social media sites and how best to use them for marketing.

Whichever social media sites you choose, use that profile space to tell prospects more about you and your business. In your bio, share your specialties or promote your blog or places where followers can learn more about you. Adding links to sites where readers can engage with you further is a huge opportunity to hang on to this audience. Don't waste it! Show a little of your personality or use emoji to gain followers' interest.

Here are two examples:

📖 Publisher @dahliabooks
✍ Editor @theasianwriter
🎬 #HE
🐝 Project lead Middle Way Mentoring
🏃 Reads, writes, eats. Views my own etc... #Discoveries2023

Non-fiction copyeditor/proofreader. Entry-Level CIEP member. Often found walking, listening to good music, reading a good book,

or watching a good show. Always learning. Words matter. she/her—
Alicia Chantal (@FreshLookEdit@writing.exchange)

Include a link to your website and provide any other contact information the profile has space for. Use your headshot for the profile picture, and don't neglect to post a background image. A background image is a great space for your brand message. Tools like Canva will help you create something on brand and eye-catching in the right sizes for the different social media sites.

Branded Stationery and Swag

In this digital age, what do you need for business stationery? Pandemics and other world crises notwithstanding, you will likely do some in-person networking, and business cards are a good way to help people remember you or pass on your information. A friend once told me he thought of business cards as little ships he sent out on the water. He didn't know where they might travel to, but the hope was that some would come back as potential clients.

A good business card must be readable. You're working with a small space, and most of it will be used for basic contact information: your name, your business name or title, email address, phone number, and website. But you also want your branding to be prominent. The easiest way to brand your business cards is to include your logo and use your brand fonts and colors for the text. If you've come up with a tagline, you might fit that on the card too. You could also use the back of the card for a short message or image, like a QR code that leads to your website. On my last batch of business cards, I had three messages printed, each on a third of the cards:

No writing is wasted.

We finished 2,000 tasks last year. What can we finish for you?

Free ebook! *How to Find the Right Editor* bit.ly/FindYourEditor

Printing on both sides of a card does cost a little more, but there are some inexpensive online printers that do a good job. I used Moo for these cards; I like the weight and feel of the paper and the rounded corners. A batch of 200 cards cost me just $80 and will last me a few years. VistaPrint and Canva are also good options.

Beyond business cards, you likely won't need much branded stationery. A simple letterhead template in Word should meet most of your needs. You can use it for proposals, contracts, invoices, transmittal letters, and the like. By having something basic on hand, anytime you need to create a custom document for a client, you can start with your letterhead.

What about giveaway items, like pens or pads of paper? These days, you can slap your logo on just about anything. Like a business card, swag can help people remember you and create a good feeling about your business because you've given them a little something. Freelance editors who have branded items often send them as gifts to their clients or give them out when they're speaking at events.

Promoting Yourself: That's the Point!

"All of this feels like shameless bragging!" you say. A lot of editors feel this way. Even when we don't, we can sometimes need encouraging to put ourselves in the spotlight. I think this is because editing is such a behind-the-scenes task. Our writers are the ones getting all the credit; our work is at its best when it's invisible. As professional editors, we understand this, so it seems a little odd to not just be visible but to actively promote ourselves.

But you've also got to find clients. It's not enough to say "This is who I am" if you want to gain a bigger audience or win new clients. People will simply walk away. Invite them to get to know you better and connect with you in some way. The more people get to know about you and your business, the more they'll remember you and trust you. And if they trust you, they're more likely to hire you. It's not just OK to show off a little—it's expected. Laura Poole, owner of Archer Editorial Services and Archer Editorial Training, says it best: "Your business is only open when your mouth is open. It's the opposite of Fight Club. It's like Fitbit: Never shut up about it."

In the next chapter, we'll look at how we can keep our mouths, and our businesses, continuously open.

Key Takeaways

+ Branding is a consistent, memorable story you tell about your business.
+ By branding your business, you'll help potential clients find you and decide to hire you.
+ Write a simple brand story by defining who you are, who your clients are, and what your USP is.
+ Once you have a brand sketched out, decide on a name for your business.
+ Make your brand story visual with a logo and a brand look and feel.
+ Get a domain name for your business website, preferably your business name.
+ Also get an email address with your domain name.
+ Let people see the real you with a professional headshot.
+ Create social media accounts for your new business.
+ Get business cards made and create a branded letterhead.
+ It's OK to feel a little uncomfortable promoting yourself, as long as you do it!

(2)

Working on Your Business

CHAPTER FIVE

Getting Your First Project—and the Next

First projects can be a rush. Someone wants to pay you actual money to do a task you've been dreaming about and training for. With your first paid project, your business starts to feel real, not just an idea in your head. You're doing it!

Marketing is a long game, but it's more sustainable because you're educating prospects about your service and who you are before they have a need for you. They will contact you when they have a project, and they'll be half sold on your services when they do. It will be less work to persuade them to hire you because they're already familiar with you. However, it takes time to build up a marketing strategy and see results. For that reason, marketing is a continuous task in your business. You'll adjust what you do as you go along, but you won't stop if you want your business to remain healthy.

In the meantime, you need paying work to get started. Searching job boards for those first projects while you work on your marketing is a short-term solution. Answering job ads can bring in business, but you'll work harder to win each project because prospects know nothing about you and you're competing with everyone else answering that ad. When prospects come to you, they're already interested in your business, giving you something to build on. Plus you'll only be competing with whoever else the prospect has reached out to, which is a much smaller pool of candidates.

Let's talk about how to find those first projects in a way that leaves you time not only to do the work but to market yourself as well. We'll look at how to strategize your search, what to do if you're not getting called back on your applications, and some red flags on job ads, all of which will apply to future projects, as well.

How to Apply to Freelance Job Ads

Whenever you apply for a job, you're in a race to get to the top of the pile. Give yourself every advantage by planning ahead with the following steps.

UPDATE YOUR RÉSUMÉ

Even though you're running your own business now, some clients will want to see your résumé, so make sure it's up-to-date. Your résumé is building the case that you're the right person for the project based on your skills, experience, and education. Revise your résumé to show that you're a business owner, highlighting the skills and experience you provide in your business. Jettison the objective and references sections; as a business owner, your objective is clear and references are a given. Revise past jobs and other sections to focus on editing, if applicable, and list your new business as your current employment.

You could also choose to recreate your résumé as a skills-based, or functional, résumé. Focusing on your skills is helpful if you don't have past work experience as an editor. Detail the skills you have and how you've used them in past work. Be sure to include any editor training and volunteer editing you've done, as well.

Make sure the design is current and reflects your brand, and include your new business URL and email address with your contact information. While the content of your résumé is most important, you have to entice people to read it first. Résumé builders can make the work easier, or you can hire someone to revamp your résumé for you. It doesn't need to be overly designed, but it should be on brand. Save your résumé in Word, plain text, and PDF so that you can send it in the desired format quickly. You can also post it directly to your website as a web page or a download.

Your Name
555-555-5555
name@yournewbusiness.com
yournewbusiness.com

[Logo]

Experience

Editor
Your New Business   Sept. 2021–present
- Copyedit and proofread academic journals
- Copyedit and proofread academic textbooks
- Copyedit and proofread NGO reports
- Clients include *Famous Academic Journal,* Well-Known University, and Respected NGO

Senior Editor, *Journal Name*
Small University Press, Location   Oct. 2009–Sept. 2021
- Manage editorial staff and contributing writers
- Assign articles to contributing writers
- Manage editorial process and schedule
- Assisted Executive Editor with day-to-day journal operations

Copy Editor, *Another Academic Journal*
Small University Press, Location   Oct. 2000–Oct. 2009
- Copyedited and fact-checked articles and other materials for the journal
- Managed the journal's style guide
- Acted as daily contact for readers and freelancers

Professional Organizations

- ACES: The Society for Editing
- Editorial Freelancers Association

Education

- Editing certificate, University of Chicago Professional Education
- BA in English, University of Chicago

FIGURE 1. Sample résumé. Credit: Erin Brenner

WRITE COVER LETTER TEMPLATES

You may need a **cover letter** when you apply for a project as well. A template you can quickly adapt will help you apply faster and should follow a similar format to the letters you'd use to find employee positions. Instead of just listing your skills in the middle section, though, focus on how your business will solve the prospect's problem. Demonstrate that you understand their needs and detail how you can fulfill them. List a few similar past projects, if you have them, or invite the reader to learn more about your service and read testimonials on your website or on LinkedIn. As well, be sure to use words from the job ad itself. These days, companies use software to screen résumés and cover letters as

[Logo]

Your Name
555-555-5555
name@yournewbusiness.com
yournewbusiness.com

September 13, 2021

To the hiring manager,
I read of your need for a freelance copyeditor for *Humanities Journal* on LinkedIn's job board and believe I would be a terrific match for the position.

As an experienced academic journal editor, I understand how important both deadlines and quality are to academic journals. While working as senior editor at *Journal Name*, I managed the production schedule, ensuring that we always made deadline. As a freelancer, I put those skills to use to deliver my edits to my clients on time, communicating any issues as soon as they appear and offering solutions to keep production schedules moving along.

I'm available to discuss your needs further at your earliest convenience. You'll find my schedule at www.calendarurl.com. I look forward to hearing from you.

Kind regards,

<signature>

Your Name

FIGURE 2. Sample cover letter. Credit: Erin Brenner

a first pass on the list of applicants. This is much less a concern when you work with indie authors, but it's still a good technique. It shows that you paid attention to what the ad says.

Because you're pitching your services as a business, you can approach the closing paragraph with a slight sales tone, urging the reader to take the next step, rather than with a supplicant tone, hoping to capture someone's attention. For example, instead of "Thank you for this opportunity. I hope to hear from you soon!" you can try: "[Business Name] is ready to take care of all your editing needs. Let's schedule a call to talk more about how we can help!" Then provide directions for how to set up a meeting with you. Meeting schedulers like Calendly and cloudHQ look professional, make setting up meetings easy, and provide an extra nudge to get the prospect going.

You'll adapt your cover letter for each project you apply to, supplying the most relevant details, but this will get you started. Most cover letters are sent either as plain text in a job system or as an email, so you may not need to worry too much about design. But it's not a bad idea to create your cover letter on your letterhead in Word for the rare times when you need to send a cover letter as a separate file. If you hire someone to create your résumé, you might add writing a cover letter template or two as well.

CHOOSE YOUR JOB BOARDS

The next step in creating an efficient job search is to choose the job boards that will give you the best listings. Especially on the bigger boards, you'll find a lot of overlap, so you don't need to regularly search them all. Refine your searches, playing with search terms and filters, until you get the results you need. Search efficiently: if a site doesn't produce good results, stop using it.

Sites like Indeed, ZipRecruiter, and LinkedIn have thousands of job postings, most of which are employee positions, so don't be surprised if you don't find a lot of matches. Broaden the geography to at least country-wide or select "remote" if it's available. It's incredibly rare for freelancers to work at a client's office—and that can be a signal that the opportunity is actually an employee position misidentified as freelance. Steer clear of these types of opportunities. Once you refine your search, save it and have results sent to you, if that's offered. Completely fill out any profile information so recruiters know what you're looking for, and upload your résumé and other documents to make applying faster.

You're more likely to find appropriate projects on job boards with a narrower focus. Many professional editing organizations have job boards, including ACES, Editors Canada, EFA, and Accidental Boston, and they often have companion directories you can add yourself to. When reviewing job boards, consider the type of projects listed, the number of postings the board usually has, and the competition for those projects. When I started freelancing, I joined EFA for the job board, directory, and email discussion list, the only benefits available at the time to folks outside of New York City. After a while, I realized that the type of work I was looking for could rarely be found on EFA's job board. I had looked at the listings devotedly for a couple of years and had applied to only two or three. Since the job board and directory weren't working for me, that left only the discussion list as a benefit, so I stopped being a member. It just wasn't worth the cost for me. These are the kinds of decisions you'll need to make with regard to memberships.[1] The downside to these types of job boards is that they're much less likely to allow you to save your searches and send results to you. You'll need to make note of your search criteria and check the boards regularly.

Related to professional editing organizations are editor discussion groups. Opportunities can be posted by fellow editors or prospective clients. Facebook group EAE Ad Space (part of the Editors' Association of Earth) is a private group[2] that allows people to post editing-related ads and is a good place to check frequently. There are a lot of editor groups on Facebook and, aside from Ad Space, most are conversational with occasional job listings. Take a look around to see if the group is a good fit for you. These groups are worth keeping an eye on (especially Ad Space, which is the busiest), but this, too, will likely be a manual search. The upside is that if you're a regular member of the community and a colleague who knows you posts the ad, you may get a referral for the project.

Last are freelance marketplaces. Rates on bidding sites, like Freelancer and Upwork, can be low because you're competing with other freelancers on price. With Fiverr, while the emphasis is on affordability, you are posting your services, and potential clients are contacting you. All marketplaces will charge you a fee for posting your profile, for each project you take on, or for both. And if the site promotes the idea that it offers high-quality work for an affordable price, be prepared for prospects who are looking for the lowest cost. As well, prospects who use freelancer marketplaces generally don't know as much about hiring freelancers or even about the editing they need, which is why they seek out a marketplace to begin with. So while there might be a lot of opportunities, you may spend more time educating people on what editing is and how much it really costs. Overall, your ability to make a decent fee with these sites has some significant obstacles to overcome.

SEARCHING AND APPLYING

Now comes the "fun" part: reviewing the job ads. Remember, this is a race to the top of the application pile. You might be the ideal candidate for a job, but if you're applicant 405, chances are that no one will ever review your résumé. It's an emotional loop: you'll get excited over all the opportunities, put in the effort to apply to them, wait for responses, and become disappointed when nothing pans out.

Automating your search as much as possible at least cuts down on the time you spend on searching. One of my favorite strategies for finding jobs quickly is to keep all of my search results in one easy-to-scan place. Create a personal job ad dashboard by saving your job searches as RSS feeds and directing the feeds to an RSS feed reader, like Feedly. The feed reader will allow you to scan several job board feeds at once instead of scanning individual boards or opening dozens of emails.

You'll have to visit those sites that don't allow you to have results sent to you. How often you visit will depend on how often new listings are posted and how long it takes for a posting to be closed to any more applicants. Busier boards may mean checking once a day; with slower boards you might be able to check once a week. Your goal is to spend as little time searching and applying as possible. Schedule the time so that you don't forget, and search and apply only as often as you have to. Spend the rest of your time actually editing and otherwise building your business.

WHAT TO DO AFTER YOU APPLY

Track the ads you've responded to so you can follow up later. Be sure to include the contact's email address or other contact point so you don't have to hunt for it. If an ad says not to follow up, however, don't. As you'll see below, following directions is key to winning a project. Wait about a week before following up and adhere to these best practices:

+ *Remain professional.* Remember that you're still trying to impress.
+ *Keep it short.* Everyone is busy, and finding the right editor can be overwhelming. Respect their time.
+ *Briefly restate your interest.* Remind them why you're the perfect choice.

WHAT NOT TO DO BEFORE AND AFTER YOU APPLY

Hiring contractors has given me a view of the freelancer experience from the other side. Candidates have done a few things that made the hiring process more difficult for me and, thus, reduced their chances of being hired. Here are a few of my pet peeves:

+ *The candidate doesn't follow the directions.* A large part of editing is following all directions. If you can't follow directions now, how well will you follow them for an edit? Those who don't follow the directions in the ad are the first candidates eliminated.
+ *The candidate doesn't have the right qualifications.* As long as the job poster understands the necessary qualifications for the project, candidates who don't have the right qualifications are wasting everyone's time.
+ *The candidate doesn't address the client's needs.* The client only knows what you tell them. You might be the best person for the project, but if that's not in the initial communication with the client, don't expect to hear back from them.
+ *The candidate follows up with indignation when they don't hear back.* While it's fine to follow up, no one owes you a response to your application. If you act as though someone does, expect silence.
+ *The candidate says, "I don't exactly fit but I figured I'd give it a shot."* This is probably my biggest peeve. While I understand the

sentiment, if you're asking me to imagine how you might be a good fit, you're already asking me to do your job. No thanks.

When You're Not Winning the Projects

You won't book every prospective project that crosses your desk. But if you're not booking any, you need to address that. Where are you losing prospects? This can be difficult to determine, and many times you can only guess. Even an educated guess, though, gives you an idea of how to adjust your approach for the next time.

Let's say you're not getting any response from your applications. Perform a basic "Is it plugged in? Is it turned on?" check: Did you send the application to the right place, did you follow all the directions, and do you have the required skills? Does your résumé or cover letter have a big typo in it? Without talking to the prospect, you can't truly find out why they chose someone else. Checking the basics, though, ensures you catch any little errors you're making.

What if you have a brief email exchange or a short meeting with a prospect and you don't win the project? Review those conversations to see if there were any hints as to why you weren't chosen. Did the client seem unsure about how you might help them? Did they seem uncomfortable with your fees or scheduling? Did you just not connect with them? You won't work well with everyone out there; sometimes you just don't click with a prospect. That's OK. Being able to identify personalities or working styles that you don't mesh with can help you identify those you do mesh with.

You can ask why you weren't chosen, though you won't always get an answer. Keep your tone professional and avoid sounding bitter or upset. One way to do this is to ask what made them choose the editor they did:

Dear [Prospect],

I enjoyed chatting with you a couple weeks ago about your upcoming project. Although I'm sorry not to have been chosen to edit your manuscript, I'm glad to hear that you've found someone great to work with.

 If you have a moment, would you mind sharing what you like about the editor you chose? That would help me improve my own offerings.

 Thank you again for your consideration. Good luck with your project!

Not everyone will take the time to respond, but if you don't ask, you'll never get a response.

 Let's say you keep getting as far as taking an editing test but you're not booking the work. Try to get some feedback on how you're doing on the tests or why they chose another candidate. You won't always get a response, but it's worth asking. If you do get a response, use the feedback to improve your skills. Ask if you can take the test again later; some publishers will let you retest after a specified time.

When a Job Ad Isn't Really a Job Ad

Q: What do you call a job that doesn't pay you?
A: Volunteerism.

I saw a job posting where the prospect announced that she and some fellow authors were starting their own publishing company and were "hiring" (her word) for all positions. She went on to say they weren't hiring for pay. The posting stated that she knew it was hard to work for free, but, golly, these nice authors want to help other authors publish their books. What bothered me most about the ad was that the author knew that asking people to work without pay wasn't right, but she neither proved why this situation should be an exception nor offered something of equal value in exchange—just a weak promise that someday everyone would be paid for future work. That's not a business plan. These authors are passionate about their dreams and are energetic about making them a reality. Good for them. But while they recognize their own need to earn money, they are blind to anyone else's need to do so.

You and I don't work out of the goodness of our hearts. Few people do. We work to earn money—money that puts a roof over our heads, food on our tables, and clothes on our backs. Asking someone to work for free in order to put money in your own pocket recognizes your needs but no one else's.

Calling the "job" an unpaid internship isn't any better. In the United States and Canada, at least, there are laws about internships. Interns who aren't paid must get something immediately valuable instead. Often the intern gets course credit at their college or university, and in all cases they get training. If you're looking at an intern position, ask a few questions first:

+ Will you get the training you're seeking?
+ Who will review your work? Are they qualified to do so?
+ Can you afford to work for free?

Working for future sales is done in some industries, but not usually in publishing. That's because selling a published piece is hard and may never actually be profitable. Skip the ads that are offering to pay you in royalties. Working for exposure is also done in some industries, but again not usually in publishing. Editors are often anonymous, and the reach an author has with other authors is limited.

Working in kind might be beneficial to you, especially as you get started in your business. You could edit someone's copy in exchange for them creating a logo for you, writing some website copy, or even just editing copy you wrote. I often encourage editors to swap services with other editors. It's so easy to miss errors in our own writing, even when we're skilled editors.

The Freelancers Union reminds people that "freelance isn't free." It's really a basic concept: we work because we need money to pay for our needs. If a client can't pay in cash and they're not offering anything else you value, take a pass on the "opportunity." Your time will be better spent talking with prospects who can pay you.

Key Takeaways

+ Searching job ads can bring in your first few clients while you get your marketing up and running.
+ Setting up a search strategy will help you spend less time searching and more time working.
+ Start by revising your résumé and creating a cover letter template that highlights your new business and your editing skills.
+ Research the opportunities on various job boards, and use the ones that offer you the most opportunities.
+ Set up profiles, save your job searches, and have the searches sent to you whenever you can. Automate the search as much as possible.
+ Set aside a regular time each week to review ads and apply for projects.
+ Wait about a week before you follow up, and do so only if the ad doesn't prohibit it.
+ Follow the directions in the ad, and be sure you're qualified for the project before applying.
+ When you're consistently not winning the work and you've followed all the directions, try to sleuth out why they chose someone else. Ask directly (remaining professional and positive) when you have the opportunity.
+ Read ads carefully, watching for red flags that a project is not what it seems. If it's not a good opportunity for you, don't respond to it. Work on your business instead.

CHAPTER SIX

What Is Marketing, Anyway?

Why is it better to do all the work of marketing rather than just applying for projects? Besides the fact that most clients aren't placing ads for their projects, marketing is simply going to produce better results over time.

When you respond to an ad, you're directly competing with everyone else who responds. What separates you from the other candidates? Unlike a permanent position, for which you can expect to be interviewed at least a couple of times, with freelancing the client may choose an editor based on just the application, a brief web search, and a quick email or call with a candidate or two. Meanwhile, you're tracking all the ads you're responding to, trying to determine which you should follow up on.

Maybe you spend extra time putting together a persuasive cover letter, and you have an extended email exchange with your prospect. Perhaps you have a call with them, making the case that you're the best person for the project. How much of your income will that project produce? At best it will be a few months and then you have to start looking again. That's a lot of work for very little return—*if* you win the project.

With marketing, you're spending your time making the case over and over, in many different ways, why you're the right person for someone's project. Even when you *do* answer an ad, you've created a brand presence through your website and online activities that boosts your argument. All this work isn't for just one client but for every client and every other person who will spread your message and lead clients your way. You're no longer making the effort for an audience of one, one at a time, but for an audience of hundreds, maybe even thousands, all at once, all the time. Your marketing efforts will work synergistically, each one building on another, creating a stronger, longer-lasting picture of your business than any one effort can do.

In this chapter, we'll look at some basic marketing principles. Understanding how marketing works will help you choose which marketing actions, or **tactics**, would work best for you. We'll look at the tactics themselves in the next chapter.

"I Get Enough Work without Marketing"

I know some successful editors who say they don't market, but I think they're wrong. It's not that they don't market—it's that they don't consider what they do to win clients to be marketing. If you're building strong relationships with a few key people at several publishing houses, university presses, and packagers, for example, you're not just being a good freelancer—you're marketing your business.

Beyond doing good work and reliably hitting your deadlines, perhaps you share what medical editor Katharine O'Moore-Klopf terms *personable information* with your project manager in your email exchanges: where you're going on vacation or that funny thing your child or pet did. You're not sharing truly personal information, like all the details of your vacation or how your child or pet nearly deleted the entire client file. You're sharing positive information you don't mind being public that gives the recipient a little insight into your personality and interests. You might build that relationship by helping your client out when they're in a jam, doing the occasional rush job or recommending other freelancers to them. You could send a holiday card or inexpensive gift in thanks for the work they send you.

You might call all of that having a good working relationship or being nice or professional, and those things are true. But those actions are also called **relationship marketing**. Because perhaps your project manager recommends you to another project manager in another division of their company or to a packager they're friendly with. They do it because they like your work and you. They trust you, and they want their colleague to benefit from your work.

That's the whole idea of marketing: building trust about the thing you're marketing so that a prospect will purchase what you're selling. And, frankly, you don't build trust by doing a poor job, being unreliable, or not being personable. You're not tricking anyone with false promises. You're not selling something your prospect doesn't need. You're doing your job well and genuinely connecting with your clients.

If you're someone who really dreads networking, particularly in person, relationship marketing can work well for you, especially if your clients already network with each other. Encouraging your clients to refer you to others and asking for testimonials are also part of relationship marketing and can help grow your business.

Many of us, though, don't work with a well-defined, closely networked client base. We work with a variety of client types who won't necessarily know each other. We'll still want to do relationship marketing with our current clients, both to keep them and to encourage those referrals, but we'll need to do more than that.

Marketing Explained

Marketing's goal is to build awareness and trust with an **audience**. Who is your audience? Clearly, it's your prospects and clients, those people you most want to build trust with and get your brand message out to. But it also includes other editors, those you can learn from and those who want to learn from you. It includes experts in the fields or industries you edit in as well as in the editing world; not only can you learn from them, but prospects will see that you are a respected editor. And it includes anyone who is interested in what you have to say, even if they would never have a reason to hire you. Anyone in your audience is a potential lead to work because if they like and trust you, they can recommend you to someone who needs an editor.

Marketing isn't shouting about your services through a megaphone, however. It's getting to know your audience and helping them get to know you. It's sharing something of yourself and your business and giving something away for free in exchange for your audience's attention and interest. It's about sending out those little boats on the ocean, hoping they make landfall in a fruitful place.

All this is done in terms of your client's need and a solution to that need, with your service either directly or indirectly positioned as that solution. Most freelance editors market themselves with their websites and social media accounts. Having a website is nonnegotiable, and being active on at least one social media site is not far from that. Clients will research you; ensure that what they find best represents you. On your website you control the message, while in your social media posts you can give your audience a sense of your personality and what it might be like to work with you. As we'll see in the next chapter, though, you can also market yourself through email, print brochures, networking, interviews, speaking engagements, and more.

While we'll talk about sales later in the book, it's important to recognize here that marketing is distinct from sales. Both aim to persuade your audience, speak to your audience's needs and emotions, and rely heavily on knowing who the audience is and what their needs are. But with sales, your job is to get prospects to become clients, while with marketing, your job is to create a relationship with your audience and build trust.

People Don't Buy Products and Services; They Buy Solutions

While many of us buy computers, we don't all buy them for the same purpose. When you buy a laptop for gaming, for example, you want a display with a high resolution and high refresh rate so you can see all the details. You want a fast CPU and high random read/write speeds because games are fast action and need power to run. If you're buying a laptop for work, you still want a fast CPU, but you might not care as much about having a high resolution. If you're buying a laptop for your child, you're likely to be more interested in durability and portability. The laptop's purpose changes the features you need—the solution changes according to the problem you're solving.

What is your prospective client's problem, and what's your solution to it? Your marketing copy will talk to clients in terms of those things.

Closely related to this is the fact that people don't buy features; they buy benefits. Probably none of us use all the features in Microsoft Word. We don't need to. But editors use Word instead of Google Docs or OpenOffice because some features, such as macros and Track Changes, make our work easier. We use it because it's what our clients use, and the process is smoother when everyone uses the same software. We choose Word because of the benefits we get from it. How does your service benefit your client?

Not Everyone Will Buy Your Product or Service

Everyone needs to eat, but we don't all need to eat the exact same foods. If I'm a yam seller and you hate yams, I'm never going to make a sale to you. I'd be wasting my time marketing yams to you. My time is better spent marketing to people who like yams or who have never tried them but might be willing to.

Not everyone will purchase your editing services. That's OK. If they did, you couldn't do all the work. Once you've identified your ideal client, your main job is to connect with them and those who could connect you with them, and then build a relationship. You don't need to market to everyone, and in fact if you do, your message will either be so broad that it won't persuade anyone or so narrow that while it will reach a lot of people, they will ignore it or conclude you don't know how to run a business. The former is a waste of your time, and the latter can hurt your brand.

But, remember, your audience also includes people who are interested in what you have to say, even if they wouldn't hire you. Your goal with marketing is to become a trusted expert who gives as much as they take. People will get to know who you are and what you do; they'll come to like you and trust you; and when the time is right, some of them will recommend you or hire you.

Attention, Interest, Desire, and Action

Marketers and salespeople spend a lot of time trying to figure out how people decide to purchase something. Research shows that 95 percent of our purchasing decisions are made with our subconscious, writes Michael Harris in *Harvard Business Review*.[1] Our subconscious mind can process millions of pieces of data. It uses emotion to communicate decisions to our conscious mind, which then attaches logical reasons to our decisions.

Research also shows that our short-term memories can hold only three to four pieces of information at a time.[2] To retain information long term, we need to move information from short-term to long-term memory. Our minds encode the information through elaboration and organization, according to John Kihlstrom, professor emeritus, Department of Psychology, University of California, Berkeley.[3] We perform elaborative rehearsals: we connect a new piece of information with something we already know, repeating it over and over.

This tells us that our prospects will make decisions largely based on emotions and will then validate them with facts and logic. By appealing to our prospects' emotions, we speak to the part of the brain that makes most decisions. By appealing to their logic, we give the conscious mind the validation it needs for those emotional decisions. We share data in small chunks, so that our prospects are more likely to retain them, at least in the short term. Finally, we repeat those facts over time, so that our prospects are more likely to retain them in the long term. How do we do all that?

Through continuous, varied marketing tactics guided by a strategy that leverages how our brains work.

One popular way to think about this is with a **sales funnel** and attention, interest, desire, and action, or **AIDA**, the steps our prospects move through before taking a desired action (see figure 3). People who have heard of your business are at the top of the sales funnel, at *attention.* Members of your audience who regularly read your social media posts, receive your emails, and otherwise interact with your marketing tactics have moved down the funnel to *interest.*

Some people will continue to engage with your marketing, with stronger positive feelings about you and more trust, perhaps by liking or sharing your posts and following advice you share. They've moved farther down the funnel to *desire.* You can talk more directly to this group about your services in a way that shows you understand the problem and have a solution.

Finally, a smaller group will take an *action* that you've invited them to take. That action might be signing up for your emails, which will build on their interest and desire. It might be to share your social media posts, which will spread your message. It could even be to call you to talk about hiring you, moving them closer to a sale. Small actions come from small decisions. It's easy to decide to share a smart tweet; it doesn't take a lot of trust or effort. Bigger actions come from the increased trust that results from completing those smaller actions, which reinforces positive feelings about you.

Let's make this all a little more concrete. Not long ago, fellow editor Amy J. Schneider had the rare opportunity to trace a prospective client's path through the sales funnel. When a prospect emailed her, Schneider asked how they had heard about her, and the prospect was unusually aware of the path they took. First, they reported, they found her in the ACES freelancer directory. The prospect had well-developed criteria for an editor, which made it easier to choose likely candidates from a list, and Schneider seemed like a good fit. They had become *aware* of Schneider.

Directory listings aren't usually enough to persuade someone to hire you, though. The prospect then checked out her LinkedIn profile, which she does not link to her directory entry. This demonstrates the prospect's *interest* in Schneider: they wanted to know more about her and made the effort to find out. Finally, the prospect went to Schneider's website. What they read gave them a *desire* to contact Schneider. After viewing her website, they took an *action*—by emailing her.

Leading prospects to you is never about being findable in just one spot; it's about being findable in many places. Where might your prospects look for an editor like you? Connecting those places to each other, like a trail of bread crumbs, can further lead the prospect along. If your prospect wanted to learn more about you, where would you want them to go? Tell them how to get there. Often, prospects are only able to tell you the last point where they found you, but it never hurts to ask. Any hints about where they saw you and your business helps you determine which marketing tactics are working.

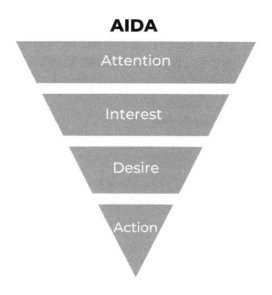

FIGURE 3. The AIDA sales funnel. Credit: Erin Brenner

Using Persuasion to Win Clients

Persuasion is the force that moves prospects down the sales funnel. We persuade our audience that the solution to their problem is editing and that we are the editor to provide that necessary service. We're addressing the subconscious, which communicates through emotions, as well as the conscious, which needs facts.

While it's true that you have to tell your audience how awesome you are, you want to do it from their perspective. You'll name their problem and validate their feelings. You'll then show them how to solve their problem. When that solution involves paying for a service, by demonstrating your understanding of their needs and your knowledge of the solution, you'll persuade them to purchase that solution from you.

Every purchase we make is about fulfilling a need or want, like that computer we talked about earlier. Don't you feel good when someone focuses completely on you, wanting to know more about you and trying to understand your problems? When we go to the doctor, we want them to listen to what is wrong and help solve it, not just throw pills at us. As business owners, when we've built trust with our audience, we can then make the case for our solution, using emotional appeals backed by facts. The following three steps will give you words and ideas to build a persuasive writing style that you can apply to all of your marketing.

1. RESEARCH YOUR CLIENTS AND THEIR NEEDS

Knowing who your client is and what they need from you is the basis of all marketing and sales. Think of how you dismiss an ad that tries to sell you something but doesn't quite get your needs. How frustrating it is to need something and not easily find the solution! We don't want our audience to be frustrated. We want them to think, "Yes, that's exactly what I've been struggling with! This person *gets* me." One way to apply persuasion to your marketing is to talk about the goal of your client's project, obstacles to that goal, and a way to remove those obstacles. For example, one

of my specialties is editing business books for professionals who
want to self-publish and then use their book to market themselves
or their companies. A web page on my site devoted to this client
type starts with the following:

> Writing a book about your business expertise is a great way to
> demonstrate your skills, grow your audience, and increase interest
> in your brand.
>
> As you push through your writing, though, it's easy to lose your
> path and get lost among all the words.
>
> Fortunately, Right Touch Editing has a map and compass—and
> we're here to share them with you.

Talk about what wakes your client up in the middle of the night
in a cold sweat. Answer those questions that prospects and clients
repeatedly ask: *How do you decide what kind of editing something
needs? Can you also make sure the extended metaphor works? How
do I review tracked changes?*

Put yourself in your client's place. Don't see your service; see
the need they have that the service resolves. What kind of pain
does that need create for them? Are they stressing out because
there have been delays and now their deadline is threatened?
What kind of obstacles do they have? Do they need to get approvals from several department heads before they can publish their
report? What emotions do you hear from them? Are they overwhelmed? Afraid? The goal is to be able to show empathy for your
client's problem within your marketing. Empathy builds trust,
and trust leads to persuasion.

If you're not sure of the answers, consider interviewing current
or past clients about their experience. Ask specific questions, like
"What was your biggest concern for this project?" Don't forget to
thank them afterward, perhaps with a small token, like a gift card
to their favorite coffee shop.

2. SHARE YOUR MESSAGE WITH FREE SAMPLES

Next, think about the types of messages you'll share. Remember, solving a smaller need builds the trust necessary for prospects to be persuaded that you can solve their bigger need. What are some smaller needs we can fulfill for our audience, a sort of free sample of our skills and knowledge?

+ *Answer your audience's questions.* How do I choose an editor to hire? How do I find a literary agent? What's a dangling participle and why should I avoid it?
+ *Offer tools to complete a job.* For example, Adrienne Montgomerie offers a calculator on her site for prospects to estimate editing costs.[4]
+ *Teach them something they want to learn.* Articles, short videos, and even social media posts can teach your audience something about writing, publishing, editing, and other related topics.
+ *Give something for nothing.* One of the most popular pages on my site is an article that reviews which style guides capitalize *black* and *white* when they're used as race terms.[5] What can you give away that your audience will find valuable and that relates to your service?

3. BUILD YOUR MARKETING VOCABULARY

Finally, you'll create a list of words that will lead to a specific response within your audience. You might think of them as your magic words, the way we sometimes teach children that using words of good manners, like *please* and *thank you*, are magic words. These magic words get your audience's attention and trigger action. Indeed, the first batch of words to put in your marketing vocabulary are those related to basic manners. The occasional *please*, *thank you*, *you're welcome*, and similar phrases show consideration for our audience.

Next, add your business-related words: your business name and brand words, the topics or genres you edit, industries you work in, types of editing you do, and so on. Let's say you're a medical editor who focuses mostly on editing journal articles and you have certification from the Board of Editors in the Life Sciences (BELS). You might include words like *medical, medicine, certification, journals, article editing, BELS, trained,* and *experienced.*

To gather some of the words most important to your business, review your client research: What words does your client use for their need? How do they describe things? What words do they put into a search engine? Dig through your branding work and the outlines of your business. What comes up a lot or is significant to what you do? *Mysteries*? *Fast*? *Supportive*? Harvest words that will have meaning for your clients.

You'll also want to include some words that are a fairly universal trigger for audiences. Some get attention, like *free* and *easy.* Some will build interest, like *premium* and *authentic*, while others will build trust, like *you* (speaking directly to your audience) and *because.* And we don't want to miss the ones that create urgency, like *now* and *last chance.* (You'll find resources for magic marketing words in Resources.)

You'll also want vocabulary words you can use in your **calls to action (CTA)**. A CTA is a statement that tells your audience what to do next. "Read more . . ." at the end of an article teaser is a CTA. "Sign up today!" on a tweet about your new email newsletter is a CTA. Your CTAs should be specific and direct. Choose standard wording whenever possible so your audience is clear about what they should do next. *Buy, sign up, subscribe, follow me, join,* and even the humble *get* are all well-understood terms for things we want our audiences to do. (Find more words and some examples of how to use them in Resources.)

This vocabulary will serve you for any marketing tactic that uses words, whether written or spoken. You'll find that some of your words will be useful in almost every message; that's a good thing for making your brand and marketing recognizable and memorable. Some of your words will be reserved for specific tactics or audience **segments** or goals. That's OK, too. It will help messages grab people's attention and stand out. Together, they'll take your marketing further and help you become more successful.

As with adjectives or adverbs, with your magic words a little goes a long way. Use a light touch when adding your vocabulary to your messages, especially those universal magic words. We've all seen *free* overused in an email or ad and decided the offer was too good to be true. When you review your copy, edit for overused words.

Marketing Is a Continual Process

When Laura Poole and I co-owned Copyediting,[6] we each continued to run our own businesses as well. I took on less work than before so I had time for the Copyediting work, and as a result I did less marketing than before. It worked well for a time, but then we sold Copyediting and I was working at RTE full-time again. Because I had done less marketing for the previous few years, I didn't have as much work as I wanted right away. I had to restart a lot of my marketing tactics, and I probably spent more time marketing than I did editing that first year.

Because marketing takes time to work, you can't stop as long as you're in business. You can ease up, but you'll need to find the right amount to keep enough business coming in. Experiment with how much marketing you need to do. If you have a big shift like I did, prepare for it by increasing your marketing ahead of time.

The best way to keep yourself marketing is to create a strategy. You'll want to create an overall strategy for your business, which has the ultimate goal of bringing in more clients. But you'll also want to create strategies for smaller activities (**campaigns**) that will feed into your larger activity, like getting more readers for your blog, which you write to increase your audience's interest. A good marketing strategy also encourages you to measure your results. Why spend all that effort to write a blog if the result is no one reads it?

Whether you're creating an overall strategy or a campaign strategy,[7] the considerations are the same:

+ What are you marketing?
+ What is the desired result?
+ Who is the audience? For a specific campaign, it might be a subset (a segment) of your full audience.
+ What are the benefits of the thing you're marketing?
+ What's the offer? An **offer** is something of value you give in order to get someone to take the desired action. It could be a free case study in exchange for signing up to your email list.
+ How does the audience get the offer? Outlining the steps now will help you identify the tasks you need to complete to set it up.
+ What are your magic words?
+ What is your CTA?
+ What is your **main message**? Your main message contains all the necessary details: the item you're marketing, the benefits, the offer, the CTA, and so on. You might use the main message on a web page and then use pieces of it in social media, an email, an image, and so on.
+ What are your **marketing vehicles**? What marketing tactics will you use?
+ What is the schedule for messaging? For events or limited-time offers, you'll want to promote for several weeks, with messages becoming more urgent and frequent at the end.
+ What are your **key performance indicators (KPIs)**? How will you measure them? In other words, how will you know if a marketing tactic has worked?

Successful marketing takes planning and review. Writing out a strategy helps make you accountable to yourself. It forces you to think through all the steps, gather all the materials and tools you need, and review what you did to see if it worked. The big piece missing here are those tactics I've been mentioning. We'll review them in the next chapter.

Key Takeaways

+ Marketing allows you to share one main message to many people at once, repeatedly.
+ Marketing builds awareness, interest, desire, and action in your audience, moving them through the sales funnel.
+ People don't buy products; they buy solutions.
+ People aren't interested in features; they're interested in the benefits of those features.
+ Not everyone will be your client, and that's OK.
+ Developing a persuasive writing style will help you connect with your audience and move them through the sales funnel.
+ To write persuasively, you need to know who your clients are and what their needs are, plan your messaging, create a custom marketing vocabulary, and write specific CTAs.
+ As long as you're in business, you need to be marketing that business.
+ Creating a marketing strategy will help keep you marketing successfully.

CHAPTER SEVEN

Using Marketing to Bring the Work to You

After the intensity of those years running both Copyediting and RTE, I just wanted to get back to editing. I was tired of business and just burned out. I didn't want to do any marketing, but I needed to rebuild my client base to get the work flowing in. It took a few years, but by rebuilding day by day, I can now say that I've reinvigorated my marketing and grown my business past the point it had been when Laura Poole and I took over Copyediting. The lesson here is that without consistent attention to your marketing, your business can founder.

If you've now done the work outlined in the previous chapter, you've taken the first steps to writing a **marketing plan** for your business. The next step is to choose the tactics you'll use and how you'll measure results. Remember that the point of all this effort is to keep business coming to you. When your marketing doesn't work, you're wasting your time. But how will you know if it works? Prospects rarely tell you where they heard about you, even if they remember. Taking a little time each month to check some simple data can be a good start.

Goals, measurement, and analysis are tied together. Goals tell you not only what actions to take (create a website, write social media posts) but also what outcomes to look for (visits to your site, comments on your posts) and what those outcomes mean (increased awareness and interest in your business). In general, your marketing goals are to share your brand with your audience, build a relationship with them, and persuade prospective clients to contact you. Let's look at several types of tactics to try and how to measure them.

Your business is as unique as you are, and your marketing

should reflect that. What works well for one editor might not work well for you. Try a marketing tactic and see if it works. If it doesn't, drop it. If it does, improve it and keep going. The value of a plan is that it multiplies the value of each tactic by allowing them to feed each other. It helps fight impostor syndrome because you can see your progress.

Create a plan, follow it, and reward yourself for doing the hard work.

Digital Marketing: The Freelance Editor's Friend

I love digital marketing because it's accessible to pretty much everyone. Many digital marketing tactics can be done on a small scale, many of the tools are inexpensive or free, and we can do most, if not all, of the work ourselves. As an individual, I'm not going to be able to afford to do radio and TV ads, a large mailing campaign, or similar tactics big companies use. But a website, social media posts, and email? Totally within my reach. I can even create videos and podcasts with more elbow grease than money. The internet provides the solopreneur with lots of opportunities.

I use what's called a **hub-and-spoke model** to coordinate my online marketing efforts. Picture a bicycle wheel: your hub is the center of the wheel, while your spokes join the outer rim of the tire, the outer world, to the hub. You use your spokes to lead your audience to your hub, where you'll be able to have deeper conversations about your business than you can on the spokes.

Your spokes are the social media posts, emails, podcasts, videos—anything you do online where you connect with others. You learn a little about the people you're connecting with, and they learn a little about you. You build awareness and interest in what you have to offer and then invite them to visit your hub, your website. It's your main office, where people visit when they have an interest in your services. Here, you'll build on that interest to move people to want to work with you and eventually take the action of contacting you.

YOUR WEBSITE: GIVE IT GOOD BONES

There are a few basic pages every business website should have. The most obvious is your **home page**, the main entrance to your office. It could be a simple front door, a modest foyer, or a grand entrance hall. Your home page gives visitors a general overview of what they'll find on your site, shares a key message with them, offers them something special, or otherwise greets them as they arrive. People who arrive on your home page are likely to be coming from a search engine or another place where they found your main URL, and they may not yet know much about you. As you plan your home page, consider how you'll greet these visitors. Like a good introduction, you may want to plan out this page last.

You'll also want an **about page**. Here, you'll give a brief bio about your company and you. And as we talked about in the previous chapter, you'll want to address the client's point of view. Answer questions like what problems your business solves and what makes your business uniquely suited to solve that problem. You don't need to give your whole résumé here; instead, link to a page or file with your résumé for those who want more information.

A **services page** is also a must-have. Outline the services you offer, noting any packages or add-on services available. If you're going to put your prices on your website, this is a good place for them. Unless you work exclusively with clients who are very familiar with editing (such as book packagers and publishers), it's a good idea to define what you mean by the different types and levels of editing you offer. If you work with clients who are totally new to editing, you might wish to use descriptive language and illustrative examples. Avoid too many industry terms, which can leave outsiders in the cold.

Finally, you want to have a way for visitors to contact you. Ideally, contact information should be on every page, such as in the footer, but you should also have a **contact page**, because visitors will look for it. How they contact you is up to you. You can simply list your email address and phone number, if that's how you'd like to be contacted. You can eliminate a step for visitors by creating a contact form for them to fill out; the form response can then be automatically emailed to you. Or you could use a scheduling tool to let people schedule a meeting with you, perhaps with a mandatory intake form so you can determine whether to take the meeting or not.

A site that has just these basics is sometimes called a **brochure website** because it contains the information you'd find in a printed brochure. You may only need a brochure website to promote yourself, such as when you're primarily practicing relationship marketing. Let's return to editor Amy J. Schneider, who works solely with trade publishers and book packagers. Her clients don't need to be educated about what editing is and why it's important, so Schneider doesn't need pages that share that information. Clients need to know a little about Schneider: her services, her skills and knowledge, and some of her past work. A brochure site does the job well, and that's what she offers them at featherschneider .com.

When you need to do more to educate and persuade prospects, you have lots of options for the type of content you share:

+ Content that helps the client identify themselves, such as case studies, lists of past clients, and testimonials from happy clients
+ Content that explains editing in more detail and the benefits of it, like **use cases**
+ Tools that help clients do their work or use your service, such as a project cost estimator
+ Information that helps visitors improve their writing, such as writing lessons or lists of writer resources
+ Answers to questions visitors have, such as how to self-publish their book or how to find a literary agent
+ Information for other editors, such as editing tips and resources for editors, which demonstrates your level of expertise

What do your clients want to know about you? What kind of questions do prospects typically ask you? What type of content would best represent your brand? Answering these and similar questions can help you decide what would benefit prospects and clients.

If you're like me and struggle to get your sales copy started, why not experiment with ChatGPT or a similar service? Ask it to write a persuasive web page that incorporates all the details you give it. Play with the wording of your question to modify results, such as suggesting different styles of writing to try or specific ideas to emphasize. An AI tool won't produce perfect copy, but it can give you a (really) rough draft to work from.

Also consider the complexity of what you want to create because you'll likely be the one to create and maintain it. If something becomes too much of a chore, I promise you, you'll fight yourself to get it done. With so many other things to do in your business, you'll find it easy to avoid doing the things you don't like.

You can create a website with a simple design using a website builder like Wix or Squarespace. Services like these allow you to create free or low-cost websites by offering many templates and simple tools. There are limitations, such as being unable to transfer content from one template within the service to another or not being able to gather data about your site, but if you want to build your site yourself and only want a simple site, this could be a good option for you. You can also use a more robust website builder, such as WordPress or Drupal. More robust services will let you track your data, expand your search engine optimization (SEO) efforts, and even build your own website template. You'll find a lot of add-on tools to let you connect to your email marketing service, take sales on your website, and more.

Consider what you want to be able to do and what your skills are, then compare different website builders to find your best option. Depending on the desired size and complexity of your site, you may want to hire someone to create your website. Professional website designers aren't cheap, but they can help you launch a website with much less stress. You want your designer to have a basic understanding of what you do and who your clients are so that they can build a site that works for your audience. Look for designers who specialize in small businesses, especially editors and writers. I've found that asking other editors who they've worked with is one of the best ways to find a designer who understands my business. For my 2019 redesign, I went with Memphis McKay because they had designed other editors' websites that I liked and knew their way around WordPress. You can also check out sites like 99designs, Webflow, and Fiverr. Be sure that you like the designer's samples and that you know exactly what's included in their service.

Blogs, podcasts, a video series, and similar publications can be a great way to lead people to your site. They're a lot of work to set up, maintain, and promote, however. If that excites you, do it, even if you think there isn't room for you. There is. There may be an abundance of blog posts on using the singular *they*, but only one written by you, with your mix of knowledge and opinions, written with your specific clients in mind. If feeding that content beast sounds overwhelming and stressful, then pass on creating a publication. Should you have strong feelings on a particular topic, you can always create a single page for it on your site or offer to be a guest on someone else's publication.

Let's look at an example of a website that makes itself a resource for its audience. Ideas on Fire (ideasonfire.net) is an academic publishing and consulting agency run by founder and CEO Cathy Hannabach. It hosts a blog, a podcast, and a resource library. Visitors can also sign up for a weekly newsletter that includes videos, podcasts, and articles to help them with their writing and teaching challenges. Visitors may not need editorial help right away, but by regularly visiting the site for information, they are also regularly reminded of what Ideas on Fire can do for them for a fee.

Take heart: you don't have to create an elaborate website right at the start. You can build it over time, releasing new pages and sections as they're completed. A new site won't get much traffic, so you're not disappointing anyone, and you'll be able to increase traffic every time you launch and promote a new site feature. No matter what type of site you create, be sure it clearly states what you do, who you do it for, and how prospects can contact you.

As the hub of your marketing, your website's main job is to be the place where people go to find out more about you. What other goals do you have for your site? Do you want people to read a blog? Fill out a contact form? Download a PDF? Whatever your goals, you want to collect data related to it and analyze whether you're making progress toward that goal.

One of the first measures you'll look at is the number of **visits** to your site. This will be a low number for new sites, but as you promote the site, that number will rise over time. Unique **visitors** (or users) is the number of individuals who have visited your site, counted only once no matter how many times they visited. Depending on the measurement tool you're using, you may be able to find out some basic information about your visitors: their geographic location, language they use on their computer, basic demographics, and so on.

You can also look at your visitors' behavior on your site. **Page views** are the number of visits to a specific page on your site, while unique page views are the number of individuals who have visited the page, no matter how many times they visited. Knowing how long on average people spend on a page can tell you whether they're reading the page or not. **Bounce rate** measures the percentage of visits that consisted of one page and no measurable interaction with that page, while the **exit rate** measures the percentage of visits that ended with that page. In other words, if a page has a high bounce rate, visitors are coming to just that page and not taking any action on it, such as clicking a link. If that page has a high exit rate, visitors are leaving the site after looking at that page.

Tools like your website's metrics feature, Google Analytics, and

Matomo can tell you a lot about your website and how people are interacting with it. But you also have to find the right questions about the data to try to figure out what's going on. The data gives you clues to what your audience is thinking; your job is to use those clues to come to as accurate a conclusion as you can and make helpful changes on your site.

Maybe you're not getting a lot of visits to your contact page, so you add a message on every page encouraging people to contact you and include a link to the contact page. Then you want a lot of visits to those pages and clicks on those links. But don't forget that sometimes people look at a page or two during a visit and make more than one visit before they take the action you're hoping for, in this case filling out your form. So the number of visits and unique visitors will also be important.

A good place to start learning about website metrics is Avinash Kaushik's "Web Analytics 101: Definitions: Goals, Metrics, KPIs, Dimensions, Targets" and "Kill Useless Web Metrics: Apply the 'Three Layers of So What' Test."[1] You may also find that a basic course on web analytics, such as Scale Your Business with Web Analytics & Conversion on the website Udemy, is helpful.[2]

YOUR SPOKES: SOCIAL MEDIA

Can you market your business without social media? Certainly, but the work will be much, much harder. People spend a lot of time on social media, where they're open to chatting with you about shared interests and learning something from you. It's a relaxed approach to networking, one that you don't leave your house for, that you do on your schedule, and that puts you in touch with far more people than any one live event can (though events have their place). By participating on social media and being helpful in some small way, you will start to build trust with your audience.

To build that trust, though, you can't post just occasionally. You need to be a regular member of the community to help people remember and recognize you. Come up with a schedule you can reasonably maintain. Experts advise that small business owners spend 10 to 25 percent of their workweek on marketing, with social media being a portion of that. Maybe it's twenty minutes a day on a social media site when your audience is most active. Maybe it's an hour a day spent among a few sites. Or maybe you pop in and out of a Facebook group or LinkedIn a few times a day, spending a few minutes at a time. Do what works best for you. I like to schedule batches of posts that share advice or links. Then during my active social media time, I can focus on having conversations with others, either on my own posts or theirs.

Conversations are where you really engage people. Comment on others' posts, contributing your ideas to the conversation. Get to know people and let them get to know you. Be helpful. Ask questions. Become a trusted, known member of the community. Then, when someone you've come to know is able to recommend you for a project, they'll be happy to do so—and you'll have a better chance of getting that project. Just remember to do so for others, too. Social media is never a one-way street.

I talked about setting up your social media accounts in chapter 4, but once you set them up, what will you say? Here are some ideas:

+   Share an insight on something you've read.
+   Reveal a tip or trick that makes your work easier.
+   Be enthusiastic about a new project.
+   Help someone else.
+   Offer to help someone with your services.

Here are a couple examples from fellow editors:

> The thing I learned this morning while editing: there's such a thing as a kimchi fridge. And I want one (stocked, of course). #AmEditing —James Gallagher, @CastleWallsEdit

> "Myriad" can be a noun or an adjective, so you can have "myriad ideas" or "a myriad of ideas." The noun version is older, and it literally meant 10,000 or, in effect, countless. Avoid "myriad" for merely "many." #editing #writing #counting —Mark Allen

You can also participate in live chats, such as ACES's chats on X, and share your conference experience through live tweeting:

> I also had to realize how many billable hours I have in me. I can't edit nonstop for 8 hours in a day—I take breaks, I have admin work, I answer email. Factor all that in. #ACESchat —Megan Stolz Rogers, @megan_stolz

> Eye-opening graph on levels of literacy to manage daily tasks—up to 50 percent in UK struggle with day-to-day reading tasks. Strong case for plain English, easy read and other techniques to simplify text #CIEP2021 —Luke Finley, @lukefinleyedit

Social media marketing is always changing and it can be a full-time job keeping up with it. The website Social Media Examiner is a good resource, and *Search Engine Journal*'s *How to Dominate Social Media Marketing: A Complete Strategy Guide* will give you a lot of tips to get started. (You'll find more suggestions in the Resources section.)

MEASURING YOUR SOCIAL MEDIA

In general, with social media you want people to socialize with you, click on your links, and share your messages with others. How do you measure if that's happening?

Audience size seems an obvious place to start, but we can become fixated on this metric. There's no magic number of followers you need. It's more important that your audience be engaged with you. Certainly monitor audience size over time. Steady growth is a sign that you're reaching people. A sudden dip could mean that your activities aren't aligned with your audience's expectations. Monitor and adjust as needed, but don't obsess.

Instead, focus on **engagement**—that is, how people interact with your posts. **Likes** are minimum interaction; getting likes on a post is a good start. What you're really looking for are comments and **shares**. Comments are what make social media social. Having a (nonaggressive) conversation with someone helps that relationship you're nurturing. It makes your audience feel heard (because

you're listening) and helps you get to know them and their needs
in order to better meet those needs.

Followers sharing your content spread your message to people
you might not otherwise reach, increasing your audience. When
someone shares your post, they're recommending that post, and
by extension you, to their audience. Their audience trusts your follower, and some of that trust will be shared with your post. It spreads
your message. And if that follower shares your posts frequently
enough, some of their followers may become your followers, too.

Beyond these basics, you can look at how to improve your social
media activities. Ask yourself the following questions:

+   *What kind of posts perform best?* Do you get more reactions
    from short videos? More shares on posts that have writing tips?
+   *What are the best times to post?* Some tools will give you
    recommendations for when your audience is most active, but
    also look at your results to judge the best times.
+   *What hashtags perform best?* You can increase your audience
    by using hashtags related to your post's topic because you may
    reach people who don't yet follow you.

You can collect some of this data, as well as data on your audience, through the different social media platforms' free tools,
such as Meta (formerly Facebook) Business Suite, or directly
from the site itself, as with LinkedIn. Alternatively, you can use
a social media management tool. These tools let you draft and
schedule posts and interact with your audience in addition to
giving you reports. Some are free, and some paid management
tools have free options with limited features, like Hootsuite. To
get data, however, you often need to pay for the service. An annual
subscription to a tool like Hootsuite or Zoho Social can be surprisingly affordable, especially when you consider the time you'll save
managing your accounts and collecting data. Consider how many
hours of work a tool saves you compared to the hourly fee you could
be earning by editing when pricing out software subscriptions to

find the best tool for you. (You'll find more tools in Resources.)

YOUR SPOKES: EMAIL

Most of us communicate with clients through email. Why not also use it to market yourself? Your branded email signature is a passive marketing tactic that reminds people of your business. But that's just the start of what you can do with email. An email list gives you a group of people who have said they *want* to hear from you. Especially right after they sign up, they're likely to open and read your messages. You've got their attention—use this opportunity to build their interest!

Email can also feel more like a one-on-one conversation than social media does. While you may be sending to dozens or hundreds of people, they're not aware of each other. Write your content with this in mind. Speaking directly to your audience and utilizing personalization features in email software can create a more personal, intimate feeling, which over time can build trust.

As with creating a blog or other publication, you'll want to send emails regularly but not overwhelmingly so. Send irregularly, and people will forget about you and likely ignore your messages. Send too often, especially if the messages aren't very different from each other, and your audience will become overwhelmed and stop opening your emails.

As with websites, you can find a range of free and paid services to create an e-newsletter, including Mailchimp, Zoho Campaigns, and MailerLite. Most services offer a variety of templates that you can work with and make designing easy with drag-and-drop tools. Check out what different services allow you to do and whether you can connect them to your website to automatically update your mailing list with sign-ups from your website.

How often should you send? It can depend on a variety of things:

+   *The content.* Newsletters sent once a week or once a month tend to do well. Emails promoting a special offer can start off once a week and then shift to twice a week as the end date gets closer.

+ *Your audience.* An engaged audience may welcome hearing from you more often.

+ *Your time.* Maybe your audience would read weekly emails from you, but you can only manage once a month. If that's all you can manage, that's what you do.

Who should receive your messages? The short answer is whoever is interested in what you have to say. To build a list of people to send to, promote your emails and encourage people to sign up. While you could just add people to your list and force them to unsubscribe if they don't want your messages (**opt-out email**), doing so can annoy your subscribers and is frowned upon by email experts.

The better route is **opt-in email**: having people voluntarily sign up to your email. **Confirmed opt-in email**, or **double opt-in email**, is the gold standard of email. Once someone signs up to be on your list, they receive an email from you that asks them to confirm that they want to be on your list. This helps prevent emails from going to spam folders and immediately engages the subscriber with your messages.

Be sure, too, that your emails follow all applicable laws, such as CAN-SPAM (giving subscribers a way to unsubscribe), GDPR (if you're emailing to subscribers in Europe), and CCPA (if you're emailing to subscribers in California). Reputable email providers like Mailchimp can help you set up your email program and guide you on following applicable laws. (You'll find more email providers in Resources.)

What types of emails should you send? Newsletters are a mainstay of marketing emails. A good newsletter shares a few short messages, making them quick to read but offering opportunities to read more, such as a blog post on your site. Descriptive headlines and eye-catching images help draw your subscribers in. Even interested subscribers won't spend long with your newsletter (fifty-one seconds, says Nielsen Norman Group[3]), so keep it short.

Twenty lines of text or 200 words is the current recommendation.

You can also send one-off messages to your audience or a segment of your audience. Messages like current schedule openings or closings, special offers, new services, rate increases, and vacation announcements can be sent just to clients or prospects. A quick writing tip or a holiday message might be sent to your entire audience. Especially sprinkled in with a regularly sent message, these short messages can help build engagement as long as they're infrequent. And don't forget out-of-office messages sent from your regular email software. Use these not only to tell senders you're not available but as an opportunity to remind them to hire you, to find helpful information on your website, or to connect with you on social media.

MEASURING YOUR EMAIL

What is your goal with email: To educate readers? Get them to click through to your website? Sign up for an event or contact you about a special promotion?

It all starts with the **open rate**, that is, the percentage of people you sent to who opened your email. It's difficult to get any other result if recipients don't open the email itself. You'll also want to track the **click-through rate** (**CTR**) or click rate. An email's CTR is the percentage of email recipients who clicked on a link in your email. Some tools will tell you which links were clicked on, sometimes called a **click map**, as well as the total number of clicks. CTRs show interest in your message. You'll also want to keep an eye on your **unsubscribe rate** (the percentage of your audience who unsubscribed from your list). If you're experiencing a rush of unsubscribes, you should adjust your messaging.

Finally, keep a close eye on your **bounce rate**. This is different from your website's bounce rate; here, it means the percentage of emails that couldn't be delivered. A **soft bounce** is a message that's temporarily undeliverable to a specific address, such as when an email box is full. It happens, but as long as it doesn't happen to a lot of emails on your list, it's not a problem. A **hard bounce** is a message that's permanently undeliverable, such as with misspelled or fake email addresses, and is more serious. It's important to keep your email list free of email addresses you can't deliver to, so that email clients don't mark your messages as spam. Your email marketing platform should remove hard-bounced addresses from your list. If you're seeing a lot of hard bounces, review your email sign-up process. You may need to find a way to prevent fake sign-ups.

If you use an email marketing tool like Mailchimp, you'll be able to get data on your email sends. It will likely also share industry-wide data drawn from all its customers' emails, perhaps next to your own data and likely in an annual report or blog post. Knowing industry averages can help you set your own goals. For example, industry open rates hover around 20 percent. As always, while comparing your results to others' can give you an idea of where you are, your audience is unique to you. It's far better to track your results over time and see how things change. If your metrics are improving, you're doing the right things. Keep doing them! If they aren't, change something and try again.

YOUR SPOKES: DIRECTORY LISTINGS

Directory listings are a way of making you easy to find and being in the right place at the right time—when a prospect is actively looking for an editor. You'll want to do your homework first: Are your clients likely to use this directory? What other benefits will you get that make paying for membership or entry into the directory worthwhile?

Start with your research with publishing-related directories. Authors ready to hire will check out directories of editors and other publishing professionals. The major editing organizations all have member directories. Sites that provide authors with hiring or publishing advice, such as the Alliance of Independent Authors, are good choices. Such sites work to educate authors, which helps build trust with those authors, some of which can be transferred to you.

Write your directory listing specifically for the type of clients you're trying to attract, and give them several ways to contact you. List your website and LinkedIn profile so they can find out more about you. Be persuasive and remember to appeal to the client's perspective in your listing. What will set you apart from others? Clearly describe what you do, and include a headshot if given the opportunity. Review your listing annually for needed changes.

One key to all digital marketing is to know your tools. We can waste so much time when we don't know how to use our tools well. Spend time learning the basics so you can do these repeatable tasks efficiently each time. Use automation when you can. Let software do what it does best and free yourself to do higher-thinking tasks.

MEASURING DIRECTORY LISTINGS AND WORD OF MOUTH

The goal of directory listings and **word of mouth (WOM)** is to get more people familiar with your business and to contact you when they need you. The only way to know if a prospect found you on a directory listing or had your name passed along to them is to ask. As previously noted, be prepared to hear that the prospect doesn't know where they heard about you. When they do, though, take note of what's working.

Physical-World Marketing

You may not have as many in-person opportunities when you live in rural areas or have a busy life that prevents you from spending a lot of time at in-person events, but wherever you are and whatever your schedule, you *can* do some marketing in the physical world. Let's look at a few tactics to round out your marketing plan.

WORD OF MOUTH: PURE GOLD

Word of mouth (WOM) is simply you telling your friends how much you like or dislike a product or service. When you tell your Facebook friends about your horrible flight, that's WOM. When you declare how much you love a book on Goodreads, that's WOM. WOM can happen in person and online, but like all marketing tactics, it takes time to work. In an interview with Editors Canada, editor and photographer James Harbeck said that the hardest thing about starting a freelance editing career was finding those first clients. "What I learned is that the best thing to do is just to make friends. The upside of this is that you will also have more friends, who will always have interesting ideas and insights and will be good for commiserating with. And sometimes they will connect you with work," he advises.[4]

To get WOM going, let people know you've started a business. Tell your family, friends, and colleagues. Announce your new business on your personal social media accounts and invite folks to connect with you on your business social media accounts if you've set up separate ones or to visit your website. When a client lets you know you've done a good job, make use of that. Ask for a testimonial for your site or a LinkedIn recommendation.

You can also write up a recommendation for a LinkedIn connection and ask for a recommendation in return. To write a helpful recommendation, start with the problem or challenge the person faced. Then describe what they did to solve the problem and the results that came from it. Be sure that the recommendation someone would write for you relates to your new freelance business. Recommendations from unrelated jobs are nice, but they don't build the case for someone to hire you as their editor.

You can also add a friendly note to your invoices and email signatures to encourage referrals. For example:

> Know someone else who needs editing help? Please share my name!

> I'm never too busy to accept new referrals. Spread the word!

> Happy with my service? Tell a friend!

To really encourage referrals, ask satisfied clients to refer you to others. Ensure that your clients understand what kind of services you provide and for what types of clients. Asking them doesn't have to be complicated, either. When a client compliments you, thank them and try responses like the following:

> Would you mind if I posted that on my website, with your name and company?

> Would you be willing to write that up as a recommendation on LinkedIn? It would mean a lot to me.

> If you know someone else I can help, please share my name!

When someone does write a testimonial or give you a referral, thank them. A handwritten note is a nice touch. If someone sends you a big client or many clients, give a gift card or other small gift to show your appreciation.

MEASURING WOM

It's notoriously hard to measure WOM. How do you know when someone is talking about you to someone else? One way is to ask prospects how they found you. If they name someone in particular and you know the person, be sure to thank them for passing your name along.

Tracking compliments and complaints made directly to you will give you a sense of what clients might say about you to others. You might even survey your clients, either as a group or individually. Not only does this give you a sense of what they might tell others, but it can provide valuable feedback on what you're doing well and what you might improve. Pro tip: Ask for permission to reuse survey takers' responses. Those compliments make great testimonials for your website.

COLD-CALLING: MAKING IT WORK FOR YOU

Cold-calling potential clients is not one of my favorite marketing activities, yet it can be a great way to win new clients. In "The Art of the Cold Call," editor Adrienne Montgomerie writes, "This is how I got my first jobs, and it's how I've broken into new markets.

Dollars to donuts, cold calls offer the single greatest return on investment out of my whole marketing toolbox."[5]

While you'll get plenty of nos, someone is bound to say yes. Says freelance writer Jake Poinier, a.k.a. Dr. Freelance, "It's much better to look at 'no' as a stepping stone than a rejection. And if you accidentally run into someone who's a jerk about it, just be glad that you don't have to work with such a nasty person!"[6]

Cold-calling doesn't mean you'll start cold, either. Identify the right potential clients. Do they use freelance editors? How do they usually hire them? Do you have the right skills and experience for them? Prepare a list of past projects that would be similar to your prospects'. Also identify the person who will do the hiring, so you can pitch directly to them. They might have titles like project manager, editorial director, assigning editor, or director of marketing. If the company website or LinkedIn doesn't turn up the right person, start with an assistant or HR to find out who to contact. Your request can be as simple as "Could you point me to the person who hires freelance editors?"

Next determine your medium. While cold-calling indicates a phone call, you could opt for an email or a letter. Keep in mind that we get so few physical letters these days, yours might stand out. Whichever method you use, respect the contact's time. For a phone call, prepare your thoughts ahead of time and practice. For emails and letters, keep these tips in mind:

+ Write a clear, enticing subject line that focuses on the prospect's problem (i.e., the need to get books edited or deadlines met).
+ Spell the contact's name correctly. Details count, and no one likes to see their name misspelled.
+ If you know someone in common, mention that person (with their permission, of course).
+ Keep it short. We're all busy. Highlight items from your résumé and items not on your résumé that make you a good fit.
+ In your email signature or letterhead template, include your

contact points and list related credentials and professional organizations you belong to.

As always, make this contact about the prospect. Put away those feelings of needing work *now, now, now.* It's OK to feel that way, but when you're engaging with a prospect, put on your business owner hat. You are a professional with something to offer the prospect. You are a language expert whose skills and knowledge can benefit the client. Keep that mindset. Now flip the text: the client has a problem. You're contacting them to help them solve that problem.

Be willing to prove yourself. This person doesn't know you, and you'll need to build trust. Taking an editing test (especially for publishers), starting with proofreading rather than editing (publishers and packagers), offering a free editing sample (up to 1,000 words), or taking a rush job are all ways to build trust.

To put it another way: Offer your clients what they need or want to make the decision to hire you. Be clear that your job is to fix their problems and make their lives easier. Let them know how working with you will be easier than working with the next editor. Figure 4 has a sample email script for you.

Since cold-calling involves contacting a lot of people, keep yourself organized. Create a spreadsheet to track your progress. List the organizations, persons you contacted, and their contact information, as well as the date of initial contact, response, any follow-up contact, and the final outcome. For calls, create a script to follow so you don't forget anything; for email and letters, create templates. Make sure you have a cover letter template and résumé ready to go upon request.

Schedule your cold-calling time. How many contacts can you handle in a day or a week? Especially if you're using the phone and you're not a phone person, you may want to do just a handful at first and give yourself prep and recovery time around those calls. Create a follow-up schedule as well. You might find that tackling follow-ups first can ease you into doing the next batch of initial

Subject line: How Can I Help You?

Dear Name,

I hope this email finds you well. I'm an avid user of Outdoor Publisher's trail guides. The details provided not only encourage me to hike more but keep me safe because of their accuracy. As a copyeditor, I know how much work it can be to ensure all those details are correct while meeting tight deadlines. (And when aren't deadlines tight?)

Your website indicates that you typically use freelance editors for your trail guides, and I would love to be considered for your roster. In addition to being a hiking enthusiast, I have several years' experience editing outdoor and adventure content, including *Favorite Hiking Magazine*, Adventure Club's monthly member newsletter, and various titles from Local Hikes Press, including *50 Hidden Hikes in Your Backyard*. Attached you'll find my full résumé, and you can learn more about me from my website, www.outdooreditor.com.

Name, even if you don't need a new freelancer now, would you be available for a brief informational call next Tuesday? I'd love to hear more about your needs and see how I could help you maintain the high quality that Outdoor Publisher is known for.

Kind regards,

Your Name

FIGURE 4. Sample cold-calling email. Credit: Erin Brenner

calls. And if you have a mutual contact who could introduce you, so much the better. It's less of a cold call and more of a warm introduction, which can make it easier for both of you to connect.

MEASURING COLD-CALLING

The goal of cold-calling is, first, to get someone interested in hiring you and, next, to actually get hired. Keep your call tracking up-to-date so you know how well you're doing. It can be disheartening to see all those nos, but since that's how cold-calling works, why not measure more than yeses, like how many interested calls turned into clients and how much your client list has increased over the course of several months or a year. Every client gained is a win; finding a way to celebrate those wins can keep you motivated.

SENDING CLIENTS CARDS AND GIFTS

Your goal in marketing, as Laura Poole, owner of Archer Editorial Service and Archer Editorial Training, likes to say, is to be "well known, well thought of, and well remembered." Cards, handwritten notes, and little gifts for current and recent past clients can help with that. Showing your gratitude for their business can create reciprocal gratitude in clients. Avoid losing that message in the rush of a season or the oddity of the gift or message. Whatever method and message you choose should make sense for your clients and your business. You can get your logo and brand on anything, but the item should connect with what you do or be something the recipient will use frequently. You'll want to consider costs and shipping requirements, as well.

Holiday cards and handwritten notes are always nice to receive, but end-of-the-year holidays can be tricky. People are busy wrapping up the year and are often away from their desks. Furthermore, you'll want to either send a general holiday greeting or know for certain which holiday your client celebrates. If you or your clients are American or Canadian, you can send something at Thanksgiving. You could also send something at the start of the year, when people are coming back to the office.

Or you could choose another holiday. Check your country's and your client's country's list of national holidays and choose an appropriate one. For example, if you work with a lot of US government agencies, you could send a card for Independence Day. Also check lists of less well-known holidays. If you work with women's organizations or your main contacts are mostly women, you might send something on International Women's Day (August 9). Additionally, you can take advantage of the language-related holidays:

+ National Grammar Day (March 4)
+ International Apostrophe Day (August 15)
+ National Punctuation Day (September 24)
+ National Dictionary Day (October 16)
+ National Novel Writing Month (NaNoWriMo, the month of November)

You can even create a custom holiday, like your business's or your client's anniversary or a client appreciation day. Remember, though, while it's fine to test things out and change things up occasionally, try to be consistent so you build that memory for your clients.

We have an advantage as editors: a lot of inexpensive swag relates directly to writing and editing, like pens and sticky notes, which can help make the connection between the item and what you do. When my self-publishing clients finish a project with me, I send them a branded notebook and pen, along with a custom notecard. It's a nice little package that can celebrate the finish of a big project. For my ongoing clients, I often send branded notepads or pens. Don't forget to toss in a few business cards, too.

Ready to spend a little more? Try items clients will use frequently, like a mug, even filling the mug with special chocolates or other treats. Katharine O'Moore-Klopf has handed out key chains with her picture on one side and a marketing message on the other. They're a big hit with her international clients.

Try to avoid items that make people wonder how they connect to your business. Over the years, my husband has brought home an astounding array of swag from security conferences, such as stress balls, Rubik's Cubes, flashlights, moldable (and staining!) putty, earbuds, and Frisbees. I couldn't tell you any of the company names five minutes after I saw the item. Everyone's trying to be different, but if I don't remember the company name, your money's been wasted.

MEASURING CARDS AND GIFTS
The only goal of sending cards and small gifts is to create goodwill. Any positive feedback from a client is a win.

NETWORKING: FINDING KINDRED SPIRITS
I feel like *networking* is a four-letter word for many freelance editors. We editors do tend to be a behind-the-scenes, introverted bunch. Go out and actually *talk* to people? No way! I'll admit that I'm a little envious of people for whom networking is natural. While I've gotten better at it over the years, it doesn't come naturally to me. Even for those events I enjoy, like editing conferences, afterward I need to replenish my energy by being alone.

Yet networking is an important part of marketing your business. You never know who you will meet and who might connect you to your next best client. More importantly, networking is about getting to know someone a bit on a personal level. When you click with someone, you start to trust them, and that trust is something you can build on. Who you know is still what gets business done.

If you're resisting the idea of networking, keep in mind that it's just one part of your marketing plan. Perhaps you'll rely more heavily on other tactics and keep networking to a minimum. You can also control what kind of networking you do. Maybe large crowds give you the willies, so you seek out small groups or one-on-one opportunities instead. Perhaps you do better on video than in person. One positive outcome of the COVID-19 pandemic is that there are more online networking opportunities. Maybe texting is your best tool, so you focus your social media efforts on conversations with individuals. The point is to balance getting to know people who could lead you to new work with honoring your needs as a human being.

Professional organizations are a good place to start. What groups do your potential clients belong to where you might fit in? Check out the members: Are they your potential clients? If you're the only editor in the group, even better; you'll be the resident authority. Participate in the group, particularly those your clients are members of. Give something. Volunteer. Let people get to know you. If they have a directory, get in it. And use it to learn more about your fellow members. Is there anyone in particular you'd like to get to know?

If you can't afford member fees, engage with the group in another way. Offer to present to the group on a topic they would appreciate. What would members like to learn from you? Your local chamber of commerce might benefit from a session on business writing or on how to choose an editor or a designer, for example. You could make this offer for conferences your clients attend, as well.

Let's say you edit novels and want to break into the self-publishing world. You might attend a writers' conference and talk about writing with other attendees. You could give a talk about the different types of editing and how to decide what kind of editing a manuscript needs, or you could hold a self-editing workshop, teaching writers a way to improve their manuscripts before handing them over to an editor.

What about getting a table or booth at the conference? You could give away your branded swag, business cards, and perhaps a printed flyer. You could create interest by having a drawing for a free thirty-minute consultation or 500-word edit. Offer a free case study you've written, which people can download when they sign up for your email list. All of this is about having an opportunity to talk to people, getting to know their needs, and sharing how you can help them. At events like these, no one is looking to buy anything just yet. It's about leads, not sales. Set your expectations accordingly.

Follow-up to networking is almost more important than the networking itself. You might have had a lot of conversations, but only a portion of them are likely to lead to a continued relationship. Of the people you spoke with at the event, who would you like to keep talking to? Connect with them after the event through social media. Reference the conversation you had and invite them to keep the conversation going. If they accept your invitation, make an effort to comment on their posts and share thoughts with them directly through private messaging. An occasional simple message like "Hey, Jane! I read this article this morning and immediately thought of you. Hope you enjoy it" can go a long way toward building a relationship with a new connection.

Make the most out of any networking events you participate in by promoting them on your social media and in your marketing emails. Invite others to join you at the event, or just share your excitement about the event itself. After the event, publicly thank the organizers or share something you learned at the event with your audience. It's a way to not only pass on good information but allow your audience to get to know you better. You're sharing a bit of your professional life with them. It may also introduce them to an event that they would benefit from attending.

MEASURING NETWORKING

The goal of networking isn't to have as many connections as possible; it's to have a network full of people who are valuable to your business in some way. They might comment and share your content, teach you valuable business or editing lessons, or introduce you to new people. As long as you're consistently building your network with valuable people, you're doing it right.

If you're not an enthusiastic networker, however, you could set goals for yourself to do the networking and reward yourself for making your goal. You could decide to attend one online networking event a month or try membership in a professional organization for a few months. Pay attention to whether you're meeting people who might help you in your business and whether you mesh well with the people you meet to determine whether an event or group works for you.

For example, the American Marketing Association has a strong chapter in my area, so I joined to see if I could meet potential clients. I attended several networking events and volunteered on the board as communications VP. Over the course of a year or so, I met a lot of interesting people and expanded my network, but ultimately I decided I wasn't meeting people who might become clients, so I left the group. Not every networking attempt works out, but each one can help you improve your networking skills. If that helps me do the networking necessary for my business, it's a win in my book.

Key Takeaways

+   Advertising pioneer John Wanamaker (1838–1922) is often quoted as having said, "Half the money I spend on advertising is wasted; the trouble is, I don't know which half." But you need to at least try to discover what works.

+ Marketing is a long-term business strategy. Create a plan with goals and ways to measure progress.
+ Digital marketing is ideally suited to freelance editors: make the most of it.
+ A hub-and-spoke strategy organizes your online activities to lead people to your website.
+ Your website is your online office for prospects to visit. Your website can be simple or complex, but it must clearly state who you are and what you do.
+ Participating in social media is like attending networking events where you get to know people and invite them to visit your office.
+ Email is a one-on-one conversation with subscribers.
+ Directory listings and WOM get the attention of people you don't yet know.
+ Cold-calling creates interest in people you don't yet know.
+ Giving clients cards and small gifts shows appreciation and enhances existing relationships.
+ In-person networking can connect you with a targeted audience.
+ To know if you're meeting your goals, measure and analyze results of your efforts regularly.
+ Some tactics are easier to measure than other. Choose tools that will help you answer the questions you have about your efforts.
+ Success takes time. Reward yourself for making a plan and working at it.

CHAPTER EIGHT
Making the Sale

While I love a lot of aspects of business, selling isn't one of them. In my head, *selling* means getting someone to do something they don't want to do or isn't right for them. Too, there's the fear of rejection—that I'll have done all this work to win this project but the prospect will decide they don't want my service. That must mean something is wrong with the service, right? That something is wrong with *me*.

I'm not alone, either. Many freelancer editors dread this part of getting work. Because selling relies on connecting with other people and many editors are introverts, editors especially can feel awkward about it. Connecting with others is hard for introverts. Frankly, though, even for the most outgoing people, selling is hard and a bit of a dark art. Yet if we don't sell, we won't have any clients. How can we get past this selling hesitancy?

Business coach Elyse Tager advises flipping your mindset from selling to inviting. "Picture an open hand and an inviting gesture, not a grabbing motion followed by a clenching, yanking movement," says Tager.[1] Let your choice of words follow that mindset. When you schedule a meeting with a prospect, frame it as an invitation: "I'd like to invite you to chat more about your project over Zoom. What time works best for you?" This approach can also help ease prospects further down that sales funnel, particularly those who have never worked with a freelancer before.

Think about this as you go through this chapter. You'll learn how to put together a sales framework that fits you and your business, with each step along the way being an opportunity to filter out ill-fitting or false prospects. How can you think about a specific tactic as an invitation to help someone achieve their goals?

And rest assured: even if you can't change how you feel about selling, you can learn to sell well enough to meet your goals.

Building Your Sales Framework

How do you know a prospect and their project are a good fit? By measuring them against your ideal client and the services you offer. You can filter out some prospects on first contact. For example, if you exclusively edit cookbooks and someone comes to you with a fiction manuscript, you know that's not a job for you. A quick note sends them on their way.

Let's say, though, that the project is to copyedit a cookbook about the latest food trend, written by a food blogger who will self-publish. That's right up your alley. You should just say yes, right? Not without some more vetting. You'll want to know whether this is a legitimate offer, whether you'll work well with the prospect, whether the manuscript is ready for editing, and more. It's really not so different from searching for employment, only you'll get to define how you accomplish each step. The key is not to spend more time than necessary. The amount of time you spend should correlate with the size of the project, but don't spend so much time vetting prospects that you can't get any work done.

As leads come in, track them somewhere. You want to always know where you are in the lead process, and having all your lead data in one place saves you the time of searching for information. A spreadsheet can be enough, especially at first, to keep you on course. But if, like me, you find yourself forgetting to follow up on leads and missing out on projects as a result, investing in a customer relationship management (CRM) tool can be a godsend. You can use CRMs to track your progress, create and send the documents discussed below, send scheduled emails to keep the process moving, and send yourself automatic reminders to follow up. (You'll find a list of freelancer-friendly CRM tools in the Resources section.)

PROJECT REQUEST FORM

Some editors start with gathering basic information through a form on their website or an email template. This can prevent time-consuming back-and-forths that come from vague requests like "I've written a book! Can you edit it?" Whether it's a required step before someone can email you or a quick response to an email, a project request form is a great way to filter out ill-fitting projects.

Some common information to ask for include the following:

+ Name and contact information
+ Title of the project
+ Brief description of the project
+ Topic or genre
+ Word count
+ Service interested in
+ Budget

As you gain experience, you'll discover other information you can ask for that will better filter out projects that aren't a good fit. At Inkbot Editing, owner and editor Molly McCowan asks prospects how many revisions the manuscript has gone through and how many point-of-view characters a fiction piece has. She also asks prospects to submit their manuscript for review before committing to the project. This gives McCowan a sense of how developed the manuscript is and whether it's a project for her company.

RESEARCH: CHECKING OUT POTENTIAL CLIENTS

The project sounds good. Is it too good? Where money is involved, there exists the potential for a scam. One of the more common scams editors see is the Frankenedit, for which the scammer contacts several freelancers about editing their manuscript, asking them to provide a sample edit. Each editor who responds is then asked to edit a specific section of the manuscript so that the scammer gets their entire manuscript edited for free via the samples. As editors, we know the results would be monstrous (pun intended), but the scammer doesn't care because they've gotten their edit for free. One benefit of being active in an editing community is being able to ask other editors about suspicious leads.

Scammers seem to hit a lot of editors at once, sometimes going down listings in a directory, so you may find warnings from fellow editors that a new scam is making the rounds.

Your next question is whether a legitimate offer will work for you and whether you can have a good relationship with the client. If you don't have enough details on the project yet, request them. Check the prospect's website and social media. For companies, you can check organizations like the Better Business Bureau and Glassdoor to see how they treat their customers and their employees. If they frequently hire freelance editors, you can ask other editors about their experience with the company, keeping in mind that what works for one editor doesn't work for all editors. You might be OK with tighter deadlines than another editor, or you might not be willing to wait sixty or ninety days for payment while a fellow editor is. Find out about others' experience, but think about it in terms of your own needs and skills.

Let's say our self-publishing cookbook author has filled out your project request form, and you want to know more about them. You check out their blog. Their articles are interesting, the recipes are well written, and there are several years' worth of posts. The comments don't reveal any big problems with recipes, and the blogger responds to reasonable criticism politely and professionally. A good start!

Next, you check out their social media. There, too, they are polite and professional, sharing information that seems accurate to you and not espousing any opinions or beliefs that would make working with them uncomfortable. You do a broader search on their name to see what the search engines dig up, and everything looks positive. They sent the manuscript with their form, and while you don't think it's ready for the copyedit they requested, you think you could help them with a line edit instead. You're ready to learn more about the project.

DISCOVERY CALLS: GATHERING INFORMATION

You could email the prospect with a list of questions that will help you get the full scope of the project. When you know the prospect personally, you're confident they're a real person and trust them to pay you, or if they've been referred to you by someone you trust, an email exchange to set up the project could be all you need.

Some prospects need more persuading, however, and sometimes you need more reassurance that this is legit. A short conversation can really help with this. And when so many editors resist taking calls, you'll stand out from the crowd as someone willing to put a little more effort into the relationship. Sales folks have a name for this conversation: the **discovery call**. Discovery calls can be a quick fifteen minutes to assess whether you want to work together, or they can be an hour or so, talking in detail about the project and the potential relationship.

These conversations give you the opportunity to connect more closely with your prospect, assess their needs, and see if they're a good fit. They also help a prospect get a sense of your personality. I've had many prospects say at the end of a call that they feel more comfortable now. They trust me and are ready to move forward. When it's not working for the prospect, it's often not working for me, either. That's a huge consideration in the writer-editor relationship. You'll be working closely with your client; for that relationship to work, you have to communicate well with each other.

Avoid a call becoming a free consulting session by sticking to the topic at hand. Some people will use a lure of maybe hiring you in the future to get free advice from you. Don't take calls like that. Point them to information on your website, if you have any, or let them know what your consultation fee is.

What if a call starts to go wrong? If you realize there's no real project or the project won't work for you, simply end the call. Break into the conversation if you have to. You can be quick without being rude: "I'm going to stop you there and say that I don't think this is a good fit for me. Thanks for taking the time to talk with me today. Goodbye." And then hang up.

When a call goes well, end it by outlining the next steps. Will you take an editing test or do a sample edit for the prospect? Do they need to give you more information? Perhaps you're ready to write up a proposal or estimate for them. Whatever it is, clarify who needs to do what and by when.

Reinforce both the good feeling of the call and the next steps with a follow-up email. Best sent immediately after the call, your message should thank the prospect for their time and mention something positive about the call. If you connected on a mutual interest or shared a good laugh, comment on that. Then remind them of the next steps and when you'll be in touch again.

TESTS: REAL OR SCAM?

Some organizations test their freelance editors and proofreaders. You'll find this with larger companies, especially trade book publishers. They're looking for specific skills and want to ensure the freelancers they hire are up to their standards.

As a freelancer, you don't have to take editing tests, though that may mean not working for the client. By taking a test, you're demonstrating not only your skills and knowledge but also your willingness to work to win a project. As Ayesha Chari notes in an article on editing tests, taking a test can also help counteract some unconscious biases, whether against a person or language usage. A test, she writes, "eliminates having to justify 'otherness.'"[2] She notes that taking editing tests has personal benefits as well, including building your self-confidence, pointing out weaknesses you can work on, improving your ability to follow directions, and providing evidence for raising your fees.

Again, be wary of scams. As with a Frankenedit, an editing test might be a way to get a project edited for free. Be cautious of unpaid tests that are complete documents or large sections, like a chapter from a book. Many editors have experience with such "tests," including McCowan, who had a packager use this ploy on her when she was just starting out. When she realized what was happening, McCowan contacted the university press where the test content had come from. The press was unaware such testing was going on, and it was clearly against its policy. The likely scenario? The packager was trying to get projects edited under budget.

Some red flags tell you that the working relationship with the client likely won't be an easy one. Long, onerous tests might be genuine, but they might also tell you that the client has big expectations, especially when the test is unpaid. A paid test is more like a trial run, which benefits both parties. Another flag to watch for is being asked to pay to take the test. That's right: you pay for the privilege of being considered for a project. This could indicate that a company is looking to make a profit wherever it can and isn't afraid to make it off potential freelancers. Yet another red flag: the sender won't answer basic questions. "I once asked a test-sender whether I should edit for US or UK English and they replied, 'I can't tell you that; it's part of the test!'" says editor Sarah Grey. "Clients should be looking for editors' ability to ask the appropriate questions before editing."

It's not unreasonable to spend an hour or two demonstrating your editing skills. Editing done well is invisible in published works, and sharing edits you've done for others is a questionable practice at best. Passing an editing test doesn't guarantee you the work, but it's another step forward, one that can be very persuasive.

SAMPLES: SHORT AND SWEET

Another way to prove your skills, one that might be more persuasive for prospects who haven't hired an editor before, is an editing sample. Providing a short editing sample on the manuscript you'd be working on can ease anxieties around editing. The prospect can see how their writing has been improved, not destroyed. It also gives you an opportunity to judge how much work is involved and what you want to charge for it.

Samples should be short, enough to get a feel for the manuscript and show your skills but not take up a lot of time or give away too much for free. I find that 500–1,000 words is my sweet spot. Ask to see the entire manuscript. You'll get a chance to review the text first and then choose a representative section to edit. If the prospect will only send you a section, request a section from the middle. Beginnings and endings have likely been heavily revised.

Some editors charge for sample edits, deducting the cost from the project fee if they win the job. Those who charge for sample edits find that doing so discourages scammers and ill-fitting prospects while reinforcing the value of editing. Other editors, myself included, provide samples for free. I don't do a lot of samples, so the time loss isn't huge for me, and I'm not attracting a lot of tire-kickers who need to be discouraged. I find that free samples build trust with the prospect and are a good way to show that I can do the type of editing called for.

Treat the sample like a real project. Time yourself, research any questions you'd ordinarily research, and write up comments as required. When you send the sample to the prospect, give them an overview of what you did. Let them know where to find the edits in the manuscript, the tools you used to make the edits, and how they can view them. Explain the type or level of editing you did, and share your professional opinion of what the manuscript will need overall.

I've had great success with editing samples. When a prospect is on the fence, this is the thing that helps them decide. Even if they don't know much about editing, they can see how it helps the writing while keeping it their writing.

Proposing a Working Relationship

After all these years, I still feel excited when someone expresses interest in hiring me or my team to edit a project. No matter how I get to that point, once I'm there, it's like Christmas. Someone wants to pay me for doing something I love! When this happens to you, dance around your office, sing, shout, whatever. But then sit down and get serious. It's time to act like a business.

With the fees you set in chapter 2, you'll use a proposal or an estimate, along with a contract and an invoice (see chapter 3), to outline your working relationship. However you've chosen to vet your prospects, *do not* take on work sight unseen. You can't accurately estimate time and fees without seeing at least a sample of the work involved, and agreeing to work on something you haven't seen can cause huge headaches later. Before creating either of the below documents, get a look at the work you'll be doing.

CREATE A PROPOSAL

Proposals are lengthy, detailed documents that define and outline a project. Most editing projects have only a few steps and a comparatively short time frame, so they don't require proposals. You might want one for large projects, such as editing multivolume textbooks or working with other editors to complete a complex project. Your prospect may require them as part of their business process. Either way, it's a good idea to at least be familiar with what a proposal is before you actually need one.

The bigger the project or the more people who need to approve the project, the longer and more detailed the proposal will likely need to be. Be clear about the steps and timeline so that people you'll never talk to can visualize how the project will proceed. A proposal is also a sales tool; it aims to persuade readers of the need for this project and for you to do the project. Keep key benefits front and center in the document.

A basic proposal should include the following:

+ Client name
+ Project title
+ Date of the proposal
+ An executive summary
+ Your bio and a brief description of your business, especially how it will benefit the client and/or the project
+ Project background, including what problem is being solved and how solving it will benefit the client
+ Project objectives and how success will be measured
+ Project methodology, including the main tasks to be done, who will do them, and an estimated timeline

+ Project budget and any resources you'll need from the client
+ Deliverables: what you will return to the client
+ Client representatives and their roles
+ You and your role
+ Signature lines

You can find many proposal templates online, including sites that also offer contract templates, like Rocket Lawyer. Choose one and create a template for your business that includes your bio, business description, and logo. Stick with the basic formula. Much like a contract and a résumé, keeping to a standard proposal format helps readers find what they're looking for quickly.

A proposal is not a legally binding agreement. Once you have agreed on the project's parameters, you'll want a signed contract, one that includes the terms and conditions of your business relationship (read more about legal forms in chapter 3). You may wish to consult a lawyer about what should go into your business templates to ensure you've protected yourself.

CREATE AN ESTIMATE

More often, you'll create estimates for a project before beginning. Estimates are like invoices, except that the final cost or some project details, such as the document's word count or the delivery date, are not yet finalized. Estimates are a quick way to outline each party's responsibilities, key dates, and potential costs.

Use your invoice template to create an estimate template. Replace the word *invoice* or *bill* with *estimate* and include an expiration date for the estimate (chapter 3 has more on invoice basics). You don't want a prospect coming back a year or two later, after you've raised your fees, and demanding your lower fee. Expiration dates can also urge a prospect to accept the estimate before it expires. Also consider adding a ceiling for the word count, as well as language about due dates being tentative until you've reviewed the manuscript. While an estimate isn't binding, it's a good idea to remind prospects of the limitations of your agreement.

Acceptance can be formal, such as with a signature or an "accept" button in your invoicing software, or informal, as with a response in an email. Do get that acceptance in writing, though, to head off any disputes down the road.

Upselling the Project

Sometimes you and the prospect may go back and forth on the details of a project to find that place where you agree. We talked about not negotiating your fee in chapter 2. Now let's look at some points where you might negotiate.

Frequently prospects ask for a copyedit or a proofread, but the manuscript needs a higher-level edit first. Samples, proposals, and estimates are all places where you make your case for the level of editing the manuscript requires. Explain the problems in the manuscript and how they will affect the project's goal. Then suggest your solution, showing the difference with a sample perhaps, and explain how the higher edit resolves the problem.

Are you still willing to do the copyedit if the prospect doesn't want the developmental edit? When a manuscript needs a higher level of editing, some editors will decline to do a lower-level edit, especially if they think the client is likely to blame them later for the manuscript's failure. You can set a policy or make the decision on a case-by-case basis. If you will do a lower-level edit, be clear about what you're responsible for and what you're not.

When Prospects Don't Respond

To keep the conversation moving, try giving prospects "homework," advises sales coach Wendy Weiss.[3] This will keep the prospect engaged with the sales process. You could ask them to send the manuscript for review, answer questions on their style, or send you feedback on your editing sample. A couple days after you've sent your proposal or estimate, follow up to ensure they received it and are still interested. I like to give prospects that grace period rather than following up the same day. Everyone is busy and I don't want to seem overeager or pushy.

A better approach is to give the prospect a deadline. When you send the proposal or estimate, let them know you'll follow up in a couple days. This can help the prospect prioritize reviewing your offer. Be sure to follow up when you say you will; you want to demonstrate that you respect deadlines.

Some prospects will be indecisive. When you sense them wavering, ask them questions to get them to share what they're concerned about. Use what you've learned about them already to make an educated guess about what might be holding them back from a decision. Is it money? Time? Questioning the need for editing? Invite them to share those concerns with you, and try to address them.

If you don't receive a response to your first follow-up or you receive only a weak response, you can follow up again. A week or so is often a good time frame. You don't need to go into a lot of detail; let it be a quick "just checking in with you" email to put the conversation back at the top of their inbox. If you still don't get a response, let it go. It's frustrating to be ghosted and it's unprofessional to ghost someone like that, but it happens frequently and there's not much you can do about it. Cross this opportunity off your list and put your efforts into the next one.

When They Say No

A prospect declining your offer might be better than being ghosted, but not much. It can bring up strong feelings of impostor syndrome. What's wrong with you? Why didn't they see your talent? Don't they understand they need this editing? Yet there are many reasons a prospect might not take on your services that have nothing to do with you. Like writers trying to get a book contract with a major publisher, we freelance editors have to be prepared for a lot of rejection and not take it as a personal affront. It's business, nothing more.

When a prospect says no, it's perfectly acceptable to ask why.

Have a template you can send that is professional and supportive. You can try something like the following:

> I appreciate your sharing your decision with me, [Name], and I'm sure your project is in good hands. Would you mind sharing with me what helped you decide to go with another editor? That will help me improve my own services.
>
> I wish you well in your project.

You may not get a response to this, and that's OK. On those occasions when you do, you could gain invaluable insight into a prospect's decision-making. You might find that another editor has more experience or a subject expertise that you don't. It could be that the other editor offered them a lower price or a faster turnaround time. Use that information to adjust your own offerings or determine that this type of client isn't a good fit for your business.

You may also discover that the prospect decided to delay the project. This happens frequently with non-publishing companies and other organizations. You might ask to check back with them in a few months to see if the situation has changed. If nothing else, it will remind your prospect that you exist. They may have a different project for you or could recommend you to someone else.

When You Should Say No

At any point before you sign a contract and take money, you can choose not to proceed any further. You may feel obligated to take on a project after investing time in trying to win it, but this is your business, not your prospects'. If the red flags start waving wildly at you, stop the process.

Upon reviewing the manuscript, maybe you find that the author advises things you can't support or holds opinions you don't want to be part of promoting. Say no. Perhaps doing the sample edit was more of a struggle than you anticipated, and you don't think you can do a good job on the project. Say no. It could be that you can't make the deadline and maintain the quality the prospect wants.

Say no. Maybe your Spidey senses are going off, even though you can't identify what's bothering you. Say no.

Do you need permission to say no to a project you don't want? OK, then, I give you permission to say no to any project that doesn't suit you for any reason. For no reason, if you can't put your finger on it. That's the *free* part of *freelancing*: you are free to say no.

Creating a template for saying no can make it easier to pass on a project. Keep it simple, such as "Thank you for your interest in my service, [Name], but I'm going to pass on this project. Good luck in your search!" You don't need to give a reason, nor do you need to apologize. You can recommend another editor or a directory if you know enough about the project and think someone else would benefit from it. But if what you've seen would be red flags for others, skip the recommendations. You don't owe it to the prospect, no matter what they say. When you do make recommendations, check with the editor first.

Most of the time, that quick message will be enough to end the conversation. Occasionally, though, you'll run into a prospect who just won't take a hint. They'll continue to ask you questions or try to persuade you. You don't need to continue to respond. If you do, be brief, firm, and polite. Don't get drawn into lengthy explanations that force you to validate your reasons. In extreme cases, you can block their email address.

Unfortunately, there are times when we must take on projects that we don't want. Maybe the rent is due or the work itself will be fine if you can find a way to deal with the people running the project. Perhaps you'll face biases no matter who the client is. Only you can judge which situations you must deal with in order to make a living. The goal here is to minimize those situations by building a business that allows you to say no.

Ways to Offer a Discount

Having a sale or offering a discount can draw new attention to your business and help nudge people to work with you. Discounts work well in retail. One reason for this is that the shopper will generally buy other things at full price, either during that trip or on a future one. That increase helps offset the loss on individual items sold.

Services don't work the same, especially for solopreneurs. You are the only one doing the work, so there is a limit to how many hours you have to sell. You have to consider how much you can reduce your income by in order to gain more clients. If you don't have any clients, then getting some income is better than getting none, but you have to balance this carefully. Be clear that this is a limited offer, and be firm about enforcing your regular fee afterward. Some folks will hire you only for that deal. If it fills your pocket for the time being, great. But if the only way you fill your pocket is through discounts, you're effectively giving yourself a pay cut.

For a price discount, you may want to limit the number of projects you take on for that fee. You can do so by promoting an end date or a limited number of people who can have this offer. You're creating a little competition for a spot on your calendar that might urge someone to decide to work with you. Encourage future work by offering a small discount on a second project with you. You could also announce a price increase starting on a specific date, but if someone schedules work now to be done after the price increase and pays a deposit, you'll let them book at the old price.

As we saw in chapter 2, you don't have to offer a straight price discount. You can also discount the work so that you're still making your desired fee, such as a reduced fee for one editing pass instead of your usual two. Here are several more discounts you can offer:

+ Give a small volume discount when the prospect purchases two or more services.
+ Charge a small fee for an editing sample, which you'll credit to the cost of editing the full manuscript.
+ Offer something extra when they book with you, like a free thirty-minute consultation or a case study you've written.

+   Discount a future project when a client refers you to someone else and that referral turns into paying work.

Whatever method you choose, be firm with your boundaries. Tell people what they'll get, at what cost, and what the restrictions are. Readers tend to ignore the details of offers, so you need to emphasize them. When you talk to the prospect, repeat those terms and conditions. When you invoice them, show the full price and the discounted price or offer to drive the point home.

Finally, we offer discounts to help our businesses grow. People will make arguments about why they deserve a discount. Whether or not they deserve it is immaterial. The question is whether you can afford it. Feeling sorry for someone is not a reason to give a discount. A grocery store clerk can feel sorry for you, but they won't discount your grocery bill. You can't spend a discount, promises of future work are not edible, and exposure just leaves you naked and cold. As the Freelancers Union likes to say, "Freelancing isn't free."

When the Prospect Says Yes

At last, your prospect said yes. Now it's time to make the relationship official. Create a checklist of everything you need to get a new client started. Your onboarding process doesn't have to be complicated, but when you standardize it and create a checklist for it, you ensure you don't miss something important and can remain organized throughout the relationship.

CREATE THE LEGAL PAPERWORK

Start with the legal paperwork. Some companies may have a specific onboarding process for freelancers, with all the necessary documentation; you just need to follow their lead. Otherwise, you'll want to prepare a contract for your new client, as well as an NDA or NCA as required. Complete any tax-related forms necessary for this client. For example, US citizens may need to complete a W-9 for US clients. (You'll find more on W-9s and other tax forms in Resources.)

PREPARE FOR PAYMENT

Some companies may also have a standardized payment process, such as direct deposit or payment through a third-party vendor. Those clients will guide you through any paperwork you need to complete and should advise you on invoicing requirements. Alternatively, you'll tell your client when you'll invoice and how payment should be received.

Add the client to your invoicing system, even if that's just drafting the invoice you'll send later. If you'll require a deposit before the work starts, send your initial invoice. Whether you require a deposit is a matter of cash flow and personal risk. Deposits can keep money flowing in while you're working on long-term projects. They can also be used to save a spot on your calendar for the client's project. And when combined with a payment schedule throughout the project, deposits can reduce the risk that the client will disappear with your edits without paying for them in full. I don't know a freelance editor who hasn't been ripped off at least once. Deposits can help minimize that.

ADD YOUR CLIENT TO YOUR ORGANIZATIONAL SYSTEM

Create whatever folders and labels you need for the client and then add their project to your calendar or task list (we'll talk more about these things in later chapters). Once you receive the manuscript, be sure you can open the file and that it's the correct file, especially if you aren't going to work on it immediately. Confirm file receipt with the client, and remind them of when you'll be in touch next; both reassure the client that you're now on the job.

Before we move on, stop and consider how far you've come. You've put a lot of effort into working on your business, and you've successfully found your first clients. Not everyone makes it this far, but *you* did. Celebrate your achievement! You'll soon be head down again, doing the work you've promised, so take a breath and appreciate this moment. In the next section of the book, we'll look at how to work in your business.

Key Takeaways

+   Having someone contact you is the beginning of the sales process.
+   You are interviewing each other to see if you'll work well together.
+   Have a framework for deciding whether the project is right for you, using the definition of your ideal client and project to measure against.
+   Research the client and consider a combination of discovery calls, tests, and samples to see if this is a good project for you.
+   Use proposals or estimates to draft the details of the project with the prospect.
+   Be willing to negotiate the details, but know your limits.
+   Discounts and other offers can increase sales but can hurt profits. Check your math before offering something.
+   Once your client says yes, complete your onboarding process before beginning the work.

3

Working in
Your Business

Preparing to Do the Work

You and Your Workspace

Organization is the key to more efficient, less stressful work and, ultimately, greater satisfaction with your business. When you're disorganized, you lose files, miss deadlines, or forget to invoice. You look unprofessional and maybe even untrustworthy. When the client's experience is stressful and hard, they may not work with you again. Even if you successfully hide any issues, you can find yourself overworked, underpaid, burned out, and unhappy.

We can't control everything in our businesses, so give yourself every advantage by organizing yourself and your space to do the work. Put the effort in upfront, and it will pay off as you go along.

Scheduling "You" Time

Multitasking was once held up as an efficient way to get your work done, but over time research has shown that multitasking is inefficient and results in poorer performance.[1] Few freelance editors can block off entire days for one task or project, however. Clients shorten deadlines, edits take longer than expected, and everyone who needs your attention reaches out to you at once. Don't forget all those business admin tasks that need to be done.

Life happens. We can minimize the effect it has on our work with time and task management.

When you can, group similar tasks or topics. Take advantage of your current mindset by blocking off a chunk of time for one task and then protect that time by limiting interruptions. According to often-quoted research by Gloria Mark, informatics professor at the University of California, Irvine, it can take up to twenty-five minutes to regain your focus after it's been interrupted.[2] If you've set aside two hours to edit, for example, turn off social media, email, and other distractions. When the two hours is up, take a break. Get up from your desk. Grab a glass of water, do a chore, take a #stetwalk—do something that gives your brain a rest.

Over the years, I've found that scheduling time in my day to look at email and social media, my two great online distractors, has helped me stay on task. It's easier to say no to checking Facebook when I know I have a scheduled time for it coming up. If the urge to check email or social media continues, I know my mind is telling me it needs a break and I'll take one.

How long should you remain on one task? That's going to vary from person to person and from day to day. Become familiar with your work patterns and your ability to focus. A physical or mental disability might mean taking more frequent breaks. Do what your body needs. What time of day is your focus at its best? Try to schedule higher-cognitive tasks for that time. When your focus is weakest, try to do easier tasks, like filing and checking email.

For example, I wrote most of this book between 6 and 9 a.m. I was not only at my most alert, but I had the fewest interruptions. Meanwhile, one of my sons does his writing between 9 p.m. and 1 a.m. That's when he's most alert and has fewest interruptions. Monitor yourself through your workday. How do your energy and focus fluctuate? Maybe your mind starts to wander after an hour or so. You might need more breaks in your day to keep going. The **Pomodoro technique** (see Resources) is good for managing this. Perhaps you can hold deep focus for several hours but then require a longer break. In that case, you might find the **Flowtime technique** more helpful. (You'll find more time-management techniques in Resources.) The beauty of freelancing is that you set your own hours; there's no boss demanding you work at a specific time or for a specific length of time. Once you find your usual rhythm, make the most of it by scheduling the work when you'll be at your best.

Your work rhythms can change over time, too. The schedule I have now would not have worked when my kids were in elementary and middle school. They needed much more parenting before and after school, and my work schedule needed to accommodate that. I've also found that as I've grown older, I can hold my concentration longer. In my twenties and thirties, I switched tasks quicker and easier than I do now, preferring to work on several short edits a day. These days I prefer working on only one or two projects in the same day for longer periods. Adjusting how I work, including the kind of projects I take on, has meant better satisfaction with my job and more energy to use outside of work.

There will be days when you have to work when you're not your most focused and need to push through to finish. There may be many weeks or months like that. You can't control everything, nor should you try. Instead, get to know yourself and adapt to the situation at hand as best you can. Some days the universe will dictate your day, no matter how organized you are. When it does, it can be less stressful and more efficient to just go with it.

Calendars, to-do lists, timers, and other time-management tools help you stay focused and on top of details. There are dozens of tools out there and hundreds of articles to help you use them well. The Resources section, found in Appendix B, lists some tools popular among editors. It doesn't matter if you use apps or pen and paper or both, as long as it works for you. Using apps that integrate with each other can make time management easier and more automated. Also helpful is being able to use different views, such as timelines and Kanban boards, or determining which view works best for you. Using color-coding or images to represent categories can make staying organized easier as well.

I'll share here how I manage and track my time, but this is just one example. If you don't yet have your own method, check out the different options and see what appeals to you. I've developed my method over years, making changes as my needs changed and new tools became available. I expect it will continue to evolve.

ERIN'S TIME-MANAGEMENT SYSTEM

Despite all the different layouts that time-management tools can give you, I still prefer calendar views and table layouts, and I love a list where I can check things off. My tool stack consists of the following:

+ A Circa Notebook and a few accessories
+ Several Google Calendars
+ Coda
+ Zoho Books
+ Zapier

MONTHLY VIEW

The monthly view is my map for the next four weeks. In our household, everyone has a personal Google Calendar that we share, and I have an additional one for work. That gives me a full view of our family life and how my work can best integrate with it. I color-code the calendars so I know who's doing what at a glance. I include meetings and other time commitments on my work calendar, along with the due dates of larger projects, such as book manuscripts and magazine issues. I don't put small items, like 500-word edits, on the calendar because it would quickly become too cluttered for me.

To track all my projects, no matter the size, I use Coda, an online app that lets you create documents that work more like web pages than print pages, allowing you to embed different types of media within them and linking them with other documents within the app. While formerly I used Word for project notes, Excel for data tracking, and Todoist for project task tracking, I now use Coda for all of them. I have one table that lists all my projects for the year. With different views, I can see what's currently being worked on and what's ready to be billed. Because my team and I might be working on a half dozen or more client projects a week, I track a lot of details to stay on top of everything, including these items:

+ Client and assigning manager
+ Project start and end dates

+ Number of words
+ Project title and file location (linking to it if it's online)
+ Team member
+ Hours (for tracking editing speed later)
+ Billed or not (to trigger invoicing)
+ Notes

Within Coda, I also create task lists for large projects, keep editing notes for transmittal letters, track project data, and a lot more.

WEEKLY AND DAILY VIEWS

From my monthly calendar and my project table, I create weekly and daily plans for my time. Years ago, one of my ClickZ authors wrote about how at the end of each workday, he wrote his task list for the following day, pulling from the weekly task list he had written up the previous Friday. I've used this method ever since, adapting it as my needs changed. I really appreciate being able to start work without having to first think about what's due that day or week, and reviewing all my upcoming commitments on a Friday has saved me from missing a deadline more than once.

My weekly and daily lists go in my notebook, which stays open at all times. No matter what's on my monitors, those lists are right in front of me. Plus it's so satisfying to cross an item off. In my most recent adaptation, I put time commitments in the left column, organized by day. I include things like doctor's appointments, fitness classes, and evening events so I can see where I'll have blocks of work time. In the main column, I list all the work tasks I need to do, organized by the size of the task, a method I learned from another of my authors, executive business coach Sabina Nawaz.[3] Nawaz recommends dividing tasks into rocks, pebbles, and sand. Rocks are big tasks, often with multiple steps, taking at least an hour to complete. Pebbles are medium-size tasks, taking less than an hour to complete. Sand are those quick tasks you may not even write down, like checking email (though we know what a time suck that can be).

Each step in a project can be designated rock, pebble, or sand.

One recent RTE project was writing promotional emails for a series of events. Each email was a rock on its own, so each was listed separately. Sometimes, though, a rock can be disguised as a pebble. The task itself may take only a few minutes to complete, but you find yourself actively avoiding it. Perhaps the task means making a decision you are uncomfortable making, like letting go of a client. It's a quick task to write the email, but making the decision is a much bigger task. Maybe you're not sure it's the right thing to do, or you're worrying about the client's reaction and how you'll need to deal with that. Instead of beating yourself up for not writing a simple email, recognize that there's a reason you're ducking it. Accept where you're at, and grant yourself the time to make the decision to let go of the client.

From the weekly list, I make a daily list. Again, I first list my time commitments and then plan the rest of my time. Listing self-care activities helps me stay accountable to myself—a lesson I've learned the hard way. While it's tempting to think you'll be editing eight hours a day, that isn't realistic. Not only will you have many business tasks to do regularly, but your focus won't remain consistent throughout the workday. Most of us can't sustain eight or nine hours of editing a day, every day, for long. Editing is just too intensive a task. A lot of editors say they're good for editing four to five hours a day. Perhaps you can edit eight hours a day a couple days a week and then only two or three hours the rest of the week. Ask yourself how many hours a day and how many hours a week you can reasonably work. This goes back to figuring out your best work rhythm and planning your schedule accordingly. I can edit or write efficiently for four to five hours a day and can spend another two to three doing administrative work. My happy place is six hours a day for thirty hours a week. That doesn't mean I've always worked that. I usually have to work more than that, especially during busy times. But because I'm a freelancer, I can put longer breaks into my day or choose to work a few hours on the weekend to space out those hours. And because I'm a freelancer, sometimes I can't give myself leeway, and I just have to power through.

It's taken me years to learn to create daily lists that I can actually complete in a day. I'm really good at overestimating how much work I can get done in a day and ignoring the plot twists life throws at me. So many lists had items moved to the next list and the next and the next. It was disheartening! It took me really looking at how long tasks take me, not what I think they should; identifying hidden rocks and accepting them; and just really learning to take care of myself first, before I was able to write a daily list I could actually accomplish. One of the key things I learned was to leave space in my day for two more items. That way, if an extra task comes along (and it often does), there's still space in my day to breathe. It doesn't always work, of course, but it does more often than not.

EDITING CHECKLISTS

Finally, we get down to the most granular view: the steps associated with each task, which can be organized and tracked through the almighty checklist. The more complex or longer term the project, the greater the need for a checklist. A checklist can be one-and-done or reusable. I use paper for those throwaway lists and Coda for reusable ones. For checklists I share with team members or clients, I use Google Docs or Word. Notion is another good app option for individuals. Use what works best for you.

More important is what goes onto your checklists. Creating a standard editing process checklist can ensure you don't accidentally skip a step. Organize tasks in the way you do them. When Samantha Enslen of Dragonfly Editorial presented this topic for Copyediting, she encouraged attendees to keep checklists brief, focusing on "killer items"—"the steps that are most dangerous to skip and sometimes overlooked nonetheless."[4] If you can keep the checklist uncluttered and to one page, you're more likely to use it.

Editing checklists customized for each client are helpful, too, especially for freelancers who juggle several clients with similar styles. While your style sheets store each client's style and quirks, checklists help ensure that you actually check those items. For example, one of my clients uses an en dash to set off phrases in the middle of the sentence and an em dash to set off a phrase that ends the sentence. While I list that on the style sheet, I also have it on the client's checklist, so that we remember to double-check all dashes in the text during the edit.

As you edit, you want your most important resources in easy reach, whether that's near your computer or within a few keystrokes to viewing. These include the client's style guide (if they have one), the project style sheet, your editing checklists, project directions, and any notes you've taken. For ongoing clients, I create a Quick Start Guide for the editing team. The Quick Start Guide includes links to these resources, editing notes, a link to the PerfectIt style sheet,[5] and examples of past work. Putting all this information in one place makes getting an editor up to speed on the client quicker and easier.

PREPARING FOR DISRUPTIONS AND CHANGING DATES

In our house, we call them plot twists: those events that change your carefully constructed plan into a tangle of stress and worry. Life has a way of happening just when you don't want it to, and we can't do much about it. You can combat it by ensuring your schedule has room for disruptions, but how do you actually handle those disruptions and keep at least some control over your schedule?

One of the most common disruptions is the client not delivering their manuscript on time. You can minimize these instances by requesting the manuscript ahead of time. Your process can include not giving the client a firm date on your calendar until they've sent the manuscript or a deposit (money has an encouraging effect on the delivery of the manuscript).

Still, there will be times when the manuscript will be late, and it's not always in the client's control. We recently edited a land survey report. I had contracted with the firm hired to do the land survey, and they had estimated delivering the file to us by late July or early August, after the firm's client had reviewed the latest draft. Early August came and went, and no report. The firm's client hadn't signed off on the report yet. I checked in every couple of weeks, and we kept moving the date out. Finally the report hit in early October, and we were able to do the job. My client was clearly stressed during the summer, though. The only thing I could do was assure them when the project came through that we'd still be available to edit it.

Stay in contact with late clients. Ask if they have an expected date, and follow up close to that date to see if they're still on track. Be professional and understanding; your goal here is to get the information necessary to plan your own work. If the client has signed a contract with you, they'll usually show up eventually— especially if they've given you a deposit. Situations like this are a good reminder to make that deposit nonrefundable. If you've saved a significant chunk of time for a big project that doesn't show, you've at least been partially paid for your time. In the meantime, take on other projects or work on your business. There's always something to do to keep yourself moving forward.

Situations like this are also a reminder not to depend too much on just one or two clients. An anchor client can keep the work flowing in, but your entire business shouldn't depend on them.

WHEN YOU RUN LATE

Those plot twists sometimes have you running late on client work. Whatever the twist is, let your client know right away that you're running late. When the problem is their project, you'll want to advise your client of the issue. Then you can work together to determine whether you should adjust your editing or the deadline.

When the problem is something other than the client's project, give them enough details to get a sense of what's going on and when you'll be back, but don't worry about long explanations. You're a business owner, not an employee. Something quick like "I'm having issues with my computer," "I've been sick," or "I have a personal issue I need to take care of" is often enough. This tells your client that the issue is genuine and not that you are mismanaging your time. You can leave out the gory details and maintain your privacy.

In the same message, let your client know when you expect to finish their project and ask them if that would work for them. By asking directly, you're showing respect for their deadlines and acknowledging the disruptions your lateness could cause. Work together to determine how to complete the project. If the new deadline won't work, could you adjust your editing to fit the remaining time? Do you have a trusted colleague who could finish the project? Is it best to stop editing here and hand the manuscript back? Being late doesn't have to be the end of the world. The world runs late all the time, and we're all still here. Alert the client right away and work together to solve the problem, and you'll often find the client continues to trust you.

Preparing Your Workspace

Where will you work, and what kind of work equipment will you have? Having a computer that does what you need it to and working in a location where you are able to focus and feel comfortable both go a long way to helping you do your best work and be happy in your business. We've all had trouble focusing because our environment was suddenly not suitable (I dread the neighborhood leaf blowers each spring and fall) or our tools weren't up to the task (an old computer that took thirty minutes to fully boot up that I held on to for too long). They don't just make us cranky, but they distract us and make us inefficient. The work takes longer, which eventually harms our business's bottom line. And we often don't recognize the situation until it's been going on a while.

EQUIPMENT

It goes without saying that you need some sort of computer to do your editing with. Technology changes so fast that any particular recommendations I might make could be outdated by the time you read this. Instead, I'll give you some guidelines to apply to the latest technology.

Most editors find editing on a full-size computer the most comfortable. Desktops and laptops generally give you enough memory to run all the programs you might need. It doesn't matter if you work on a Mac or a PC. Some editors struggle a little more with Word on the Mac, but otherwise it's down to personal preference. Whichever you go with, do as editor Lori Paximadis advises: Always get as much memory as you can afford. Even if you think you'll never use all that memory, buy it. You'll use it all eventually.

The decision between desktop and laptop also comes down to personal preference. Desktops can be cheaper (though not necessarily), but they lack portability. What are you more comfortable on? What fits your lifestyle best? When my kids were younger, I had a laptop so I could work anywhere in the house. This was great at homework time, because I could sit at the kitchen table working and be available for nudges to focus on homework. These days, I have a desktop and three monitors in my office, where I work most of the time. But I still have a laptop devoted to work so I can work elsewhere when I want to.

Also get as big a monitor as you can afford and you have room for. Working with text on a screen all day is hard on your eyes. The bigger the monitor, the bigger you can make the text or the more files you can have showing on the same screen. Also look for the highest resolution you can get. The better the image on your monitor, the easier it will be on your eyes. Consider getting an ultrawide monitor, a vertical monitor, and/or multiple monitors to increase your productivity.[6] An ultrawide monitor lets you have more than one document next to each other on one screen, like your working document and the style sheet. A vertical monitor (or a horizontal monitor set to display vertically) lets you see more of the manuscript at once and scroll less often. Multiple monitors not only give you more screen real estate but also let you organize everything you have open. I keep email and project management tools on my left monitor, my current task on the center monitor, and social media and other browser tabs open on my right.

For those with physical disabilities, tools like screen readers, magnifiers, dictation software, and specially designed keyboards and mice might be just what you need to work comfortably. Consult with an occupational therapist or other medical professional to find the best tools and techniques for you.

Consider eventually maintaining a backup computer so that you can keep working if your main machine goes down. An older computer can be a good short-term backup, as can one of those Black Friday specials. It doesn't have to be a perfect replacement, just something to keep you going while your main machine is being repaired. A tablet computer, such as an iPad, can be a good backup as well. They can also be handy devices to keep your business running while you're traveling. While I don't know of an editor who runs their business solely on a tablet, my older son does almost all of his work on his iPad, including writing, project management, and invoicing.

A mobile phone is pretty much a necessity these days. Even phone-phobic editors occasionally have to talk to clients. The good news is you likely already have one and at least a portion of it may be tax deductible as equipment for your business. (Check with your accountant.)

Printers are less necessary than they once were. What do you anticipate printing for your business? You might get away with a cheap printer or no printer at all. If you're not sure, try using your local office supply store's printing and copying services (also a potential tax deduction). If it becomes too much of a pain or too expensive, you'll know to add a printer to your must-have list.

None of this technology is cheap, of course. You'll be balancing your need for tools with your budget. Seek out deals and any discounts you might be eligible for. If you can, start a technology fund to help with future purchases. Also, seek out a trustworthy computer repair service. Like a good car mechanic, having a repair service that knows your machine can be a lifesaver when it breaks down.

SOFTWARE

We've already talked about a lot of software tools that can help

your business. You'll choose ones that work best for you, along with an email program and web browser. Those are personal choices. But what about editing software?

Microsoft Word is still the most common and best tool for editing. It's the legacy program; most people have it or work in software whose files can be easily imported into it. Word has many features to help the editor, especially Track Changes, customizable Auto-Correct, and macros, which competitors have yet to duplicate well. And there are add-ons, like PerfectIt and Editor's ToolKit Plus, that increase efficiency and accuracy and aren't available for other software. If you're working for publishing houses and others with deeply embedded publishing processes, you're very likely going to be asked to edit in Word.

For proofreading, you may be asked to work on PDFs. Acrobat Reader is free and sufficient for proofreading. The paid Acrobat DC Pro allows you to actually edit a PDF file, changing text, moving content boxes around, and other advanced tasks. If that's something your work will require often enough, it could be worth the subscription. For occasional PDF editing, you can try an open-source option like LibreOffice Draw editor or PDFedit. (See Resources for more options.)

Editors who deal with mathematics and math-heavy subjects like physics, machine learning, and economics might run into a program called LaTeX, which publishers use to typeset such manuscripts. LaTeX uses code tags to format the document, which helps with presenting complex equations. Most editors use LaTeX editing software to edit the manuscript, with Overleaf being one of the most popular. It allows you to track your changes and collaborate with others in the document, while handling all the coding, notes editor Tasha Rebekah Bigelow. (See Resources for more.)

Among self-publishing authors, you're likely to see Word files, but you might also see Google Docs files, as well as files from programs aimed specifically at book authors, like Scrivener. Generally, you can import these files into Word, but watch for hiccups when importing and exporting.

Among companies, you may be downloading Word files from a cloud storage space rather than receiving them by email. Share-Point and Dropbox are common options, with SharePoint letting you work in Word in the cloud. If you're not getting Word files, you might see one of the flavors of the month in documentation software, like Quip or Notion. Some companies are rethinking their workflows and looking for more internal efficiencies. Here, too, you can generally import the text into a Word file for easier editing, but watch for those translation quirks, especially when exporting Word back to the original software.

Working on web content, you may be working directly in the client's content management system (CMS), such as WordPress or Drupal. Most, if not all, have "what you see is what you get" editors, so you shouldn't have to deal with coding.

Really, you could be asked to edit in any program that deals with text. Who your clients are will tell you what software you might require. While the expectation is that you'll supply your own software on your computer, when you're working in cloud software, the client should be providing you with access to their system. And if it's an unusual request, the client may offer you access to their software license or you could bill them for a portion of a software license you have to buy, as an extraordinary condition.

Many editors refuse to edit in anything other than Word, for reasons shared earlier, and if you stick with working for clients with mature publishing processes that use Word, this won't be a problem. University presses, publishing houses, and book packagers have well-honed processes and are unlikely to upset that with new software anytime soon. But there's a whole world of words out there to be edited. If you're looking to get into that, you'll need to work within the client's process, and that might mean working in something other than Word.

While I work in Word whenever I can, I've found that being adaptable has brought me more opportunities. I've edited in Excel, PowerPoint, Google Docs, InDesign, Acrobat, Dropbox Paper, and several CMSs, including WordPress and Drupal. I've logged into SharePoint, Quip, Fluxx, and not a few now-defunct file systems. Being willing to work with a client's software has landed me better-paying jobs, and I've learned that different programs that do the same task work on the same principles. Word processors tend to operate similarly and have similar features; the work is in noting where they differ.

Whatever software you use, there are three important rules to follow. First, *know your software*. Working in a program you don't know well enough can, at best, slow down your editing and create frustrating situations for you. You could spend more of your time troubleshooting what the program did that you didn't expect than actually editing. At worst, you could create huge headaches for your clients when they have to recreate files you've damaged. You should have at minimum a working understanding of all the features you'll use in any program you edit in. It's not the client's job to train you; as a freelancer, it's yours. Take the time to learn your tools so you can get the most out of them.

Keeping your software up-to-date is also imperative. Not only does this give you access to the latest features, but updates almost always include bug fixes. Many flaws are minor, but the more serious they are, the more you want those updates. Serious flaws can lead to corrupt files, computer crashes, and security risks. Maintain secure, up-to-date tools, because your business depends on it.

Finally, *stay current with advances in software*. I've shared what's current in software as of this writing, but that's almost guaranteed to change. Advances are happening all the time, and younger generations bring their software preferences with them as they enter the working world. To stay relevant as an editor, stay conversant in the latest software developments.

One development that currently has editors' attention is AI software like ChatGPT. As of this writing, it's not yet ready for the generic "Edit this" request. Technology can change quickly, of course, and we can't predict how it will develop over time. It's important to stay informed about AI development as it relates to writing and editing and how you might apply it in your work.

Check out the *Right Angels and Polo Bears* blog by editor Adrienne Montgomerie (scieditor.ca) and the *CyberText* blog by editor Rhonda Bracey (cybertext.wordpress.com) for experiments on how AI can be used in editing.

OFFICE SETUP

A few freelance editors I'm aware of rent office space away from their homes. Especially if you're someone who needs other people around, renting coworking space could be a good solution for you. Perks can include better Wi-Fi, access to a printer, a well-stocked break area, and even a private office. Most editors, though, prefer to work on their own, with the occasional excursions to coffee shops and libraries.

Whether your work area will be a dedicated room or just an area of the room, make it work for you. Employees who suddenly became remote during the COVID-19 pandemic learned the hard way that sitting at the kitchen table forty-plus hours a week was not good for their bodies. Sore backs, overly stressed wrists, and kinked necks are common in a setting not made for long use as a workplace.

Your workstation should fit your body's needs as much as possible. The US's Occupational Safety and Health Administration (OSHA) offers a wealth of information on how to set up a workspace for able-bodied people (see Resources for a list of links). If you have a disability that your workspace will affect and you're unsure how to create a healthy workspace, talk to your doctor, occupational therapist, or other medical specialist to determine what your body needs and what tools will support you best.

OSHA outlines recommendations for several workstation postures, including seated upright, seated reclined, seated declined, and standing. Common to all of them is preventing the body from overreaching or twisting while you're working. Neutral positions, such as feet flat on the floor and straight wrists, are best for preventing injuries.

When possible, spend the money on a comfortable workspace,

including chair, keyboard, and mouse. The long-term effects of working on a computer all day are no joke, and freelancers, who often lack long-term disability insurance, need to protect their hands and arms from permanent damage. Test-drive them in stores or at home (make sure they're returnable) to find the style that works best for you. If you have the resources, you can hire an ergonomics specialist to help you create a healthy workstation.

Wherever your workspace is, if at all possible, reserve it just for work. Especially if it's in a common space in your home, you want at least a mental divider between work and home. An inexpensive room divider might help you put work aside at the end of the day. Living in the same space you work can make it easy to always be working. There are fewer barriers between work and life, and we need those barriers to maintain a healthy mindset. When you walk away from your workspace, you want to walk away from your work, too.

Editing is a focus-intensive task. Noise-canceling headphones or earbuds can be a sanity saver when you're unable to control noise in your environment, and a music playlist with your favorite focus music can help you find your editing zone.

Put tools you need most often in easy reach. If you do video meetings, think about whether you want to create a nice display behind you or use a pleasing background in the software. The balance of your workspace should please you: candles, framed pictures, action figures, posters, swag—whatever makes you feel at home in your space. And if you're a minimalist who prefers uncluttered surfaces? Then create an uncluttered space. You have only yourself to please.

Key Takeaways

+ Prepare yourself to focus on your work by getting to know your work rhythms and energy fluctuations.
+ Schedule your work to take advantage of your work rhythms and your personal needs.

+   Use tools like calendars, notebooks, and to-do lists to keep on top of your schedule.

+   Use checklists to help track all the tasks to be completed for each project. Create checklist templates to make the task easier.

+   When you're going to be late with a project, tell your client right away. Work with them to find the best solution.

+   Your work computer should be reliable and have more than enough memory.

+   The bigger the monitor, the easier reading on the screen is.

+   Multiple monitors can increase your efficiency.

+   Microsoft Word is the industry standard for editing, but it's not the only software clients will ask you to use.

+   Being adaptable to new software can increase project opportunities.

+   Know your software, or you'll spend more time trying to figure out the software and less time editing.

+   Keep your software up-to-date to avoid nasty tech surprises.

+   Create a workspace that supports you physically and mentally.

CHAPTER TEN

Handling Work Files and Keeping Records

As freelance editors, we don't need big, expensive warehouses to store all our work product. Our work is primarily stored in bits and bytes and relatively cheaply. Saving data is easy, too, with so many apps saving automatically. Still, we need to organize our data in a way that helps us quickly find what we need, avoid editing or sending the wrong file, and show the work we've done. We also need to keep some data for a specified time, finding it easily when it's time to delete it.

None of that is possible without a good file and folder structure. In this chapter, you'll learn about document version control, file-naming conventions, and folder structures, as well as backups and archives, all of which will help keep your business and client data organized and in your control. The focus here will be on the software editors most use right now: Microsoft Word and Excel, Acrobat, and Google Docs and similar cloud software. Because methods can vary by technology, always use the method that works best for the software and client.

Document Version Control

In order to maintain a record of the changes made to a manuscript and know you're looking at the latest version of a file, you'll want your work files to utilize **document version control**—copying the last version of a file and appending identifying information to the file name, such as stage, actor, and date (I'll talk more about this in a moment). Version control is especially helpful when the publishing process involves many people working on the manuscript. It will give you a clear record of who made what changes to the file and make it easier to go back to an earlier version of the manuscript, if necessary. Let me give you an example.

A client sent us a Word file to edit. The client's file names don't seem to follow a standard naming convention, but we always create a new file to edit in and appended "edited" and the editor's initials to the end of the file name. By making a copy of the client's file, we always have the original to go back to, in case something happens to our working file. We completed the work and sent the client the edited file. A short time later, the client let me know they had sent the wrong file and wanted to know whether we could edit the correct file (for a fee, of course). Because they didn't have a standard way of naming files, it was easy for them to send the wrong version. The client paid twice to have the file edited.[1]

We can't tell clients how to name their files, of course, but we can gently recommend. And we don't want to change file names so much that we interfere with any naming conventions the client does use. The best solution is to add something to a file name that will make it clear who was last in the file and what they did, like *edited EB*. When you're doing multiple rounds of editing, you can add something like *R1* and *R2* as well. By placing this information at the end of the file name, you can sort files alphabetically and all of the versions of the manuscript will be grouped together.

Some cloud software offers a limited kind of version control for you. Microsoft's SharePoint, Google Docs, and Dropbox all save past versions of a file under the same name. How many past versions are stored and how you access them vary from software to software and are apt to be updated quietly. Become familiar with how the software you use can help you store and retrieve past versions and what its limitations are.

Setting Up Your Filing System

When every device and app has a search function and that function keeps improving, why do you need to know where a file is stored? You don't—until a search doesn't turn up your file.

Finding the right file via search requires using the right keywords and having a powerful enough search engine. Using a file-naming system that helps you predict the most accurate keywords for that file will help you find what you need and identify it in a search results list, whether locally or in the cloud. Creating a well-organized folder structure will also help you find the right file, whether through search or just knowing where the file is stored. We'll look at both in this section.

FILE-NAMING CONVENTIONS

File names should be comprehensible to file users today and in the future. For those files you keep for years, you want to be able to look at the file name and have a good idea about what's inside. File names should also be unique so that if they are moved to a different folder, you won't end up with two files with the same name, advises the Wisconsin Historical Society.[2] And you want to keep your file names as acceptable for different environments as possible. That means avoiding special characters (\$, ^, &, etc.), spaces, and periods before the extension, because they're not universally accepted in file names.

Keep your file names fairly short, too, because some apps limit the character count. Abbreviations can help here. For example, whenever I sign on a new client, I immediately give them an abbreviation, trying for the most obvious abbreviation I can. The University of Chicago Press, for example, would be *UCP*. Avoid using *draft* in the file name, as there are likely to be several drafts. Use a version number instead, with or without a *V* before the number. You can also skip any words that indicate the app type or the date the file was last opened, as those will be in the file metadata. If you're tempted to put *final* in the file name, be prepared to add a number after it for those inevitable revisions after something is "final."

Also include the subject or a description of the file. This might be a shortened form of the title of the manuscript, like *Handling-*

WorkFiles. When a longer manuscript is broken up into sections, you could include the section number, such as *C10* for chapter 10. Next, consider how you want the files organized within the folder. When you want to organize by date, use the ISO formula: YYYYM-MDD. An expenses spreadsheet might be titled *YYYYExpenses*. Your résumé could be *YYYYResumeLastname*. Meetings notes might be *YYYYMMDDMeetingClient*.

Version numbers should be at the end of the file name to keep all the versions of one manuscript together: *GreatReadsV1*, *GreatReadsV2*, *GreatReadsV3*, and so forth. When assigning numbers to projects or versions, consider how many you'll have in total and add one or more leading zeros to your number scheme. This will allow you to order the files numerically in an alphabetical system, giving you *PROJ001*, *PROJ002*, *PROJ003* and not *PROJ1*, *PROJ11*, *PROJ111*, *PROJ2*, *PROJ21*, and so on.

Make a record of your file-naming system, along with any abbreviations you use. Even if you're the only one to use the files, should you need someone else to jump into your business to help out because of an illness or other catastrophe, they'll have a guide for understanding your file names. (And, honestly, if you write it down, you don't have to struggle to remember it.)

FOLDER SETUP: GETTING ORGANIZED

Folder organization and names should also follow a pattern that's easy to navigate and easy to search for. Years ago I learned a method from Paul Lagasse, a writer and editor with a master's degree in library science. With slight modifications, it has served me well. Lagasse's system is divided into three parts: before a project begins, during the project, and after the project is completed. Extending your folder setup to email, physical folders, and any other digital space where you keep work files will help you find things in any location with ease. You'll spend a little time setting up a new project, but it will take only a minimal effort to stay organized.

When you sign on a new client, start with your email program:

+ *Create a folder or label for every client.* Create subfolders or sublabels for administration and projects as necessary.
+ *Add all contacts for the client to your contacts list.* Fill in all the information you can, including any important notes.
+ *Create a mail group for the client's or the project's contacts.*
+ *Assign a color to the client.* This might be flags, folders, or labels, depending on your software. (We'll talk about color-coding in the next section.)
+ *Create rules or filters for the client's emails.* Allow your email program to put all mail into the proper client folders.

Next, create a client folder on your computer. Whatever color you assign to the client follows through to your e-folders and physical folders. Label the folder with the client's name or your abbreviation for them.

Within the client's main folder, you'll create another series of folders, which can be divided into more folders as necessary.

+ *Administrative:* This folder includes contracts, correspondence, tax forms, and similar files.
+ *Project:* Put the actual work of the project here, such as the client's original manuscript file and your edited file.
+ *Notes & References:* Any project-specific notes, such as notes from meetings, go here.
+ *Graphics:* Put any graphics specific to the project here.

The bigger the project, the more you want to organize that project folder. Each one might have several folders within it, such as stages for the project, old versions, and notes.

Once the project is done and you've handed your edited files to the client, what do you keep and for how long? Some contracts will stipulate that you destroy any copies of the files you have, so be sure you know what the client expects first. Otherwise, Lagasse suggests holding on to files for six months. Any file you haven't needed after that you can delete except the final project files (such as your final edited file), any notes (including style sheets), and any files you're legally required to keep. To make this process easier, you can move completed project files to a top-level archive folder, adding the completion date to the project folder. Once a month, go through folders that have hit the six-month mark and delete anything you don't need.

Duplicate the structure as much as necessary with your physical folders. Use the same naming convention and put a starting and ending date on the folder to help narrow your search in the future. For example, when I was teaching online courses, I kept backup paper records of my contract, student grades, and similar important documents. Each folder was labeled with the university name, course name, and semester and year. If I needed to look up a student's grade, as long as I knew which course and when, I could immediately go to the right folder.

One of the ways I adapted Lagasse's system was to follow this structure for my business as a whole. I also moved his suggested clippings folder out of each client folder and into this top-level structure. Within my files folder, I have folders labeled RTE Admin, RTE Clips, RTE Graphics, RTE Notes & References, RTE Projects (where all client folders live), and RTE Tech (a folder I added to keep all my tech-related files, like custom Acrobat stamps). Each folder contains several other folders, organized by category. For example, within RTE Admin, I have a folder called Invoices. RTE Graphics has folders for my logo, client logos, my headshots, and so on.

To quickly set up a new client, create and color an empty set of subfolders within a folder with other templates. When you sign on a new client, copy and paste (don't drag and drop) those folders into your new client's main folder. Now your client's folder is ready to go. The goal is consistency in structure and labeling. If you have a map, you know where to look first, and if you have to search, consistent names will bring up the right results. Setting up a structure at the beginning will help you spend less time looking for things and more time actually working.

COLOR YOUR WORLD

Having a color scheme can help you identify categories quickly. Many apps that have folder or label features will let you assign a color or an icon to them. Windows, however, does not. To make up for this glaring oversight, I use an app called Folder Marker. The free version gives you a short list of colors and icons you can apply to your Windows folders; the paid versions give you more colors and icons.

When you have only a few clients or only a few active at once, you can give each of them their own color. Because my client list is rather long, I categorize my clients and then assign each category a color. Across clients, the subfolders are colored according to type. For example, my admin folders are black and the graphics folders are red. It amazes me how applying both structure and color across systems has given me one less thing to think about. When I started using Google Drive more often for work, I duplicated the folder structure I use on my desktop. Clients that have me work in Google Docs have a folder in my Drive with the same label I use on my computer. It makes using multiple systems so much easier.

Be sure to record your filing system with your file-naming conventions so you can remain consistent. Add to that a client onboarding checklist, which will ensure that you have everything you need to start a new project.

Backing Up Your Hard Drive

Many apps autosave the file as you work on it, but what happens if a crash corrupts a file? Or you get the dreaded Blue Screen of Death and all your data becomes unretrievable? The short answer is that without a backup plan, you're out of business. A well-thought-out backup plan will keep you working and minimize recovery efforts. At the very least, you want a copy of all your important work files, like your active client files, invoices, and contracts. In the case of a complete computer meltdown, you'll be happy to have an exact copy of everything, including macros, templates stored deep in an app's folders, and all other system files.

File-syncing services and **backup services** can create backups automatically. File-syncing services make a copy of your files that you can access online. Dropbox, Microsoft OneDrive, and Google Drive are familiar examples. As noted earlier, in some cases, you can access previous versions of a file from the cloud. However, these services require you to add each file or folder to their folder on your hard drive in order for it to be backed up. That leaves anything outside of that folder (like your systems folder) unprotected. Think of this as a short-term backup for your most-used files.

Backup services create a copy of everything on your computer and make it easy to restore data after a big loss. Options here include IDrive, Backblaze, Carbonite, and Acronis Cyber Protect Home Office. They can back up on a schedule or continuously (that is, after the initial backup, they back up a file whenever it changes). There are a lot of options available among all these services, including the ability to create a local backup, heightened security with encryption, and backup for additional digital devices. Shop around for the right combination of features, price, and ease of use for you.

Cloud software won't work for everyone, though, especially if your internet service is unreliable or doesn't offer enough bandwidth. Instead you'll want to create a local backup. You can do a light backup by putting all your important files on a thumb drive or an external hard drive. You'll want to back up at least your day's work at the end of each day. To do a full backup that includes all your system files, you can try **disk mirroring** or **disk cloning**.

Disk mirroring will create a complete copy of your main hard drive on your computer. If your main drive fails, you'll be able to retrieve your files from the mirrored drive, though you'll want to replace the failed drive as soon as possible. One thing to know about disk mirroring is that once created, if you delete a file from your main disk, it will be deleted on the mirrored disk as well. (You'll find directions for Windows 10 in Resources.)

Disk cloning means creating a copy of your hard drive to a second drive. Your desktop computer might have a second drive within it, while a laptop is unlikely to. If you don't have a second drive in your computer, you can put the clone on an external drive. (An article that gives directions for creating a clone for both Macs and PCs is in Resources.)

Once you have your method, create a schedule that ensures your files are backed up often enough that the backup files aren't outdated if you ever need them. Your most important data should be backed up weekly, if not daily. The gold standard of backup strategies is the 3-2-1 strategy. You want three copies of your files: the one you're working on and two backups, using two different media, such as in the cloud and on a thumb drive, with one copy located offsite. You may not need to go to such lengths for every file, however.

To put together a backup system for your business, first consider what files you consider critical to back up. Active client files and all your work files would be critical. Without those files, you're out of business. After that, decide what would be easy enough to recreate or you wouldn't bother restoring. Do you also want to back up all your photos or music files? How about your system files?

Next, consider your level of risk tolerance and your budget. You can put together a solution that fits both. For example, you could use Microsoft OneDrive as your short-term backup for your work files and then manually back up your most important files weekly. With a subscription to Office 365, you get a certain amount of free storage space, so costs are minimal. Or you might use Dropbox for all your work files, purchasing extra storage to include your music and image files. You might then buy a subscription to a service to back up your entire system or clone your drive monthly to protect against calamities. When shopping for solutions, make sure it will work with your hardware.

Backing Up Emails and Other Files Not on Your Computer

Don't forget about your emails and files you have in places other than your hard drive. How you back up your email will depend on your email software. Check with the provider to learn how to back up and download emails to one or more folders on your computer and then back up those folders regularly. By labeling your emails, you'll be able to quickly identify those you want to save and those you can safely delete.

To keep your email messages from overwhelming you, editor Lori Paximadis recommends creating a "Temporary" folder or label and filling it with emails that you need only for the short term, like meeting invites, out-of-office messages, and shipping notifications. Then periodically delete the oldest files from the folder. If you hold on to messages for six months, you'll be on the same review-and-delete schedule as your computer files, making the task easier to remember to do. I've found this was a great way to avoid using up all the storage in my email program.

If you're using cloud software like Google Docs or Quip for work files and want a backup, download those files as you complete them to a folder on your computer that you regularly back up. This way, you'll create a backup that has everything all in one place.

Archiving Data

Once data is no longer actively being used, you need to decide what to keep, how to keep it, and for how long. You could save every bit of data you've ever created with enough storage and time, but do you need to? And if you do, will you actually be able to find it again? Archiving data generally means storing it in one or more places away from your active files. For digital files, this could mean one or more external hard drives, freeing up space on your devices for new files. For paper files, this might mean moving them from a drawer of active files to a drawer or box set aside for inactive files, also creating room for new files. If you've put the recommended folder structure and a backup plan in place, you'll have already started weeding out what you don't need long term. For the rest, you'll want to create a schedule you can easily follow.

Legal and financial paperwork is one of the most important categories to keep safe. In the United States, your tax return can be audited up to three years later and up to six years later if you haven't claimed 25 percent or more of your gross income. Hold on to your tax returns and all supporting data, such as invoices, 1099s, and expense receipts, for at least as long as you can be audited. You can keep digital records of these documents as long as all the information required is clearly shown. Keep in mind that if you take a home office deduction, you'll want to keep items like your utility bills for the same amount of time. Always check with your local government for its requirements.

You'll also want to hold on to contracts, business permits, articles of incorporation, and insurance documents, at least while they're active. The Small Business Administration (SBA) recommends the following schedule[3] for some common business documents:

+ Invoices and receivables: 5 years
+ Checks and payables: 5 years
+ Contracts: 7 years
+ Annual statements: permanently
+ Copyrights: permanently
+ Tax returns: permanently
+ Tax bills and statements: permanently

SBA recommends holding on to those tax returns permanently in case of litigation. Check with a business lawyer or accountant to see what your specific situation requires.

That leaves a lot of other business records, like business tracking reports, and client-related files to deal with. You can likely toss project schedules as soon as you're done with them, but you may want reports that show annual business results, like a profit-and-loss statement, for several years. You could keep files for that client that comes around every few years, but do you need the files from that one-off client you haven't heard from in a decade? Probably not. I like to keep style sheets and style guides as a resource, but even those become outdated after a while. Make a schedule that works for you. Add a year to the folder name to help track how old the data inside is.

Archiving old files annually helps keep space in your computer and filing cabinets for new files, and using the 3-2-1 strategy for your most important papers helps ensure they're safe. When you add new files to your archive, take a moment to remove those you no longer need. By setting up a good system at the start, you'll save yourself time searching for the right file later and maybe even save your bacon.

Key Takeaways

+ Creating a filing system for electronic and paper files will save you time now.
+ Backing up and archiving your files can save your business in the future.
+ Maintaining document version control can prove which edits you made and which errors you're not responsible for.
+ Don't change the file names for files you'll send back to the client. Instead, append *edited* and your initials to the end of the file name.
+ Names of files you keep for yourself should be comprehensible to present you and future you.
+ Use the topic of the file and version numbers in your file names. Avoid using special characters and spaces to ensure portability across systems.
+ Create a folder system that you can use in all environments, including email and paper.
+ Use a naming system that will tell you what's in the folder, such as *admin*, *graphics*, and *projects*.

+ Colors and icons can make folders instantly recognizable.
+ Backing up your work can save your business from tech catastrophes.
+ Choose a backup system and create a schedule for backups—and then *stick to it*.
+ Common backup options include cloud backup services, disk mirroring, and disk cloning.
+ Don't forget to back up files that exist other than on your hard drive, like email.
+ Archive inactive files that you need to keep for a specified period or indefinitely.
+ For your most important files, use the 3-2-1 strategy for archiving.
+ Check with a business accountant or lawyer for advice on what you're obligated to save and for how long.

CHAPTER ELEVEN

Increasing Your Work Efficiency

No matter how we bill our clients, we spend our time performing services for them, as well as running our businesses. And as freelancers we are the only ones managing our business. We do all the client work, but we also do all the business work, and as we've seen, our task lists can quickly grow beyond our control. When we spend more time trying to figure out how to do something than actually doing it, we're increasing our work time without increasing our earnings. And if we're increasing our work time, we're equally decreasing our personal time, which puts us in the high-speed lane to burnout.

With a new business, you have an excellent opportunity to build in efficiency at the start, but efficiency is also an iterative process. As you and your business evolve, so should your systems. Small improvements may hardly seem worth it, but saving a minute here and a couple minutes there during the course of a workday, day after day, adds up. I typically save three to four hours a month just by using phrase-expanding software. Large improvements can take more effort and time to implement, but if you work on them a bit at a time, you not only gain the results but also train yourself to reach for efficiency whenever possible.

For example, at the beginning of 2021, I focused a lot on team and client onboarding processes. I created templates for proposals, contracts, and emails and set up a process to better track leads and alert me to follow up on them. I organized my Google Drive to be a knowledge center for my team, creating materials for them to better acclimate to new clients. It took months and some outside help to do all this, but by the end of the year, I had a smoother, more professional process for prospects and team members.

Before you can create a system that benefits you, you have to know how you work. Consider how you think and how you evaluate information, pay attention to your habits and rhythms, and make notes of the pain points and the repetitive tasks you do. As you create a working system, write it down. You'll be more likely to follow steps you've created if you've recorded them somewhere. Our needs and habits change over time, as does technology, so review your processes regularly. One of the worst reasons you can give for not changing is "That's the way I've always done it." Be willing to ask whether the way you've always done something is still working. If it is, great. If not, adapt it until it does work or get rid of it.

Business Management Efficiency

There's no one right way to run your business, only the way that works for you at any given moment. It's all trial and error. You may apply what you learn here, as well as what you learn from other resources and freelancers, and you'll adapt it as you go. As you define your business processes, think about what makes the most sense for you. Efficiency isn't about what you do so much as doing it the same way every time.

Say you work exclusively on student dissertations. You have a new client for each project, which means you'll spend a lot of time **onboarding** and **offboarding** clients. You'll want efficient processes to do so to avoid spending more time doing those tasks than doing the actual editing.

You determine that once a student has decided to use your services, you will do the following:

1. Send them a contract to sign and an invoice for the deposit, and request the manuscript for editing, if you don't already have the final version.
2. Enter the invoice into your tracking sheet.
3. Enter the project on your calendar.

4. Create your client folders.
5. Place the contract in the client's Admin folder upon receipt.
6. Log the payment upon receipt.
7. Put the manuscript in the client folder upon receipt, and open the file to ensure it opens and appears to be the correct file.

You'll open the client file even if you won't edit it immediately. If there's a problem with the file, you can contact the client immediately to resolve it. Once you complete the edit, to offboard the client, you will then complete the following:

1. Invoice for the balance of the fee.
2. Log payment upon receipt, and send the edited manuscript and a cover letter.
3. Send a follow-up email a few days later, thanking them for their business and asking them to complete a satisfaction survey.
4. Log survey results upon receipt, or mark the survey as not completed if you don't receive a response.
5. Mark the project as completed.

Further, you create templates for the contract, invoice, survey, and common email messages to increase the efficiency of these processes. As you go through these processes for each client, you find more efficient ways to do some steps. Perhaps you switch to invoicing software that will automatically send late-payment reminders and record payments through gateways like PayPal. You like that, so you change your process.

Any repeated business task can become a standardized process, though not all tasks are worth the effort. Tasks that are low priority or take only a couple of minutes to do might not be worth standardizing. Those that are standardized should be recorded somewhere. Writing down your processes will help you remember how and when to do them. Editor Lori Paximadis advises recording all your business operations in a **business book**—a folder on your computer containing all the necessary information about your business (properly backed up, of course). If you're a hard-copy person, you can print it out for easy reference. Paximadis notes that creating a business book can be invaluable if you have an emergency and a trusted person needs to step into your business for you; all the information they need will be in one place.

As well, create lists of business tasks that need to be done and add them to your business book. Include tasks that help keep your business running, such as invoicing, recording expenses, and archiving old files. By following a regular schedule, you can avoid using large chunks of time to catch up on them. Task lists can be created according to the frequency the tasks need to be done, such as daily or monthly. Here's a starter list[1] that you can add to as you develop your business:

DAILY

+ Respond to any urgent emails.
+ As you work, track your time.
+ At the end of the day, back up today's files (if not using an automated backup system).
+ At the end of the day, create a to-do list for tomorrow.

WEEKLY

+ Create a task list for the following week.
+ Respond to any outstanding emails.
+ If you bill according to project timelines, send any due invoices.
+ Record any payments received.
+ File any papers in your outbox.
+ Update any lists or processes that have changed this week.

MONTHLY

+ If you bill clients monthly, send your invoices.
+ Record your business expenses, including home office expenses.
+ If you're an S corp, pay your business taxes.
+ Review your business strategy (see chapter 12).
+ Make any necessary adjustments to your business processes.

+ Plan for the coming month.

QUARTERLY

+ If you're a sole proprietorship or LLC, pay your business taxes.
+ Catch up on any outstanding business tasks.
+ Review your website content for any needed changes.
+ Review your goals list for the previous quarter.
+ Plan for the coming quarter.

YEARLY

+ Review your business from last year. How did you do?
+ Create goals for your business for the coming year, dividing them into quarterly and monthly tasks.
+ Create goals for your professional development, identifying when and how.
+ Plan vacation time for the coming year and block it off on your calendar.
+ Start organizing your tax files. Make an appointment with your tax accountant.
+ Review your personal and business finances, and make an appointment with your financial adviser.
+ Review your online biographies, directory entries, and profiles, and update as necessary.
+ Archive last year's emails, e-files, and paper files.

As you build your standard business procedures, adapt your lists accordingly. Schedule time to take care of business tasks, and you'll find it easier and more profitable to run your business.

Project Tracking

Most of us start out tracking our projects with a calendar and a task list, and that's a good start for getting the work done. But as time goes on, you'll likely need to juggle multiple projects at once, and you'll want to know things like how many words you edited last quarter or how many projects you worked on for your anchor client last year. Having a way to track all your projects will help keep your work on track.

If you're a rows-and-columns person, a spreadsheet can be the perfect project tracking tool, with Katie Chambers's Project Data Tracker being a readymade option for you. I like Coda as an advanced spreadsheet option that also lets me see my projects in different views. If you decide to invest in a CRM, you could choose one that tracks projects as well. Or you could go with a dedicated project managing solution, like Asana, Trello, or monday.com. Many of them present your projects in different views, like calendar, timelines, and cards, which is handy for visualizing the information in a way that works best for you.

Task Efficiency

It's a challenge to do everything that needs doing in your business to keep it alive and growing. I often have more ideas for promoting my business and services to offer than I have the capacity to do, so identifying tasks that would most help me reach my goals is critical. On *I Done This Blog*, Matthew Stibbe teaches a great way to evaluate and sort all the tasks we have to do to run our businesses, adapting the **growth share matrix**, more commonly known as a **Boston Box**.[2]

CREATE A PRIORITY GRID

Start by creating a list of all your work tasks and how much time you spend on them. You might split the list into business tasks and editing tasks if it helps with the next steps. Do you track your time? Pull those time sheets to build your list. You can also use the business task lists in the previous section, but then dig deeper: list your marketing tasks, technology updates, sales tasks, file backups—everything you can think of. Answer the question: How do I spend my work time?

Next, create a Priority Grid using the Boston Box model (see figure 5). Label the x-axis "Value" and the y-axis "Time." Sort your work tasks in the following quadrants according to their value and the time it takes to do them:

+ Upper left: low value, time consuming
+ Upper right: high value, time consuming
+ Lower left: low value, little time
+ Lower right: high value, little time

To determine the value of the task, ask yourself how it benefits the business and you. Does the task help you grow the business or improve a client's satisfaction with the job you do? Does it help make you a better editor or business owner? "Value" can mean whatever you want it to mean, but be sure to define it closely so you know how to categorize your tasks. For me, a task that has the most value is one that helps my business grow, pleases a client, or brings me joy, often because it results in more time off. For low-value, time-consuming tasks, you want to find a way to do fewer of them or do them less often. For high-value, time-consuming tasks, your goal is to do them better so that they take less time. Those tasks that have a low value and take little time, you want to be able to ignore. And those tasks that have a high value and take little time? Those you want to do more of. Now let's look at how to tackle those tasks.

DO ONLY THE WORK YOU'RE BEING PAID FOR

First, free yourself from low-value, little-time tasks by simply no longer doing them. You are your business, and if you're doing tasks that don't help your business, you're wasting your time. You're not an employee who has to do things because your supervisor or some upper-level manager wants it done. You are in charge of your own time; do those things that help you reach your goals rather than reach someone else's.

This includes extra editing the client hasn't asked or paid for. All too often editors say things like "I couldn't help myself! I just

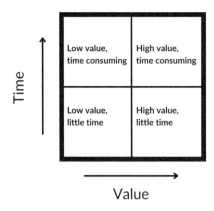

FIGURE 5. Priority grid. Credit: Erin Brenner

couldn't leave those errors!" We *must* help ourselves. We must learn to control the edit to give the client what they paid for. If we compulsively edit to an unlooked-for higher standard, we are working for free and, over time, that reduces your income. We also risk dissatisfying the client, who may have had reasons for wanting a lower-level edit or who may be unhappy that the edit took longer than it was estimated to. Those are sure ways not to succeed with our businesses. Do your best work, by all means, but do the work that's being paid for.

DELEGATE OR AUTOMATE

Many of the tasks on our list can be put on someone or some*thing* else's list. For tasks that need the human touch, consider hiring someone to do them. Look at all the quadrants in figure 5. Are there items on your list that you're not very good at or that you hate doing that someone else could do? In *Virtual Freedom*, Chris Ducker advises making three lists of tasks to potentially out-source: tasks you don't like doing, tasks you don't have the skills to do, and those low-value tasks.[3]

Sometimes, we need to hire an expert. Hiring someone else to do an important job better than you can will benefit your business in the long run because you won't waste your time doing a so-so job when you could be doing what you do best (editing) and earning the money to pay for these advances to your business. For example, even if you do your own bookkeeping, you'll likely find hiring a tax accountant worth the expense. Not only can it save you hours of effort and aggravation, but it can also help keep you out of trouble with the government.

Even when your business is up and running, affording professional services can be a struggle. Another way to get some important jobs done in your business is to swap services with another freelancer. Maybe you've written all the copy for your website, but now it needs editing. Could you swap services with a fellow editor? Maybe you need a logo, so you do some writing or editing for a designer in exchange for a logo. Whatever you swap, be sure to outline the details of the exchange so that both parties know what to do and what to expect. A contract can make both parties feel more secure.

When you can afford it, a virtual assistant can do a lot of those low-value tasks for you, sometimes for less than you might realize. College interns and older teenagers are also good candidates for helping you with these tasks.

Melanie Padgett Powers of the *Deliberate Freelancer* podcast and blog recommends another set of tasks you might hire out: household chores.[4] While she doesn't mind cleaning, she does mind the time it takes from her business and personal life. Once she hired cleaners, she not only had more time for her business, but she was happier.

Think about those tasks you need to do that prevent you from doing what you want to do. Maybe grocery shopping and running errands isn't your thing; delivery services and curbside pickup could save you time for little to no cost. How about yardwork? A local teen might appreciate a little extra money in exchange for mowing your lawn. Or perhaps cooking is a struggle. Check out one of those services that sends you prepped ingredients and easy recipes. Whatever tasks you hire out should free you to do more of the work that you enjoy and brings in money.

Technology is another little-to-no-cost solution for getting things done. I love letting software do tasks for me. Once the task is set up, I can essentially forget about it. There's no one to manage, and software doesn't take a vacation. Things just happen, as if by magic. How cool is that? We'll talk about examples and software later in the chapter.

IMPROVE PROCESSES AND CONSOLIDATE TASKS

Still, there are tasks only we can do or we can't or won't hire out, so we have to get creative. First, look at your high-value, time-consuming tasks. How can you reduce the time it takes to do them? Review your processes to find opportunities for efficiency. Is there a step you can let software do? Are all the steps necessary? Invoicing has always been time consuming for me, but I'm not ready to let someone else do it for me. Over the years, I've modified the process, a step at a time, to make it less of a nuisance. It's still not perfect, but at least I'm making progress.

Would learning to use the tool better help you complete the task easier? Sometimes watching a short tutorial or learning new keyboard shortcuts can make all the difference. For me, it was taking the time to better organize my Google Drive space. For years, I used Google Drive as a dumping ground for shared documents. I never took the time to set up folders or learn how to best use Drive. Once I determined I would use it as a knowledge base for my contractors, I knew I had to do better. I created a folder structure that mimicked the one on my hard drive, with separate folders for family, volunteering, and hobby files. I learned that even when a file is shared with me, I can move it to any folder on my Drive. That's because it's not the actual file I'm moving but a shortcut. The file only exists in the file owner's Drive; everyone else receives a link they can access, which shows up as a shortcut in their Drive. Now instead of avoiding Drive and having to do long, painful searches, I'm using Drive to get repetitive tasks done quicker. It's such a relief not to dread going into my Google Drive.

Consolidating tasks helps you use your time more efficiently, as well. We've already noted that multitasking really doesn't help us get more done. We're actually more efficient when we focus on just one thing at a time. The length of time we spend on one task or one type of task matters, too. Each time we switch tasks, we spend time adjusting to that task. It makes sense, then, to chunk our tasks to work more efficiently.

I'm sure you do this already with your editing, settling in to work on a project for a few hours, and taking breaks as needed. Your focus is fully on that manuscript, right? You can do the same thing with other tasks in your business. Blocking out time for invoicing or answering email can not only get those tasks done but put them out of your mind while you edit.

It's critical, too, to block out time to think strategically about your business, what I like to call my CEO time. To keep an eye on where your business is and where it's headed, you'll want to set aside time regularly to review your progress and plan next steps. In a word, *strategy*, just as the CEO of a big company would do. I'd recommend doing this at least monthly and perhaps weekly when you're first starting out or making a big shift.

DO MORE OF THE THINGS YOU LOVE

By doing the above steps, you really will create more time to do those things that you do best. In addition to the services you offer, what else in your business do you love doing? What are you really good at and enjoy doing? That's where you should be spending the bulk of your time. From the beginning, I've really liked writing a blog. It's a task that I resist letting go of, even when I'm busy. I don't want to outsource it, I resist guest posts, and even when I'm not actively blogging, I'm collecting ideas of what to write about next. So I've made it a key part of my marketing plan, and I make sure I have time to do it.

While working with a coach to find the things she loves to do in her business, Powers asked herself the following questions:

+ What work do I absolutely cherish in my business?
+ What am I really good at and like to do?
+ What am I OK at but don't really love to do?
+ What am I not good at?[5]

It's a variation on the Boston Box we've been discussing through a lens of enjoyment. If you're struggling to identify which of those important tasks you should be doing, these questions can help. However you get there, though, you need to prioritize that endless task list and get help where you can.

Workspace Efficiency and Organization

Your workspace is another place where you can create efficiency. It's easy to say you work well in a mess, but when you can't find what you need immediately or you frequently misplace things, you are not working well. Professional organizers advise getting rid of anything that doesn't belong in your workspace. If it's broken or worn out, get rid of it, they say, right down to rusted paper clips. Anything else you keep must have its own home.

File organizers, drawers and drawer dividers, and shelves can all help keep your things in reach and findable. Store items by category, putting all your papers to file in one place, current papers in another, frequently consulted books in arm's reach, and so on. File papers regularly—before they outgrow their temporary home. Whiteboards and bulletin boards are handy for temporary notes, as are sticky notes on monitors, but be sure to review the notes periodically to remove outdated ones. Cables can be labeled and tied to prevent a rat's nest from tripping you or causing a fire. Keep both trash and recycling bins nearby and empty them regularly.

Many organizers advise not having personal items on your desk, apart from one or two small things. Instead, they say, use the space around your desk for personal items. That seems a bit extreme to me. The key is to give yourself enough space to work. If you set up your space first with your work tools and space to do the work, you can then decide whether you have room for decorative items, keeping in mind that the more items on your desk, the more items you have to keep clean and organized. In the end, your workspace should not just be functional but also make you feel good.

If you're overwhelmed with how to create order in your workspace, check out professional organizers' websites for tips and best practices you can use. Tova Weinstock of Tidy Tova, for example, has a free checklist on her site that you can download.[6] If yours is an extreme case, consider hiring an organizer to help you out. It will be worth the expense to have a workspace suited to you that you can keep organized.

Tool-Based Efficiency

Tools are only as good as their users. Learning to use your tools and how they can best complete a task is key to working more efficiently. Get to know all your tools, study tips and techniques, and keep both your tools and your skills up-to-date. Automate tasks and integrate tools to work together to save you even more time.

Of course the main tool we're concerned about is the computer and all the related software, both on the hard drive and in the cloud. It bears repeating how important it is to keep all your software up-to-date. It will run smoother, and you'll reduce the risk of security breaches—that's an efficiency you can't do without.

Disabilities and injuries notwithstanding, keep your hands on the keyboard and off the mouse as much as possible. Switching between the two may not cost a lot of time, but over the course of a workweek, it can add up. Keyboard shortcuts are a great help here. Get to know the keyboard shortcuts for the actions you do the most in different software.

Text expanders are also great for staying on the keyboard, as well as for avoiding typing long chunks of texts, such as comments you make frequently in your editing. A text-expanding app stores any text you enter and assigns it a keyboard shortcut that will work in almost any program. If you're frequently typing the same long comment in a manuscript, put it in your text expander program and assign a shortcut. Then each time you need to make the comment, put your cursor in the comment balloon and type your shortcut. Voilà! Your long comment will appear in the balloon.

There are several text-expanding apps available, some for free. Although I pay a small annual fee, I like PhraseExpander because I can do things like create shortcuts to open folders on my computer and websites in my browser. The app comes programmed with shortcuts for several dictionaries, social media and news sites, and searches for Google and Amazon. I've added online style guides, folders and files within Google Drive, and more.

Related to keeping your hands on your keyboard is switching apps less often. Recent studies of knowledge workers show that the more often we shift between apps, the more keying mistakes we make and the more time we spend adjusting for the new environment, known as **context switching**. In a 2021 report, software company Asana notes that knowledge workers switch apps 10–25 times a day, hampering their ability to prioritize their work.[7] By performing more tasks in one app and integrating apps to automate tasks, we'll context switch less often, working more efficiently and with fewer mistakes as a result.

As you choose the software to run your business, consider how you might use one app for several tasks. CRM software Dubsado integrates with several email and calendar programs, allowing users to contact prospects and schedule meetings within the software. Users can also create email templates and form templates within the software so that creating a new proposal and sending it to the prospect takes less time. Balanced against this, though, is the time it takes to set up and learn more complex software. Dubsado takes some work to set up and learn. No one wants to abandon a tool they've spent a lot of time trying to make work. Research and test bigger software packages before making a full switch. If too much of the app would go unused or you're struggling to make the software do what you want, keep shopping. Don't trap yourself in software that you don't like and that doesn't work for you.

Connecting, or integrating, apps you already use can be a good alternative to using more complex software. More and more cloud apps are integrating with each other to help users save time. You could integrate Facebook with Mailchimp so that Mailchimp announces the latest edition of your newsletter on your Facebook page, for instance. Check out the apps you use already to find opportunities.

For apps that don't offer integration, you can try a service like Zapier or If This Then That (IFTTT). Following simple setups, you can trigger an action in one app when a specific action happens in another. For example, when I download a new document for editing to a specific Dropbox folder, Zapier will list predefined details about the document in my project management table in Coda. And when I publish a new blog post, Zapier will create a new row in my blog post table in Coda. While these are small tasks, they're tasks I don't have to even think about. Watch your work habits. What do you do repeatedly that doesn't take much thought? For those mechanical tasks, let software do what it does best: exactly perform a series of steps, quickly and as often as necessary.

What about the actual editing work? What can we do within our editing software aside from using keyboard shortcuts to increase our efficiency and productivity? Let's look at three major apps you might use.

WORKING IN WORD

Editors hold on so tightly to working in Word despite all its aggravations and limitations at least partly because of the amount of customizing that can be done. Wildcards in the Find and Replace feature that let you perform more complex searches, macros that automate tasks like swapping first and last names, customized AutoCorrect items, and other features can have Word working for you while you focus on higher-cognitive tasks. If you repeat a task three times, it's worth trying to automate it instead, even if it's for just one manuscript. A quick macro or a robust Find and Replace with wildcards can save you hours of work in just one manuscript.

You'll find a lot of resources for using Word more efficiently. Jack Lyon's excellent *Wildcard Cookbook for Microsoft Word* and his blog, *Editorium Update*, will teach you how to use wildcards. Rhonda Bracey is also a wonderful resource for learning how to use Word better, particularly her *CyberText Newsletter*. Software integrations (called "Add-ins" in Word) like PerfectIt and Acrobat can boost your productivity even further.

If you spend most of your editing time in Word, become intimately familiar with its features and add-in software that can help you work more efficiently and consistently. Lyon offers a package of macros especially suited for editors working on long manuscripts at the Editorium, and you'll find even more resources and tips for working in Word in the Resources section. As long as Word is your main tool for editing, you owe it to yourself to get the most out of it.

WORKING IN ACROBAT READER

PDF isn't the most efficient format for editing and proofreading, but it's become common, if not standard, for proofreading. Some editors, including myself, even copyedit in PDFs. I don't recommend it, as it's clunky and time consuming. However, for particularly clean files or for clients who are willing to pay for extra effort, it can be done. Whatever type of corrections you're making, you want to use the software as efficiently as you can.

Acrobat Reader, Adobe's free software for reading PDFs, is generally enough for editing PDFs. You'll use the annotation tools, such as the drawing tools, inserts, and deletions, as well as sticky notes and comments to mark up the file. You can also install proofreading marks as custom stamps. The stamps often take fewer clicks to use, and many immediately tell another user what correction to make with no further explanation needed. Several editors and publishers have created proofreading stamps you can download and install on your version of Acrobat (you'll find popular ones in Resources) or you can create your own. Everyone has their own preferences for which tools to use to mark up a PDF. Play around to see which suit you best.

To learn to use Acrobat efficiently, check out Adrienne Montgomerie's proofreading course at Archer Editorial Training and her tips on her website, scieditor.ca, both of which are listed in Resources.

WORKING IN GOOGLE DOCS

About a third of my work happens in software other than Word, and most of that is in Google Docs. I'm not surprised my corporate clients have gravitated to it. It allows collaboration, has a change-tracking feature, and is available to anyone who has access to the internet. Editors' complaints are valid, however. It doesn't run macros and sometimes requires too many clicks to do things, with few keyboard shortcuts that help editors. It lacks Word's robust features and customization options. And how do you keep writers from making changes while you edit?

I resisted using Docs for editing for a long time, but I'd rather fill my roster with my desired client base than lose money protesting a change I have little control over. *Google Docs for Editors* by Karin Horler helped me adapt to an environment an increasing number of people outside of editors are embracing. One compromise is to convert Doc files into Word files to edit in and then convert them back. No conversion is perfect, so review the file after both conversions to fix any resulting issues. Remember, too, that the upload will be a new file, not the client's original file, and you will be the owner of that file. That may be fine for the client's purposes, but make sure the client understands that it works this way.

If you'll work in Docs, this process has worked well for me:

1. *Determine with the client the mode you'll work in.* Suggesting mode is like Track Changes, which I recommend using. But even in Editing mode, you can see past versions of the document, so version control is less of an issue.
2. *Request that clients not open the document while it's assigned*

to you. Clients making changes or responding to queries while you're editing can cause overwrites and derail the editing process. Ask clients to wait until you're done editing.

3. *Tag the person next in the process.* I ask clients to tag me when they're ready for me to edit, which sends me an email with the file link. When I'm finished, I tag the client, so they know it's ready for review.

4. *Download a copy of the edited file to your hard drive.* This will provide you with a local copy of the changes you made. It's a good resource to have in case something happens to the file later. (Be sure your contract doesn't prohibit keeping a local copy of the document.)

I also recommend learning keyboard shortcuts and finding software add-ons, such as Consistency Checker, EasyBib, and Doc Tools. You can find these and more in Google Workspace Marketplace.

All efficiency starts with some upfront work, which we sometimes resist. How do we know spending time now will save us time later? We don't always, which is why we record our processes and track our time. Also, trying to implement all the efficiencies at once can be a huge hurdle. Start with one efficiency, recording as you go. You'll soon see the results.

Key Takeaways

+ Efficiency matters, even when you work hourly, because it frees up time to do other things.
+ Efficiency should be an iterative process; let your systems evolve with your business.
+ Your exact processes matter less than your ability to do them the same way each time.
+ Collect all your processes in your business book.
+ Create a list of business tasks to do according to a regular schedule.
+ Prioritize your tasks by their importance to your business.

+ Delete tasks that don't add value. Delegate, automate, or consolidate tasks that add value.

+ Focus your time on tasks that only you can do or that you do best, and that add value to your business.

+ Set up a workspace that puts what you need the most in arm's reach, give everything a home, and get rid of anything that doesn't serve you.

+ Keep your hands on your keyboard by learning keyboard shortcuts and using phrase-expanding software.

+ Make your software work for you by setting up automation and integration.

+ Learn Word's more advanced features, like wildcards and macros.

+ In addition to using Acrobat's editing tools, check out customized proofreading stamps.

+ Don't be afraid of Google Docs. Create a process that limits its downsides and improves your workflow.

CHAPTER TWELVE

Creating Goals and Working toward Success

The first time I called myself a CEO, I felt like an impostor. I was the only one in my business at that time. It took some help from a smart business coach to see that I wasn't just an editor; I was also the leader of my business. My success depended entirely on me, the same way your mindset relies entirely on you.

Here's the tricky part: What does success mean to you? You set your first financial goal in chapter 2, but success is about more than money. Only you can determine what your business goals are. To do so, you need a clear understanding of what you're setting out to achieve. When you're just starting out, it might be to land a regular client or to see your name on an acknowledgments page. Once you've been freelancing for a bit, you might have other goals for your business, such as attracting a new type of client, offering a new service, or increasing your profits.

Most CEOs are good at writing goals. To be a successful freelancer, you must put your CEO hat on and take the time to dream about what you want to do and make a plan for getting there. In this chapter you'll work on creating SMART goals for your business (more on SMART goals below). You'll ask yourself questions like "What steps will I take to reach my earnings goal? How will I know I'm on the right path?"

It's not enough to set goals, as you might have already realized. You'll also want to do the following:

+ Create a workable plan that includes timelines, steps, and metrics.
+ Follow the plan, step-by-step. If you get stuck on a step, work through the difficulty.

+ Continually monitor results.
+ Make minor adjustments as you go along.
+ Periodically review progress. What could be improved? What works and what doesn't?
+ Apply what you learn from your review and keep going.

Here's the thing: no plan is guaranteed to work. Growth is a messy process, with mistakes being an important way that we learn. Ignoring problems won't change the results. Only by acknowledging when your plan isn't working, learning from your mistakes, and actively changing what you're doing can you resolve problems and reach your goals. And the only way to know if you need to change course is to ask questions and measure progress.

Be Your Own CEO

As the owner of your own business, you must be your own CEO. You might be thinking, "But I'm just a freelancer. It's just me in my business." I thought that too. But CEOs focus on a business's operations, looking at how the business runs and gathering input from department leaders to determine where it can be improved. They create a unified vision, charting a path and giving their employees a map and compass for getting there.

You need to do those things, too, even if you're the only one in your business. Schedule time at least monthly to work on your strategy and review your progress. Add the time to your calendar to help you stick to it, and set an agenda to keep you on track. Checklists can be helpful here. Give this block of time an inspiring name, and maybe coordinate a time with a fellow freelancer to keep each other accountable.

Start each session with a review: what you accomplished, what you didn't, and what obstacles you faced. Some periods are busier with client work than others, and you can't accomplish as much strategy work. That's OK. Look ahead and consider what's realistic to accomplish in the near future. Then spend the rest of your scheduled time actively working on that strategy. Monthly, you might create social media posts and schedule them, reach out to clients you haven't heard from in a while, or research new services to offer.

The end of the quarter is the time for a bigger review. If you continue to struggle to accomplish your monthly goals, can you break down the tasks into smaller ones that are easier to do? Are you hitting an obstacle, such as a lack of information or training? You'll want to tackle those things first. It can take practice to figure out how to break down a goal into doable steps, and obstacles are often unpredictable. If you can learn from the struggles, strategy will become easier over time. Then use the rest of the time to work on your goals.

Your CEO time is about being the business owner. Shift your thinking from nouns and verbs to goals and metrics. Block off the time and protect it as strongly as you can. Without regular reviews, it's difficult to move your business forward. You also might find it helpful to adjust your environment when you do your reviews. Try a different music playlist. Use pen and paper rather than the computer. Work elsewhere in your house or in a coffee shop or library. Put on a crown or tiara. Do whatever it takes to shift yourself into that owner mindset. Then put that time to good use. In the rest of this chapter, we'll look at how to choose your goals and how to write goals you can actually work toward.

Choosing Your Goals

There are no hard-and-fast rules about what you should set for your business goals, nor what you should measure to track your progress. Start by being curious about your business. How many hours do you have to spend editing, and how many words do you have to edit to earn your income? How much time do you have to put into administrative tasks to keep your business going? Into marketing and sales tasks? By tracking these things, you'll learn something about how your business operates and where you can improve it. Let's look at some metrics you might track and the goals you can create from them.

FINANCIAL GOALS

We freelance to earn a living, so financial goals should be part of any goals list. Tracking your income and looking at it through various lenses can help you understand the health of your business. You're tracking your annual revenue and net income for tax purposes already. Take the next step and compare the current year with the previous year to monitor growth. Reviewing quarterly earnings can also show you times of year that are typically busy or slow for you. If you always experience a slowdown in July, for example, you might create a goal to increase projects for that month—or schedule time to work on bigger projects within your business.

Combine income data with project data to discover what your average fee is. Are you making the fee you're aiming for? A good financial goal is to increase your average fee, especially for project fees. What percentage of your income comes from each service you offer? Is one service more profitable than another? You could create a goal to increase the percentage that comes from one service or to phase out a less-popular service to focus more on the rest. You can do the same with clients: knowing which types of clients are more profitable can guide you to looking for more like them.

Dig into your invoice data, as well. Accounting and invoicing software are great for alerting us about clients who are habitually slow or late in paying. Make a goal to resolve those issues and keep revenue flowing in. And if you grow to a point where your goal is to cull your client list, you'll know who to put on the top of the list. How are you at sending out your invoices? Maybe your goal could be to set up a process for sending out invoices on a schedule, again to keep incoming payments consistent.

Expenses can help lower your tax bill, but they can also get out of hand quickly, especially if you tend to easily spend a lot. Review how you spend money on your business to ensure you're always spending wisely. I wish I had looked at the different expense categories sooner. It wasn't until the COVID-19 pandemic that I realized exactly how much I was spending on traveling to conferences—money I could have been putting into growing my business or into my retirement. As a result, I'm setting new goals for travel spending and professional development.

SALES GOALS

Closely related to your financial goals are your sales goals. The overall number of leads can tell you how visible your business is and how interested people are in it. When you have few leads, you could set a goal to increase the number of people who fill out an interest form or take a discovery call with you. When you've got plenty of leads but not enough of them become clients, you can set a goal for increasing the quality of leads.

You'll always lose leads because of factors outside of your control. But what about those you felt you should have won? Looking at how much time you spent on each lead, how the interactions went, and how much time passed between interactions can tell you how attentive you are to the prospect. Could you do better? Would a goal to create a better process or get more training help?

MARKETING GOALS

We talked a lot about metrics for measuring your marketing activity in chapter 7. Keeping in mind that marketing takes time to work, how well is it working? Don't be afraid to set goals that change or even cut a marketing tactic that isn't working.

Maybe you hate marketing and want to do it more efficiently. Your goal could be to automate more of your marketing tasks or hire them out. It could be to reduce the number of marketing tactics you use, putting your efforts into the ones that remain. Knowing which tactics don't bring in a lot of results can tell you which to cut.

PROJECT GOALS

When you're looking for the right balance between work hours and income, you want all the project data you can get. The metrics to look at here include editing hours, editing volume (like words/year or average project length), and editing speed. You want to know what type of projects are the most profitable and which drag down your average fees. You want to know which types of content you edit the fastest and which are a slog. All of this will help you set a goal to take on more of the best projects for you, while steering clear of those that give you the biggest headaches.

Is your goal to better diversify your service offerings? Find out how your income and projects break down by service, and set a goal to increase one of your offerings. As you look at the percentage of new and repeat clients on your projects list, your goal could be to gain more repeat clients.

OPERATIONS

How many hours do you spend editing compared to doing administrative and marketing tasks? The latter are unpaid time, so the more efficiently you complete those tasks, the better. A goal to reduce your administrative hours, for example, might include updating to business tools that offer more functionality, creating more processes and templates, and adding more of the automation we talked about in chapter 11.

You might also create an annual goal for professional development, looking at your editing, business, and tech skills. Improvement in any of these areas will improve business results overall. Your department reviews can highlight areas where you need to improve, and tracking the training and hours you put in can help you identify the types of learning that work best for you.

Check the data reports your tools offer for more inspiration on ways to improve your business. Setting goals for the year and breaking them down into weekly and monthly tasks, with quarterly check-ins, can keep you and your business growing over time. Applying the SMART goals formula and using reviews and data dashboards will help you get there.

Creating SMART Goals

Freelancers are usually self-motivated people, so chances are that you've achieved at least some of what you set out to do. But what makes a good goal? Vague goals like "I will earn more money next year" can be hard to act on. While earning any more money would mean you met your goal, how helpful is it if you earn just a few hundred dollars more? It's likely that you have something more specific in mind, like increasing your earnings enough to help you afford a new car. How will you earn more? Without a plan of where this money will come from and how you'll get it, the goal is really just wishing.

Creating a goal that will have the results you want and that you know how to achieve is critical to success. **SMART goals** offer a reliable structure to writing goals that will work for you. A common feature in business planning, SMART goals are *specific, measurable, achievable, relevant*, and *time bound*. The formula helps you write realistic goals and create the plan for achieving them. They don't guarantee success—nothing does—but SMART goals can help you track progress toward your goal and even provide early indicators that you need to make adjustments. They take time to create and put into action, so determine how much time every week or month you'll spend on this project.

Let's look at each variable in the formula using the example of your business attracting a lot of leads but most of those leads aren't turning into paying clients. You're spending a lot of time working on those leads, talking to the prospective client, doing a sample edit, creating an estimate, negotiating the details, and so on, only for them to walk away. Yet you need more projects to grow your business and increase your income. Your draft goal is to turn more leads into paying clients. Now we'll apply the SMART structure to it.

SPECIFIC: WHAT DO YOU WANT TO ACCOMPLISH?

To create a specific goal, think about what you want to accomplish and why. What makes this goal important to your business?

How does it fit into your overall strategy? This one's easy: turning more leads into clients will grow your business and increase your income. To know how to turn more leads into clients, you first have to discern why people aren't hiring you. After reviewing leads that didn't work out, you realize many of the leads weren't a good fit for your business for one of three reasons:

+ The lead doesn't have the budget for your services.
+ You don't work on the type of project they have.
+ You don't do the level of editing the project needs.

Your goal could be to increase the number of leads that come in, but then you'd be sifting through an even bigger pile, hoping to find a good match. Instead, make your goal to increase the number of leads that fit your service and that, as a result, you're more likely to win.

Goal: I will attract leads that better fit my service.

MEASURABLE: HOW WILL YOU MEASURE SUCCESS?
Making a goal measurable ensures that you'll know whether you're making progress toward your goal and when you reach it. You'll ask questions like "How much?" and "How many?" How do you know what a good number is? This can be particularly challenging when you're setting a new goal. You may find it helpful to set the other variables first and come back to measurement. Even then, you may still be taking only an educated guess. That's OK. You answer only to yourself with your goals, so adjust them as needed. Let's say you decide on 10 percent.

Goal: I will attract 10 percent more leads that better fit my service.

If numbers give you anxiety, set nonnumerical measurements instead. For example, once accomplishing the tasks for the goal, do you feel less stressed or less resentful? More satisfied with your leads? Capture your feelings with regular journaling, remembering to review the previous journal entry to note any progress, and let that be your measure.

ACHIEVABLE: WHAT'S POSSIBLE?

To ensure your goal is achievable, think about the steps it will take to get there and how realistic they are based on constraints you have, such as time and money. To attract better-qualified leads, review where your leads are coming from now. In chapter 4, you began collecting this data, asking each lead where they found you. You'll now group them by results to determine next steps.

Poor sources provide leads that never work out, so you decide to stop using these sources or responding to leads from them. Maybe one directory you list in only brings you fiction clients, and you don't edit fiction. That directory would be a poor source of leads, so you decide to remove yourself from the directory. While you're at it, you decide that one of the first questions you'll ask a lead is whether this is a fiction project, and you create an email template turning down fiction work.

Mediocre sources provide some good clients and some leads that didn't pan out. You'll study these sources closer to see if you can improve the leads that come from them. Maybe a networking group you're in sends you some leads that can't afford you. You decide to clarify the types of fees you charge to help others in the network understand how much your services cost. Keep in mind some changes will take time to make.

Excellent sources provide leads that generally become good clients. You'll study these sources to determine whether you can increase the number of leads coming from there. Can you become more active in that space? Create a special offer for just this source? Be wary of changing too much, since these sources already work for you.

Also research new sources for leads, especially ones that look like your excellent sources, and spend time developing them. If it's a directory listing, create your listing and be active within the group that supplies the directory, if possible. Ten percent is

starting to feel a little ambitious, so you lower it a bit and flesh
out your goal.

> Goal: I will attract 7 percent more leads that better fit my service by
> analyzing and revising the sources the leads come from.

RELEVANT: HOW WILL THIS HELP YOUR BUSINESS?

Next, ask whether this goal is relevant to your business. How does
it help your business grow? Does it blend well with the other efforts
you're making right now, or should you do this another time?

In our example, your goal aims to help you get more clients
by reducing the number of poor-quality leads and increasing the
number of good-quality ones—clearly relevant to your business.
You also decide that you can create two more goals to help you
increase the number of clients, which you'll flesh out later.

> Goals: I will create a better way to qualify leads sooner in the sales
> process and improve my sales skills to turn more of those leads into
> clients.

TIME BOUND: WHEN WILL THE EFFORT END?

Now the last part of the SMART goals formula: *time bound*. How
long will revising your lead sources take you? Let's say this is your
business's slow season, so you determine you can make these
changes within a month, but you realize seeing results will take
longer. You decide you'll track changes over the course of a quarter, measuring the quarter's results against the same quarter last
year, which brings you to your final goal.

> Goal: I will attract 7 percent more leads that better fit my service by
> analyzing and revising the sources leads come from. I will com-
> plete the analysis and revisions within one month and monitor
> results for the following quarter, comparing results to the same
> quarter last year.

Make your goals challenging enough to motivate yourself but
not so challenging that they're unachievable. (You'll find help in
Resources.)

Bolstering Your SMART Goals

Psychologists Edwin Locke and Gary Latham have spent decades studying goal setting, developing a set of five principles that can help you achieve your goals: clarity, challenge, commitment, feedback, and task complexity.[1] As you develop your SMART goals, aligning them with these five principles can help you stay on task.

CLARIFYING YOUR GOALS

Clearly defined goals are easier to achieve because we know what steps to take to achieve them. Using the SMART structure to write your goals is a good start, but the website Mind Tools encourages digging a little deeper: "Once you've set your goal, examine how it makes you feel. . . . If you don't feel strongly about the goal, you might need to clarify it or change it entirely." For example, maybe your goal is related to increasing interest in one of your social media accounts, and part of that is posting to LinkedIn every day. But you frequently have to force yourself to read and post on LinkedIn. You find yourself making excuses and pretty soon you don't go to LinkedIn at all. Go back and clarify that goal: Why do you want to increase interest in LinkedIn specifically? If increasing interest in one of your social media accounts really is important to your strategy, does it have to be LinkedIn? Maybe you decide you'd rather use Instagram instead, so you revise your goal accordingly.

CHALLENGING AND REWARDING YOURSELF

To make your goal challenging but not impossible, identify specific milestones within your goal, says Mind Tools, and reward yourself when you meet them. Especially for longer-term or more complex goals, this will help you stay motivated. A reward can be as simple as posting a humble-brag on social media or something bigger, like an extra day off or that additional monitor you've been wanting. Choosing rewards ahead of time can keep you on course.

COMMITTING TO GOALS

You'll need a good dose of commitment to stick to your goals. Visualizing your goal and keeping that image in mind can help here. Try creating a **vision board** to help. While the science is uncertain on whether and why this works, many people find that taking the time to do a vision board helps them focus on what their goals are. I did one for the first time in 2021 as an exercise for one of my mastermind groups (see figure 6). It represented my big goals for the year (clockwise from the top left):

+ Expand my team of contract editors.
+ Write this book.
+ Increase the amount of marketing I do.
+ Increase the amount of automation in my business.

FIGURE 6. My 2021 vision board. Credit: Erin Brenner
with stock photography from iStock

All of these would lead to the center image: more time for my favorite activities, like hiking.

I used a Canva template, stock photography, and a favorite hiking picture to create my vision board. You can create a digital or physical board, and you'll find lots of inspiration on Pinterest. I chose to print out my board and post it where I could see it every day to keep me motivated.

FEEDBACK: REVIEWING YOUR PERFORMANCE

Feedback means measuring your progress and taking the time to review it. Mind Tools recommends breaking down larger goals and reviewing progress at regular milestones. How you track your progress will depend on the precise goal. I'll cover some specific ideas below, but here I'd like to share an idea from productivity strategist Sagan Morrow.

In an Editors Canada conference session, Morrow encouraged attendees to create performance reviews for their businesses, creating departments and subdepartments based on the tasks they do in their businesses.[2] For example, Morrow divides her business into growth, creative, and operations. The creative department includes her courses, short-story contests, romance novels, and business books.

To keep performance reviews manageable, set the maximum number of subdepartments to five, advises Morrow. If you come up with more than that, consider which projects could be categorized together and which take up more time than others. For each department, create a performance review form based on the department's goals and tasks. Gather the data and fill out your forms ahead of time, then during your CEO time analyze the result and decide on any needed changes. I like to include journaling as part of the review process; it helps me identify problems or results that my questions and data didn't anticipate. It also gives me context for the metrics I'm reviewing, helping me determine what's really a problem and what's just my perfectionism getting in the way of progress.

COMPLEXITY: MAKING GOALS ACHIEVABLE

The final principle is task complexity. We do our best to design goals that are achievable, but it sometimes takes actually doing the tasks to discover whether the goal is appropriate. Says Mind Tools, "If you start to feel stressed about meeting your goals, they might be too complex or unrealistic. Reassess both of these areas and modify your goals if necessary." You can break a goal down into smaller goals to focus on more manageable tasks. You can also lengthen the timeline and introduce more milestones.

If you find yourself feeling like a failure if you don't reach milestones in the time you set for yourself, remember that none of this is set in stone. Rewriting your goals to make them manageable isn't cheating—it's discovering what's realistic. It's OK to scrap a goal completely if you realize it's not benefiting you or your business.

Key Takeaways

+ It's not enough to set goals. You need to create a plan for achieving them. This includes monitoring results and making adjustments as you go along.
+ Be open to recognizing when you're not reaching your goals. Growth is messy, and we learn best from our mistakes.
+ The right mindset will help you achieve your goals. Think and act like the leader you are.
+ The SMART goal formula—goals that are specific, measurable, achievable, relevant, and time bound—can help you write goals that will expand your business.
+ In addition, you will need to be committed to your goals. Vision boards can help you maintain that commitment.
+ Performance reviews for each department in your business can help you spot weaknesses before they become big problems for your business.
+ You don't need anyone's permission to adjust your goals. If something's not working, change it.

+ Create a short list of SMART goals for the coming year. Be sure financial goals are part of the list.
+ Increasing your annual income, increasing income from a particular service, or increasing income from a particular client type are common financial goals.
+ Sales goals to work toward include improved lead quality and a higher percentage of lead wins.
+ For marketing, try goals related to automation and an increased focus on successful tactics.
+ Use project data to discover the best projects for your business, and set a goal to increase the number of those best projects.
+ Use time tracking to discover how you spend time working on your business. Set goals to work more efficiently, and create more processes to reduce work overall.
+ Review data reports available from your tools to inspire the best goals for you. Create a set of goals to work toward each year.

CHAPTER THIRTEEN

Handling Difficult Client Situations

One of the advantages of working as a freelancer is more control over your work life. When you're an employee, you can become stuck in difficult situations. You can't choose your colleagues, dictate the publishing process, or choose the work you're assigned. Sometimes you can resolve issues or conflicts with the help of your manager or HR, but when that doesn't work, you have to either put up with the situation or find a new job.

You've already shown that you're brave enough to take risks by becoming your own boss. Now be brave enough to accept when things don't go as planned and do something about it. It starts with having the right mindset. As a freelancer, you choose who you work with and on what. You work with the client to create a process that will benefit both of you. And when things get out of hand, you can fire your client without losing your entire income.

Every client situation is different, though, and there's no one right way to handle problems. You'll develop methods that work best for you and the type of situations you're in over time. To start, below you'll learn about some of the more common red flags and methods for dealing with them that other editors have found to be successful.

Act Like a Business

The best way to deal with difficult clients and projects is to avoid them altogether. By always acting like a business, you'll protect yourself from many problematic situations. It starts with doing things we've already talked about:

+ Defining your services well and communicating that with prospects and clients
+ Using well-thought-out contracts and other legal forms
+ Acting professionally and being respectful of others
+ Communicating clearly and regularly with prospects and clients in a professional voice
+ Setting client expectations for both your editing and your business processes at the beginning of the relationship

Following a **code of practice**, sometimes called a code of ethics, can guide your professional behavior and give you something to share with prospects when you need to build trust. Several editing member organizations have codes you can follow even if you're not a member, including CIEP, EFA, Institute of Professional Editors Limited, and BELS (see Resources for more about these groups).

The most robust comes from CIEP, which also has a complaints procedure that clients can use to help settle disputes with editors who are CIEP members. The code outlines such practices as accurately representing your skills in your advertising, only taking on jobs you have the skills and knowledge to complete, and using your work time wisely to avoid wasting the client's fee. CIEP's code also covers conduct freelancers should expect from their clients. While you can't control what a client does, you can direct them on what you need, such as clear directions on the level of editing and a house style guide.

Acting like a business doesn't mean acting like a doormat, however. Giving clients whatever they want just to appease them isn't a healthy way to run a business and can make you extremely miserable. Know "your bottom line in the way you operate," says freelance editor Lisa Cordaro. "Over time you will have a number of clients coming to you, and you'll develop your offer. It's essential to know what you are—and are not—prepared to accept in a business relationship."[1]

You can't protect a bottom line that keeps falling. Once you've defined it, you'll know what to look for in client situations.

Record your bottom line in your business book and refer to it as needed.

To avoid taking on clients who will become problematic, do your homework on all leads. It can be tempting to say yes immediately, and those clients who would mistreat or scam us count on that. Get basic information from the client upfront—such as telephone number, mailing address, and website—to research them. Also get at least a brief outline of the project before you start a deeper discussion. Consider having prospects fill out a short intake form before you spend any significant time on a lead.

Research them online: Do they have a legitimate-looking website, with well-developed content? If they participate in social media, have they been participating long or is this a new account? Do they talk to their connections, or are there just a couple of posts or memes? Can you find complaints about the prospect online?

For companies, try the Better Business Bureau and Glassdoor. For published book authors, check Amazon and other booksellers for reviews. With individuals, what do you find when you do a search on them? Consider how what you learn fits with your ideal client and project and your bottom line; prospects need to fall somewhere in that range.[2]

As you talk further with the prospect, get as many details as you can about the project. Repeat back what you've heard, outlining how you envision the project working. Set expectations for how you work and what editing can—and can't—do for a manuscript. Especially for indie authors, clarify your public office hours and response time. If you don't answer client communications on weekends, for example, let them know that. Repeat the most important points to the client in conversations, emails, and legal documents. In a new situation it's easy to be overwhelmed with the details and miss something that later becomes important. Targeted repetition from you can help the client catch the most salient details.

Review the entire manuscript whenever possible and do a sample edit, if only for yourself. It's easy to skim a section or two and feel confident about what the edit will be like. It's not until we spend a little time with the manuscript, reading and editing, that we start to see what the work will really be like. Watch for red flags as you go along, and be willing to walk away at any point before you sign a contract. Talking to trusted colleagues can help you decide whether you should accept a questionable project. It's a fact of business that we have to take on less-than-perfect projects to keep the money coming in, but we should always take the time to calculate the risk first. Some situations can be improved by negotiating better terms or getting a nonrefundable deposit, but if your gut says something isn't quite right and you can afford to, listen and let the lead go.

DURING THE PROJECT: UNEXPECTED PLOT TWISTS

Even a promising new client or project can provide a plot twist during the edit. One way to avoid dissatisfied clients is to write respectful queries that clarify your thinking and guide the author to successfully addressing the issue. *Respectful Querying with NUANCE* by Ebonye Gussine Wilkins and *The Subversive Copy Editor* by Carol Fisher Saller are two excellent resources for writing queries. Also be sure to review all your queries before handing the manuscript back. Editing can be a long process, and we get tired and cranky along the way. That's OK, as long as you remove any crankiness from the comments before the client reviews them.

During the edit, you may find problems that you can't address and that will affect the rest of the editing. When those occur, let the client know right away and, if you can, offer guidance on how to resolve the issue.

If you're going to miss the deadline for any reason, let the client know right away, preferably with an estimate of when you can deliver the manuscript. Try to work with the client to get the project done as close to on time as you can. When the problem is personal, such as with an illness, consider letting your client know in broad terms what's going on. Everyone experiences personal crises, and most people will be not only understanding but willing to make concessions they wouldn't otherwise.

Sometimes, though, you realize that you can't complete a project. Are you stuck with it? Depending on the reason, a termination clause in your contract may allow you to stop mid-edit. In addition to a personal or work crisis, reasons you might stop a project include the following:

+ Plagiarized content
+ Triggering or objectionable content
+ Late or missed payments
+ Nondelivery of required materials

With triggering content, let the client know at the beginning what you won't work on, but don't be surprised if they don't recognize that what's in their manuscript is triggering. Humans are really good at justifying things that benefit themselves. You don't need to convince them of anything; just enact your termination clause and move on.

When it comes to the fee, you keep the nonrefundable deposit, but you can also keep any additional portion of the fee that you've earned, especially if you're handing back some edits or professional feedback. The unearned portion of the fee should be returned.

AT THE END: GETTING PAID AND RESOLVING ANY ISSUES

Once you've completed the project, invoice for the balance of the fee as outlined in your contract. For indie authors, I like to receive the final payment before delivering the edited manuscript. I don't generally have that option with companies, but I do submit invoices as soon as I can with new clients to help ensure I get paid.

If the client has an issue after you've submitted the editing manuscript and you've been paid, don't ignore it. Being paid doesn't relieve us of responsibility for the work we've done; the terms of our contract and of any professional code of conduct we follow make us responsible for our work. Deal with the issue in a timely and professional manner, resolving the issue as best you can.

Identifying Common Red Flags

While acting like a business can help us avoid many problematic situations, we won't avoid them all. Becoming familiar with common red flags can help you spot them early. Below are some of the most common red flags freelance editors might experience, sorted into broad categories.

PERSONALITY RED FLAGS

The author-editor relationship is much like the therapist-patient relationship: the professional's and the client's personalities have to mesh. There is so much trust involved in editing someone else's work, and personality clashes make that trust difficult to create and hold on to. If you've communicated a few times with a lead or client and your personalities aren't meshing well, they aren't a good fit for your business. Sometimes, though, clients will have personality traits no editor should put up with, such as with the following examples:

+ The client claims they can take criticism while complaining about small issues or grossly limiting the editing with odd rules.
+ They complain about criticism from a past editor or others in broad terms without offering examples.
+ They make broad accusations about you personally: "You think I'm a substandard writer!" "You just want to write your own book instead of edit mine!"
+ The client is extremely negative or completely lacks confidence about their work or themselves.
+ They yell at you or otherwise speak to you with disrespect.
+ They blame you for their own failings or errors.
+ They ask for editing but give conflicting or impossible directions.

BOUNDARY RED FLAGS

An editor is often their writer's cheerleader and supporter, but we cannot be their therapists. Nor is a freelancer a client's employee. These are boundaries we must enforce. Editing for family and friends and clients who become friends provides another boundary to enforce because you're balancing two relationships—personal and professional—and the other party doesn't always realize how to balance them. You can set a policy to never work for family and friends. Otherwise, you'll want to carefully think out the process for working with family and friends, clearly communicate the boundaries, and work to protect those boundaries. Be upfront about potential issues and occasionally repeat them as needed. Here are some more issues to watch for:

+ The client wants 24/7 access to you, contacting you outside of your stated business hours.
+ They otherwise make claims on your time, such as by continuing to talk after you've indicated your meeting time is up or peppering you with email questions.
+ When family or friends send you something to edit, they expect that you'll do it for free. Whether you do it for free is a decision, not a given.
+ The client treats you like an employee, such as making demands that aren't part of the project, demanding you work on their project first without paying for the privilege, and dictating your work times.
+ The client makes unreasonable contract demands, such as an indie author demanding you not work for anyone else in their genre.

PROFESSIONALISM RED FLAGS

You are a skilled, knowledgeable professional, and you should be treated that way. You have been hired to perform a service, and there are accepted metrics for measuring the quality of that service—perfection isn't one of them. Being treated with respect and having your work evaluated on fair terms are important for good client relations and your mental health. Here are some red flags to watch for:

+ The client hasn't done their work on the manuscript, expecting you to do it without consulting you first.
+ They embroil you in office politics or blame you for problems on their end.
+ They miss a deadline without good cause and without communicating it to you.
+ They miss a lot of deadlines.
+ They frequently pay late.
+ The client owes you money but continues to send you work, expecting it to be done.
+ They blame you for things you can't control.
+ They expect zero errors in the edited manuscript, even after you've educated them on that impossibility.
+ They are unhappy with the number of hours the project took, even though they adjusted the scope during the project and you advised them of the time the extra work would take.
+ They find a significant amount of "errors" that aren't errors and refuse to accept that fact.

PROCESS RED FLAGS

I have encouraged you to create processes that work best for you, but negotiating your process with a client to make the project fit their needs is a good business practice. Being flexible within reason can help you win more projects and give everyone something of what they need. Yet there must be a line. As Cordaro advises, you must know your bottom line. If a client needs a process that will ask too much of you or your business, affecting your health or income, that client is not a good fit for your business. Here are some other potential process red flags to watch for:

+ The manuscript is not ready for the level of editing you're supposed to do.

+ The manuscript for a second pass has significantly changed beyond the boundaries of your original agreement.
+ The directions are vague or you're missing necessary pieces of the project.
+ The client refuses to follow your process without a good reason.
+ They repeatedly adjust the project's goals or parameters, creating an unworkable situation and negatively affecting quality.
+ They repeatedly hand you updates to the manuscript while you are editing, confusing the process and forcing you to redo work.
+ The client's process involves more than one publishing stage happening at once, such as you editing while the writer is still writing or you proofing while designers are still designing.
+ The client doesn't know how to use their software to such a degree that it threatens your ability to do the work.

PROJECT RED FLAGS

Each project is going to have its own quirks and needs. Your goal is to evaluate whether you can handle them. There may be nothing wrong with the project itself, but it may not be one that fits within your business. It could include too many disruptions to your workflow, require extra attention you can't or don't want to give, or simply be a topic you don't want to edit. All of these things are personal considerations, which you can make on a case-by-case basis.

To make those decisions, though, you need a thorough idea of what the project is. When the client doesn't provide it, you must draw it out of them. When they resist defining it and you take on the project anyway, you risk not being able to do the desired job because what's desired hasn't been communicated. Other project-related red flags to look for include the following:

+ Midproject the client demands work that wasn't part of your original agreement and won't renegotiate deadlines or fees.
+ The client is unsure of what they want even after you explain your services and/or provide a sample edit.

+ They set an impossible goal for getting the work done.
+ They keep asking for more and more beyond the original brief.
+ The client wants a refund or to withhold a percentage of payment based on "errors" found after the edit.
+ They offer criminally low fees. If you could earn more in a fast-food drive-thru, the fee is too low.
+ They send you a file "just for a quick glance." What does a "quick glance" mean to them?
+ The manuscript arrives, but it's not as advertised. It's longer than expected, in worse shape than expected, or something similar.
+ The manuscript includes libelous copy or other text that could lead to the author being sued.

You can find more red flags by reading articles by other freelance editors and talking to fellow editors, especially in closed forums.[3] One red flag may not be enough to reject a project; it can depend on the context. The more red flags, though, the more strongly you should consider walking away.

Listening to the Red Flags

Financial concerns aside, you don't need to accept or continue with any project you don't want to do. You don't have to, nor should you, put up with anyone's poor behavior. Nor do you have to make up for it. Defending your boundaries and respecting your own needs are important parts of running a business that you're satisfied with.

HOW TO SAY NO

When a lead throws up too many red flags, some editors will quote an obnoxiously high fee in hopes that the prospect will be the one to say no. While that can work, you may end up cursing yourself should they accept your fee (though your bank account may thank you). If you go this route, be prepared to take on the project if the prospect says yes. Other editors will say that they don't have room in their schedule for the project. This too can work, particularly if you don't mention how long you're booked for, but be prepared for them to negotiate getting on your schedule later. You may find yourself struggling to turn them down a second time.

I prefer to shut down any chance of negotiation if I really don't want the project with a more direct but polite response:

> *Dear [Name],*
>
> Thank you for the opportunity to review your proposal. Unfortunately, it's not the right fit for my business. Good luck with your project!

I keep it brief and factual. I don't apologize because I did nothing wrong, but I also don't accuse, because that can lead to a defensive response. I don't hedge with "I think" because that can be argued. And I don't use my schedule or a fee as a shield because they can be negotiated.

Note, too, that I didn't recommend another editor or an editing directory. If a lead is not a good fit for me but it could be for someone else, I'm happy to recommend fellow editors with their permission or recommend a directory or other resource. If I'm turning them away because of something troubling, like abusive behavior, however, I'm not going to assist the prospect in finding an editor to abuse.

Whatever approach you decide to take, make saying no easier by saving your response as an email template or a text snippet in text-expanding software. Then it's just a couple of keystrokes to create your response and hit send.

WHEN AND HOW TO LET A CLIENT GO

If it's difficult to say no to a prospect, it's even more difficult to say "Stop!" during a project or when you have an ongoing relationship with a client. When I was editor of *Copyediting* newsletter, a reader had outlined the following situation to me. She had been editing a client's periodical for several years. At one point, the publisher's policy changed to allow writers to ignore house style and common sense, resulting in a publication that no longer looked consistent or, to the editor, professional. She had been trying to keep in mind the copyeditor's mantra: "It's not my publication," but she was struggling and couldn't decide whether to keep editing for this client.

It's easy to say that you won't allow an author to plagiarize or that there are certain subjects you won't edit, especially those that go against your spiritual or political beliefs. This situation was less clear. How comfortable should an editor be with working with a client who is fine with reducing quality? This is less a matter of ethics and more of personal comfort.

When you're seeing red flags with a project or client, ask yourself these two questions:

+ *How aggravated am I?* Do I strongly avoid working on this client's projects? Do I turn in sloppy or late work because of my resistance? Does working on the project ruin my day? If so, it might be time to let the client go.
+ *What am I getting from this client?* Do I get more than money that makes the irritation worthwhile? For example, does this client send me a lot of new clients that I love? Do I get other benefits that I wouldn't otherwise get, such as free training or software, and is it valuable to me? Do these things make keeping the client worthwhile? If not, let them go.

Firing a client means losing the income. That's not always a choice you can make. When it's not, make it a priority to replace that client so you can afford to fire them. I kept a client for perhaps six months longer than I wanted to because I couldn't afford to lose them—and it had probably taken me the previous six months to accept that I didn't want to work for them anymore. That's a long time to be unhappy with a client I had to work with for a couple of hours every day.

I made it my mission to replace them. I increased my marketing and started searching job boards. I asked my mastermind group to keep an eye out for opportunities for me. When I at last had built up enough business, I let the client go. I felt lighter immediately. It had been worth all the effort to replace them just to feel that relief.

Give your client advance notice on when you'll terminate the relationship. You don't have to explain yourself if you don't want to. Tell the client in broad terms that the situation no longer works for you. For example:

> *Dear [Name],*
> Thank you for opportunity to work with you. [Add something positive here if you wish.] However, I'm finding that the work no longer fits well in my business. My last day will be [date], on which I'll also send my final invoice. [Add anything additional required to end the relationship, such as returning materials.]

You can give details about why you're leaving if you think the recipient will hear them and take them well. But be cautious: it could burn a bridge you don't want to burn. Unless you want to burn it. Then, by all means, do. Why else be a freelancer?

When Conflict Arises

Few people like conflict, and many actively avoid dealing with it, but the health of your business—and its good reputation— depends on you dealing with conflict in a professional manner. That's not to say you won't feel negatively about the situation and won't want to avoid it; those are normal human reactions.

Immediately let your client know when to expect a response from you. Keep it simple, like "Thank you for letting me know about this, [Name]. I'll review the situation and get back to you within the next couple of days." Then take a break from the situation and let yourself feel those reactions. Maybe it's just a few minutes, maybe it's a day or so. Don't let it go beyond the time frame you gave your client.

Once you're calmer, review the situation, talking to a trusted colleague for objectivity. Honestly consider whether you are at fault in some way. Did you fail to clarify something? Did you make the errors the client is claiming? We all make mistakes, and there are few situations in which we have no responsibility for the outcome. Own your actions and do your best to resolve or make amends for them.

Whether you're at fault or not, offer a solution, preferably one you can both live with. Following good customer service principles can help here. Continue to treat your client with professionalism, respect, and kindness. Really consider the client's complaints, even when it's difficult to do so. Is there stress or worry behind their anger?

With one client recently, I misunderstood the project deadline, and we delivered the edit a couple hours later than the client wanted. She seemed unreasonably angry, but when I thought about the fact that the project was a proposal for a large project she was bidding on, I realized that those couple of hours might have made her miss a submission deadline and miss her chance for new business. It put her anger into perspective for me, and I have since taken extra care to know exactly what time she needs a project delivered.

Try not to take any issues too personally. Humans are complicated, and we can't always know what's motivating a person or what else is going on in their lives. Dealing with problematic situations is just part of running a business. Once you've decided on an action, take it and find a way to let go of the emotions. Vent privately to confidants, scream at your monitor, take it out on a literal punching bag, have a good cry—whatever it takes to release the emotion and get back to business.

How to Write an Apology Letter

You've decided that the client's issue is at least partially, if not fully, your fault. The problem might be something that wasn't completely in your control, such as a major hardware failure that put you out of work, but it's perceived as your fault. Your client's project is now at risk, and they may never hire you again. It's time to write an apology letter.

Let's say you didn't fully review a book manuscript before accepting a project. The editing involved more work than you thought, and the references were particularly rough. Sure, the client's assistant sent you an updated references list, but you were already running late and the references didn't add that much time. Your delivery was so late that the client may miss their publication date. Now that you've handed everything in, you want to write an apology letter.

Particularly if your client is still angry, a little throat-clearing can engage their attention and get them to hear you:

> *Dear [Name], I want to take a moment to discuss what happened with your project.*

Outline the situation and state your part in it as soon as possible. Don't drown your client in details, however, especially if they already know them:

> *I took far longer than I had estimated to finish the edit on your manuscript. I realize that the timetable for getting your completed manuscript to the printer is now in jeopardy.*

Now comes the hard part: a sincere apology. Too often, we're ashamed or defensive (again, normal human behavior), and we hedge our words. We say we're sorry but follow it with why it's not really our fault: "I'm sorry it took me so long, but I did the estimate quickly so I could get started right away for you." Or we never actually say we're sorry for what we did: "I'm sorry you're hurt." Or we state that we want to apologize, but we don't actually do so: "I want to apologize." We need to actually say "I'm sorry" or "I apologize."

In your apology, don't go into endless detail. At this point, frankly, your client doesn't care. They care about solving the problem:

Because I failed to review the entire manuscript before I started editing, as I usually do, I didn't accurately estimate the time the project would take. I'm sorry about that.

Next, be honest about your responsibilities. Don't take responsibility for things that weren't your fault, however. Your client might see this as desperation or a lack of professionalism. They might also use it to take advantage of you. And if someone else has mistakenly received the blame, absolve them of fault. You'll demonstrate humility as well as responsibility.

I'd like to clarify that the extra hours I spent were not the result of your assistant Felipe sending an updated references list during the edit. The original and updated lists were not significantly different, and Felipe sent me the list in a timely fashion.

Now it's time to tell your client how you're going to help them out of this situation, if you can. Keep the focus on your client and their needs.

To help you meet your publishing deadline, I can prioritize proof- reading your manuscript, cutting the time needed to complete the project by a week.

If you can't resolve the issue, acknowledge that and consider what you can do instead. Will you offer a refund? Preferential fees or scheduling for the next project? Choose something that will solve another of the client's problems.

I realize my error will push your publishing date back by several weeks. While it doesn't fix the issue, I'd like to do the proofreading round for 20 percent less than we originally agreed to.

If part of the solution is to offer discounted or free work, be sure to note that on the invoice, along with the original price. This will reinforce the value of what you're offering your client in a positive way. As you wrap up, don't just reassure the client the mistake won't happen again: tell them how you'll avoid it.

In the future, you can be assured I will not rush through an estimate and that any estimate you receive from me will be as firm as I can make it, based on the manuscript reviewed.

For those errors that were outside your control, such as hardware failure, try to adjust your processes to prevent them from upsetting your deadlines again. It's not always doable, of course. Life likes its plot twists. But resolving outstanding computer issues and coordinating with trusted colleagues to step into each other's work in times of crises can up the professionalism and reliability of your business.

Finally, for major problems, apologize a second time, reiterating your important points:

Once again, I'm sorry my actions caused delays in your manuscript. I will do my best to help minimize the delay and ensure costs as outlined above.

After you've sent your apology email, if the client decides not to work with you again, accept their decision gracefully, possibly with a quick email: "I understand your decision, and I wish you well." Not every situation can be saved, nor can you make the client forgive you. Yet a well-written apology—one in which you focus on the client's problem, sincerely apologize, and do your best to fix the situation—often leads to the aggrieved client regaining trust in you.

Let AI Write Your First Draft

When you're struggling to write these emotionally difficult communications—or any professional communication—you can let a generative AI tool like ChatGPT write a draft for you. Enter your ideas and ask it to write the copy for you. Follow up with directions to make it more formal, friendlier, sterner, or another adaptation that would suit. These tools aren't ready to write all on their own, but it can be easier for us to see how to adjust faulty writing than come up with the initial writing. And the AI will do it for you in seconds.

When the Client Won't Take No for an Answer

Sometimes no matter what we do, a client will not be appeased. Maybe it's a mistake you made or maybe they're being unreasonable, but now they just won't let the matter drop. Writing for the *CIEP Blog*, academic copyeditor and CIEP Advanced Professional Member Sue Littleford offers two important pieces of advice. First, "keep full records of the complaint and your response." In a follow-up interview, Littleford explained that writing up the events "slows you and makes you think more clearly, perhaps putting the complaint into perspective to help you respond in a more mature, considered way."[4] The perspective you gain can help you handle the situation better rather than just react defensively. Additionally, it gives you a written record of your side of the situation. Some organizations, like CIEP, offer conflict resolution between its members and clients. Your record will outline your side of the conflict rather than forcing you to rely on memory, which, as Littleford points out, may be "selective about unpleasant things, shying away from them, or blowing them out of proportion."[5]

Littleford's second piece of advice is to know when to stop engaging with the client. If you've attempted to resolve the complaint but they keep making demands or continuing to argue and insult you, "you simply have to tell the client that you won't engage in any further correspondence," she says. "You'll have to decide for yourself when the time has come to put an end to the exchanges. Nowadays, that does involve the risk of being attacked on social media, sadly, but you can't be held hostage."

When you've decided to end all communications with a client, stick to it. Send their messages directly to the trash unopened. Block their email address and mobile number in your devices. Block them on social media. Do what's necessary to prevent receiving or seeing any further communications.

Key Takeaways

+ Freelancing allows you more control over difficult work situations.
+ By acting like a business, you can avoid many conflicts in the first place.
+ Research your prospects before agreeing to take on their project. Be alert for common scams and difficulties.
+ Act professional throughout the project. Write clear, respectful queries, and let the client know when there's a problem that stops your editing.
+ When possible, invoice for the project before returning the edits. In any event, invoice in a timely manner to help ensure prompt payment.
+ Your personality and the client's should mesh. A lack of trust or easy communication can cause problems throughout the relationship. But remember that you aren't the client's employee or therapist. Maintain proper, professional boundaries to avoid problematic demands.
+ Try to ensure the client understands how your relationship will work and what to expect from editing.
+ Do *not* put up with abusive or manipulative behavior from the client.
+ Know what your minimal needs are regarding process and resources, and ensure you get at least those.
+ Stick to your agreement. If the client wants changes along the way, adjust your agreement and make sure you are compensated for any additional work.
+ Unless it's financially impossible to do so, reject projects that bring up too many red flags. One red flag can be enough, but sometimes it's two or three smaller red flags that can lead you to say no.
+ When turning away work, do so firmly but politely. If you don't want to negotiate, don't leave room to negotiate. And don't apologize. You're not obligated to accept every offer that comes along.

+ As long as your contract has an escape clause, it's OK to fire a client midproject if the situation becomes intolerable.

+ When trying to resolve an issue with a client you want to keep, remain professional and respectful. Apologize for your mistakes but not for others'. Try to resolve the issue and in a timely fashion. When you apologize, do so sincerely.

+ When a prospect or client starts to harass you, end all communication.

Beyond the Beginning

CHAPTER FOURTEEN

Continuing the Learning and Getting Help

Staying current in both editing and business trends is crucial to business success and satisfaction with your career. I've worked with both clients and editors who haven't stayed current, and it's painful. Outdated software causes compatibility issues. Outdated processes, like hand-marking printed pages, takes more time than current ones, raising costs and causing delays. Outdated language can create dissatisfaction at the least and a firestorm from readers at the worst. Such situations become a choice between spending extra time to work out the issues and educate (and charging accordingly) or passing on an otherwise good project or contractor.

You might reason that you can attract clients who fit within your limitations, and maybe you can. As time goes on, though, there will be fewer and fewer clients who fit, shrinking your income. And you may miss out on some great projects because your learning is so far behind that you can't catch up in time to take on that tantalizing project.

Don't get into a situation like that. Your business is your livelihood. The better you take care of it, the better it will take care of you. Build a habit of keeping up-to-date so that you'll never struggle to catch up. The best way to stay up-to-date is to plan to do so. Create a customized program of continuing professional development (CPD) to keep all your skills updated. Not only will it make your work life easier and more productive, but you'll increase your self-confidence and satisfaction with your work. Let's look at how to keep learning while continuing to work.

Putting Together Your Own CPD Program

Setting training goals for yourself at the beginning of the year will motivate you throughout the year. Make a list of what you want to learn, prioritizing those lessons that will help you reach your business goals. What are your biggest pain points right now, and what kind of training would help ease them? Maybe you want to use Word more efficiently so you can complete editing projects in less time. Set a goal to learn Word better. Early in your business, one goal is likely to be expanding your client list. You might benefit from learning more about increasing interest for your social media posts, networking, or closing a sale. Look for training in one or more of those areas.

Let's look at several categories of skills to nurture to help you create your own CPD program.

EDITING SKILLS: KEEPING UP-TO-DATE

It should go without saying that professional editors should continue to study grammar and usage, not only staying current but also going deeper. Grammar is complex, and grammarians and linguists don't even all agree on how it works. Seek out both basic and advanced training. The former will refresh rules for you, while the latter will increase your knowledge.

Another area to focus on is manuscript assessment. How can you better assess how much editing will be needed? Seek out training that will help you better review those incoming manuscripts. For example, the Efficient Editing: Strategies and Tactics course from CIEP teaches experienced editors how to analyze and record editorial work and create a methodical plan for doing the editing.

It's also well worth keeping your fact-checking skills up-to-date. With the rise of fake news and other media manipulation, it's critical that editors be able to spot problems and verify authors' statements as far as their responsibilities for facts go. In addition to Brooke Borel's informative *Chicago Guide to Fact-Checking*, check out resources from media literacy organizations like Media

Literacy Now, and increase your searching skills through programs like Google Search Education.

To help prevent clients from sounding outdated or inconsiderate of others, keep up-to-date on changes and trends in language. For example, the rise of conscious language should have every editor considering how a text's readers will view the author's language use. Editors weigh reader expectations in their editing decisions as a matter of course. Becoming familiar with these trends and how they affect the work you do is critical for helping the manuscript be the best it can be.

When you edit, stay alert for the struggles you have or things about language that interest you but that you don't have time to dig into. Add those items to your CPD curriculum, too.

BUSINESS SKILLS: INCREASING EFFICIENCY

After more than a decade in business, I thought I had my business processes locked in. Then I joined a mastermind group for editors who run agencies, and I discovered a whole new set of tasks I hadn't previously recognized as repetitive and new software to help me complete those tasks. I was able cut my administrative time in half within eighteen months. That's time I can spend on winning more clients, working in my business, or taking more time off.

New trends in how we work crop up continually. While in ten years you can run your business just the way you do today, without exploring what's new, you won't know if you're missing out on something that could be valuable to your business. Skills related to executive functions are also often overlooked. If you find yourself consistently struggling to prioritize tasks, organize your workflow, or manage your time, you might benefit from working on these skills. Whether you work with an organizational coach or independently, improving your executive functions will directly benefit your business.

There's so much more you can dig into: finances, project management, marketing and sales, time management, strategy and goal setting, and so on. The more you put into your business skills, the easier it will become to run your business.

TOOL SKILLS: INCREASING PRODUCTIVITY

Your computer aside, software is probably your most important tool. Learning to use your software more efficiently should be a regular part of your CPD. So, too, should keeping up with those never-ending changes that software companies make. I've known freelance editors to tear their hair out in frustration because they could no longer use their software the way they had been for years. They hadn't kept up with software updates, and now when they were finally forced to update, the changes were overwhelming.

Don't delay updates longer than you have to. Not only will there be more changes to adjust to, but you'll be at increased cybersecurity risk. When the software is updated, get to know the changes, especially for major updates. The loss of favorite features is no fun, and the time spent learning yet another change to a critical program can seem wasted, but we rely too much on our software to let our skills become outdated. At the minimum, seek out trusted sources of tips and tricks for your software choices, especially those that focus on an editor's needs (you'll find a few sources for Word and Acrobat in the Resources section).

Explore new tools, as well; you might be surprised at the results. Phrase-expanding software, knowledge management platforms, and workflow automation all sounded like tools my little business did not need. I thought it was all too fussy and more effort to use than would be worth the results. Boy, was I wrong! I started small with PhraseExpander, Coda, and Zapier, trying one task at a time, and now I don't know how I would run my business without them. They save me a ton of time and put information where I need it. Not every program will be for you, and that's fine. Some people love Kanban boards like Trello's, but they don't work for me. Trying out new things can lead to new ways of doing things or reinforce your current processes.

Don't neglect your reference works in your CPD program,

either. Spend a little time reading your dictionary's front matter, for example, or learning how words get in the dictionary. Read about new words and analyses of how we use words. While I don't recommend trying to memorize *The Chicago Manual of Style* in its entirety, brushing up on sections of a style guide that you haven't used in a while will help you retain that knowledge.

Exploring and vetting other resources for your work is CPD, too. What reference works would help you in your editing? Maybe a reliable book or website of quotations? How about a source of geographic information? A database of common abbreviations or a glossary of industry terms? Spend a little time getting to know what new-to-you resources offer and whether their information is trustworthy.

WHERE TO FIND TRAINING

Once you know what you want your professional development program to look like, search for the training. Start by understanding how you best like to learn:

+ *Virtual.* Look for webinars, online courses, and virtual or hybrid conferences.
+ *In person.* Plan to attend conferences, workshops, and courses happening in person.
+ *Self-guided.* Seek out books, articles, podcasts, and videos. Form study groups and plan retreats, whether on your own or with colleagues, in person or virtually.

It's likely that you do well with a mix of training options, depending on the skills and the instructor. Cost and availability can also be key factors. Use the Resources section to get your list of training resources started, and talk to colleagues for more ideas. You'll find an abundance of options.

Once you've gotten a few years' experience in editing and running your business, you may find that teaching others also helps you learn. When I was teaching copyediting for UCSD, my students would regularly ask questions I hadn't anticipated, sending me off on a research expedition. They'd also come up with edits that I hadn't considered but worked well, sometimes even better than what I had. Consider sharing what you know with others, and be open to learning as you go.

Community involvement, whether as a frequent participant in a forum or volunteering with a professional organization, can also be a way to continue learning. The more we listen to each other, the more we learn from each other. Stay curious! Ask questions, seek out new sources of information, and be open to new ideas. These things will help you continue to grow and improve.

Targeted Support

Why do people have so much trouble asking for help? Certainly, we have a responsibility to try to do things independently, but at some point we all need help. The trick is recognizing that point. It's sometime after you've identified a problem and tried the solutions you've researched. It might be as small as scratching your head over how to fix a sentence or paragraph. It could be a client situation you've never come across before or wondering how to approach a business task, like tracking projects. When you've tried what you know, it's time to reach out to others for support.

We all need an outside perspective, honest criticism, and encouragement. In a book about J. R. R. Tolkien's writing group, the Inklings, Diana Pavlac Glyer identifies what made the Inklings work so well for decades. The members offered each other praise and encouragement, as well as opposing viewpoints, pressure to complete tasks, and modeling and editing of texts.[1] Editors have built rich communities that offer these things, and it's common to belong to more than one community. Let's look at some options.

PROFESSIONAL ORGANIZATIONS

The professional organizations I keep talking about also provide editors with colleagues to bond with. Chapters or branches—such as those offered by CIEP, EFA, and Editors Canada—give you a chance to see other editors in person and can offer programming like lectures, networking events, and social hours, both online and in person. Some professional organizations also have forums just for members, including CIEP, EFA, and ACES.

Joining a professional organization can boost your career and make you feel like part of the community. As you think about which organization you might like to join, consider your specific needs. Many professional organizations offer one or more of the following:

+ A job list
+ A member directory
+ Discounts on or free training
+ Networking opportunities
+ Discounts on conferences (the organization's and other groups')
+ Group insurance
+ Increased visibility within the membership
+ Increased visibility with the general public
+ Status

To compare organizations, consider how many of the benefits you will realistically use. It's great when an organization offers group insurance, but do you need it? You shouldn't join a more expensive organization just because it offers insurance you don't need.

Here are some more questions to consider:

+ *Does the job list have the kind of jobs you're looking for?* Are the ads usually for the types of jobs or clients you want? Or are they jobs you wouldn't apply for?
+ *Does the directory get a lot of visitors?* Being listed in a directory is great—as long as your target audience actually visits the site and finds you.

+ *Is the proffered training something you want to take?* And if it's
  not free, is it affordable?
+ *Are the networking opportunities ones you can participate in?*
  If networking events are always Wednesdays at lunchtime and
  you're never available on Wednesdays, the events won't help
  you.
+ *Will the people you'd network with help you reach your goals?* It's
  fine to get to know lots of editors for camaraderie and support,
  whether it's within an organization or in a discussion group.
  But if you're counting on the networking you do within an
  organization to produce career results, you need to think about
  the makeup of the group.

An organization may not fit your needs perfectly, and that's
fine. You're looking for the best fit, not the perfect fit. Weigh the
options and determine which organization will give you the best
bang for your buck. If you have more bucks to spend and more than
one organization will help you, join more than one.

That isn't to say you can't join an organization simply because
you like the people involved and you'll have fun being with them.
That's a perfectly legitimate reason to join a group. When you're
watching your finances, though, it's important to know why you're
joining an organization and ensure you get what you want from it.

UNAFFILIATED EDITING COMMUNITIES

You don't have to join a professional organization to hang out
with like-minded colleagues. The digital world offers us so many
socializing spaces. Email discussion list Copyediting-L (CE-L),
run by medical editor Katharine O'Moore-Klopf, is one of the oldest. Launched in 1992, CE-L continues to be very active. Messages
are not publicly available, giving members a private place to ask
questions and vent a little.

At the time of writing, many editing groups were on Facebook,
including Editors Alliance, Editors' Backroom, Editors Who Talk
Tech, the Editors' Association of Earth and associated subgroups,

Conscious Language + Design, Ask a Book Editor, and Binder Full of Editors. Each group has its own style and culture, so be sure to read the welcome information and rules and get a feel for the group. Groups come and go frequently, so look around your favorite social media or group communications platform to see what's available.

Wherever you land, remember that communities thrive on give-and-take. Being helpful and social as well as asking questions will help you become a valued member of the community. When we only ask and never offer, we quickly wear out our welcome.

BUSINESS COACHES AND MENTORS

Business coaches are a great resource when you have a specific problem or goal you want to tackle. While there's generally a cost involved, a good coach can help you make your investment back many times over. Most engagements with a coach are short term, with a goal of helping you resolve the issue you came with. That said, you may find a coach who will take you on for the long term, if that is what you need.

One reason coaching can be so successful is because generally you're working one-on-one with the coach, who is getting to know your unique business and your unique needs. Some coaches also create small private communities for the people they coach as part of the service, which can be a good way to make connections and not feel like you're the only one with this problem.

Business coaches Elyse Tager and Malini Devadas both helped me with my business, particularly with my mindset. With Tager, I was part of a small coaching group that focused wholly on mindset, particularly traps that women fall into. I learned that I wasn't the only one who thought a particular way and began to focus more on my mindset. I worked with Devadas one-on-one, which was helpful for working on challenges particular to my business. The fact that Devadas is also an editor gave her insight into my business that other coaches often lack. (See Resources for more business coaches.)

Mentoring is similar to coaching in that you work one-on-one with a skilled expert to help you in your business or career. Mentoring will focus more on your development as an editor or business owner rather than on a particular concern you have. Where coaches usually ask you questions to help you discover your own answers, you will usually do the asking with a mentor, tapping into their expertise. The relationship tends to be longer term and less formal than coaching. Mentoring also tends to be a volunteer activity, something to keep in mind when you consider how big an ask you're making.

When you work as an employee, someone senior to you might act as a mentor. Historically, this is how new editors learned to become better editors, and it still happens in those corners of the industry where teams of editors exist. For freelancers, though, we're once again on our own. Some professional organizations offer mentoring as a benefit of membership, and some local business groups offer mentoring programs. For example, the Small Business Administration (SBA) here in the United States provides free counseling for small business owners (that's you!) through several programs, including SCORE Business Mentoring and Women's Business Centers. All advisers are business experts, and sessions can generally take place in person or online.

I was one of those lucky new editors to work on a team and benefit from formal and informal mentoring. My editorial manager read behind newer editors until they reached a certain level of expertise, and then she assigned senior editors to read behind those editors. I learned so much from discussions about why an edit didn't work. I also learned how to help others once I became more skilled. At the beginning of my freelancing career, I worked with O'Moore-Klopf, who had been in business for a while. She made herself available for my questions about running a business. My job was to come up with clear questions she could answer. In return for the mentoring, she asked that I someday mentor someone else, which I have eagerly done.

As with clients, you want a business coach or mentor to be a good fit. Their expertise should match your problem or goal, and their approach should work for you. If your issue is marketing, for example, and you don't like aggressive tactics, then steer clear of coaches who focus on such tactics. Those tactics aren't bad— they're just not for you. Find a good match to get the most out of the relationship.

As you grow in your career, consider mentoring someone else, especially if you benefited from mentoring at some point. Our community thrives when we all give to it in some way.

MASTERMIND GROUPS

A mastermind group offers its members "a combination of brainstorming, education, peer accountability, and support to sharpen your business and personal skills."[2] Unlike group coaching or mentoring, there's no leader or hierarchy in a mastermind group. Everyone has an equal share in learning *and* helping other members. These are private communities with a purpose and goals, as determined by the members. You could belong to a mastermind group with other freelance editors who have businesses similar to yours or who have different types of editing businesses. You might also belong to one where all the members run different types of businesses.

I belong to two mastermind groups, the Quad and the Exchange. The Quad was formed in 2015 and has seven members. We had gotten to know each other through editing conferences, and Laura Poole suggested creating a group chat to stay in touch, where we quickly gelled into a cohesive unit. We all edit, but our businesses are fairly different, and one member now works as an employee rather than as a freelancer. Each member's goals have changed over time, but we've continued to be able to help one another. We have an annual business retreat, a monthly call, and many, many chats every day. We've also presented at conferences together, talking about our group and how to create one. The Quad, I think, is something special. The trust we've built over time is breathtaking. These women aren't just colleagues; they're my best friends.

The Exchange was formed in 2020 by Inkbot Editing owner Molly McCowan, who wanted to create a group of four women who run, or want to run, editorial agencies. We have a monthly meeting that focuses on issues related to running an agency, and we use Slack to chat between meetings. The Exchange has helped me dig deeper into the CEO mindset and focus on expanding my business.

Have a facilitator for your group, recommends the Success Alliance. The facilitator is a member with their own needs, too, but in the facilitator's role they manage group dynamics, such as creating meeting agendas, facilitating conversation, and helping create trust in the group. The Exchange has a facilitator, while the Quad doesn't; instead, we work cooperatively and take turns with leadership and planning duties when they arise.

Although mastermind groups seem to be becoming more popular among freelance editors, it's difficult to know how many exist because the groups are private. And since membership is generally closed, at least among freelance editors, you can't request to join one. If belonging to a mastermind group with other freelance editors interests you, your best bet is to create your own with freelancers you have something in common with.[3] You can also search online for groups with more open membership; remember to look for a group that you can both learn from and contribute to.

Training Others

When you're itching to give back to the community that fostered you, consider sharing what you know in a blog, podcast, or video series. Even if you think the topic is well covered, your unique experience could be valuable to someone else. You can also help others by volunteering your time with one of the editing organizations. Speaking at a conference, presenting a webinar, and mentoring a new member are all ways to support other editors. Some organizations will pay a small honorarium or offer a discount on the conference to acknowledge the work that goes into presenting.

CONTINUING THE LEARNING AND GETTING HELP

You might even teach a course on editing or business through an organization like EFA or a program like UCSD's Extension School. These should be paid opportunities, due to the time and expertise required for them, which boosts your bottom line while helping the next wave of editors enter the field.

Supporting other editors can support your brand as well. Letting clients know, directly and indirectly, how you support other editors gives them more confidence in you. They'll understand that you must be a strong editor if you're teaching others and you must be trustworthy if you're willing to volunteer. You'll expand your network by helping others, too, which can lead to referrals. Editors will get to know you and what kind of editing you do, appreciate the work you do, and be willing to send work referrals your way.

When to Say No

There's a line, however. As with any kind of helping or teaching, you can't do the other person's work for them. Recognizing unreasonable requests is important to avoid being taken advantage of, even unintentionally. Many people who come to you with unreasonable requests don't realize that they're unreasonable. They may just be so new that they don't know what's a reasonable request. It could also be that they're from a place of such privilege that they are blind to the work they're asking for. And, yes, a few folks are just demanding and selfish. You may be able to distinguish between the different types of requesters through the request itself, or you may need to treat a request at first as though the person is just misguided. If they reveal themselves to be otherwise, you can shut them down.

When someone is looking for free help, it should be specific and not require a huge amount of time. How much time you want to give away is up to you, but unexpected requests should take only a few minutes of your time. For frequently asked questions, especially those very basic ones, I've written up short responses in PhraseExpander, making it easier to give an answer. When possible, I point people to further resources, including my blog, to move them forward on their research.

It's not your job to build someone else's business or to train them to edit—unless they hire you to. Learn to recognize the difference between asking for a little guidance and asking you to do their work. You're the person they meet along the road when they're lost. You're giving a little direction to help them to the next step.

One way to recognize an unreasonable request is a resistance to answering it. If it seems like a lot of work to answer, it's probably too broad a question. Questions like "How much should I charge for my services?" and "How do I find clients?" are big questions. I take a chapter for the first and several chapters for the second in this book, and I've only scratched the surface. You can politely decline to answer these types of questions, pointing to a resource if you'd like.

You might feel obligated to respond to someone when they ask you for something. Not only are editors in the business of serving others, but you also might remember how you needed help at the beginning of your career. Give what you're comfortable giving. If someone is making an unreasonable request, however, *you can say no.* Creating a polite "no, thank you" template can make the moment easier:

> *Dear [Name],*
> Thanks for your email. However, this is not a request I can fulfill.
> Good luck in your endeavors!

You're not being rude or harsh; you're simply and clearly saying no. Beating around the bush can lead to misunderstandings, and you don't owe anyone an explanation. Give one if you want ("That's not my field of expertise") or point them in a better direction ("Try the courses offered by . . ."), but you are not obligated to.

Helping other editors can be incredibly rewarding, but it can also be draining and can quickly take away from your paying work.

Finding the right balance will make our community even better, preventing a few folks from burning out while ensuring everyone can get the help they need. In the last chapter, we'll talk more about the self-care that will help you enjoy your new career.

Key Takeaways

+ The best way to maintain your business's health and your satisfaction with it is to continue to develop as a professional and seek out advice when you need it.
+ Plan to continue developing your editing, business, and tech skills. Staying up-to-date will help you remain relevant in a world that moves much too fast.
+ Create a program of continued professional development for yourself, taking advantage of the many offerings now available, including on- and off-line courses and conferences, webinars, workshops, and training materials, like books, articles, and podcasts.
+ Ask for help when you need it! Do what you can to research and resolve the issue yourself, only afterward reaching out to someone else.
+ Professional organizations offer CPD, as well as many other benefits that can help your new business. Compare benefits and join organizations that best meet your needs.
+ Unaffiliated editing communities are a great place to network with like-minded colleagues. Remember to give as much as you get.
+ Business coaches and mentors can provide targeted help for you and your business. Most relationships are relatively short term.
+ Mastermind groups are a powerful way for people in business to help each other. They require trust and confidentiality to run well, however.
+ The editing community is a supportive place that depends on all members giving back in some form.
+ Answering quick questions is a great way to give back. You can

go further by creating content for new editors and teaching.

+   You may find helping others personally rewarding and
    beneficial to your business.

+   It's OK to say no to requests that you're not equipped to handle
    or that are unreasonable.

Taking Care of You

In my teens, I worked at a local McDonald's. Fast food is all about constant motion. If you're not waiting on customers or cooking, you should be restocking or cleaning. Idleness is strongly discouraged. That worked just fine with my type A personality and the work ethic I'd been raised with. The problem was how detrimental such thinking was to my mind and body. I was always tense and stressed. I suffer from migraines, and the more stressed I was, the more migraines I got. I was often underrested and unpleasant to be around as a result. I took that constant-motion mindset into my professional life, working myself into illness on more than one occasion, only in the last several years really understanding what I was doing to myself.

The more we understand about stress, how it affects us, and how we can manage it, the better we can take care of ourselves and our businesses. Let's dive in.

The Long-Term Effects of Stress

It's tempting to work all the available hours to get your business off the ground and keep it going. But you are your business, and if you don't take care of yourself, you can't work and you won't earn a living. The effects of overworking and not taking care of ourselves are well known. In the short term, we lose our ability to hold our focus. Licensed counselor Suzanne Degges-White, PhD, writes:

> Stress overworks the brain and when you're constantly overloading and dividing your limited attention span between computer screens, cellphones, conversations, and worries about what you should be doing that you don't have the time to do, you lose the ability to pay attention to what is going on around you.[1]

With intense tasks like editing, we may find our minds wandering while we work, and we can miss obvious errors in the text—not a good look for our businesses. Stress can also lead to a hyper-focusing state called tunneling that has us focusing on the wrong things, like email instead of the edit that's due to a client. "We get captured by whatever's in front of our face, and we don't give ourselves the space or introspection to think about what might be more meaningful to do," says Anandi Mani, professor of behavioral economics at the Blavatnik School of Government at University of Oxford.[2]

Many people have been conditioned to believe that we "must always be productive," says Matthew Glowiak, PhD, clinical faculty at Southern New Hampshire University. "[That] comes with significant consequences, which may include but are not limited to burnout, depression, anxiety, resentment, and a whole host of other negative implications."[3]

It gets worse.

Working too many hours over the long term can lead to serious health problems and even death. According to a World Health Organization (WHO)/International Labour Organization study, working fifty-five hours or more per week can result in a 35 percent higher risk of stroke and a 17 percent higher risk of ischemic heart disease compared to working thirty-five to forty hours a week, and in 2016 long work hours led to 745,000 deaths from stroke and heart disease.[4] The result isn't immediate, either. The study noted that while deaths occurred in people aged 60–79 years, they had worked long hours when they were aged 45–74.

The solution, then, is twofold: keeping a handle on your work hours by managing your time and workload (see chapters 9 and 11) and reducing stress by practicing a self-care routine. *Self-care* might be a bit of a buzzword right now, but what it describes is something vital to our health. Says Glowiak, "Self-care includes anything you do to keep yourself healthy—physically, mentally and spiritually."[5] Self-care is not being selfish; it's being responsible by meeting your individual needs. While it doesn't mean self-indulgent, what's indulgent for one person might be manda-tory self-care for another. Sleeping long hours every day might be indulgent for healthy people, but for those with a debilitating illness it might be the only way they can lead their lives.

But does it work?

Yes. Glowiak notes that self-care "has been clinically proven to reduce or eliminate anxiety and depression, reduce stress, improve concentration, minimize frustration and anger, increase happiness, improve energy, and more." It can also reduce the risk of heart disease, stroke, and cancer, and it can give your spiritual life a boost.[6]

Creating a Self-Care Routine

Maybe you engage in a little self-care once in a while, such as occasionally getting a massage or diving into a good book. What's needed, though, is routine. "When self-care is regularly prac-ticed," says Brighid (née Courtney) Sullivan, director at Wellable Labs, "the benefits are broad and have even been linked to posi-tive health outcomes such as reduced stress, improved immune system, increased productivity, and higher self-esteem."[7]

Several years ago, I wanted to lose a little weight. I was strug-gling to manage my eating on my own, so I signed up with Noom, a weight-loss program that focuses on the whole person using positive psychology to help you better understand yourself and create healthier habits. I didn't work on just my eating habits but also my sleep and activity habits. I learned how to manage stress better, too. When it was time to figure out how to create an exer-cise regimen, I restarted my yoga practice, this time with a stu-dio that emphasized all eight limbs of yoga, including breathing (pranayama), meditation (dhyana), and spirituality (niyama), as well as the physical poses (asanas). Through these experiences, I've built a routine of self-care, consciously monitoring when I need to adjust something.

What should your routine look like? Everyone's needs are dif-

ferent, of course. Something that helps me relax might cause you
stress. What matters is that whatever you do for self-care you consistently enjoy. There will be times when getting up for a morning
run might be difficult, but if you feel good once you're running,
that's self-care.

Our routines can't become set in stone, though. We need to
keep an eye on our changing needs. *Everyday Health* advises the
following to successfully build a routine:

1. Determine which activities bring you joy, replenish your
   energy, and restore your balance.
2. Start small by choosing one behavior you'd like to incorporate
   into your routine in the next week.
3. Build up to practicing that behavior every day for one week.
4. Reflect on how you feel.
5. Add more practices when ready.
6. Get support through sharing practices from loved ones, a
   coach, a licensed professional (like a therapist or dietitian), or
   through your healthcare plan, community, or workplace.[8]

Especially if you haven't regularly practiced self-care in the
past, you might find it helpful to sketch out your ideas and track
progress. Consider whether you consistently enjoyed the activity
and *how* you can fit it into your life, not whether you can. Once it's
a habit, how often do you think you can practice it? I love hiking
mountains, for example, but it's impractical at this point in my
life to hike them as often as I'd like. Instead, I plan trips to the
mountains several times a year and try to hike the woods around
me as often as I can.

When building your self-care routine, consider the potential
for longer-term effects. For example, changing your eating habits to align better with your body's needs will not only help you
feel better now, it may prevent diseases later in life.[9] Regularly
practicing meditation can not only help you feel calmer in the
moment, but it can help you stay calmer longer during stressful
times. Both of these activities have become a large part of my

routine. Pay attention, too, to what makes you feel stressed. For instance, my office is accessed by going through my bedroom. If my bed is unmade, it irks me every time I pass it. So while a chore, making my bed in the morning helps me feel a bit less stressed throughout the day.

It's a fine line between discipline and subjugation, however. I've long kept a journal to help me process thoughts and feelings, but I don't journal every day or even every other day. I've found that I don't have the urge to journal every day, and I become stressed if I make myself do it when I don't feel that urge. Sometimes it's because I'm processing in a different way, such as by talking to loved ones or working with a therapist. Other times, it's because I just don't have anything I need to process at the moment. I use journaling when I need it, and I don't force myself to journal when I don't because that's what works for me.

Not everything you try will work out, of course. Health experts often recommend setting a goal of 5,000 or 10,000 steps a day to ensure that you move enough during the day, and many editors have a goal of a short walk outside every day to get away from the desk and get moving (search #stetwalk on many social media channels). I've tried several times to do these things, with no success. I do take a break from the computer every hour or so, and I exercise three to four times a week, so I know I'm moving enough. I've decided that these recommendations don't work for me and that's OK.

Frequent breaks are an important part of self-care, though, and maybe more so for people with mental, emotional, or physical challenges. Maybe your break from work is staring blankly out a window or spending a little time with your pet. You might sit in the sunshine or work on a puzzle. You could wash a couple dishes or fold a load of laundry. It could be playing an instrument or completing another row of knitting. Consider what would take you out of your work headspace for a few minutes, giving your mind a chance to rest. You might even create a list for inspiration on those tough days.

If you're getting stuck on building a habit, ask yourself why.

Small changes could make the difference. For example, if you're struggling to work out, would changing the time of day help? I've learned that I have to work out first thing in the morning or right before dinner. These are reliable times when I don't have other responsibilities to distract me. And I need accountability, such as by working out with someone else or signing up for a class I'll have to pay for even if I skip it.

When you're consistently getting stuck in creating a self-care routine, it might be time to bring in an expert in the area you need help with. If it's exercise, work with a fitness coach. If it's food based, a dietitian could be helpful. And if it's mindset, a therapist or spiritual adviser is a good resource.

UPDATE YOUR SELF-CARE PLAN

We evolve as people, and so do the challenges we face. We sometimes go through intense or stressful periods. Starting a new business is a good example. So is a worldwide pandemic. With COVID-19, our lives changed seemingly overnight. Social events were canceled, schools and workplaces went remote, even grocery shopping became a challenge. For many of us, our self-care routines were suddenly disrupted just when we needed them most. Even as the pandemic eased, our needs likely remained in flux as our favored public activities were on-again/off-again and we continued to spend energy on negotiating what's doable and what's not. It may feel like a routine doesn't last for more than five minutes, but the effort is worth it.

Apart from knowing a period is unusually stressful, how can you tell when your self-care routine needs a refresh? "When your self-care starts to feel like work," says clinical psychologist Seth J. Gillihan. "If something has become a 'should' that you feel you have to do instead of something you're looking forward to doing," you need to adjust.[10] Or maybe you've gone all type A on it, hyper-focusing on how you do it or the results of it. Goals are fine, but you can't become fixated on them. If you're fixated, it's no longer self-care.

To revamp your self-care routine, ask yourself where you're

struggling and what feels like work. "Once you've understood that a formerly enriching practice is now becoming fatiguing, keep an open mind about what else you can look to that may provide you with the soothing coping mechanisms," says *Everyday Health*.[11] There's no ideal set of self-care practices you need to do. Do things that relax you, relieve stress and tension, or rejuvenate you. It's normal to need to adjust routines and find new sources of joy from time to time.

WHAT GOES INTO A SELF-CARE ROUTINE
Self-care starts with the basics of good health:

+ Eat a healthy diet.
+ Go to bed and get up at a consistent time.
+ Get enough sleep to feel refreshed.
+ Exercise regularly.
+ Regularly visit medical professionals, such as a primary care doctor.
+ When you're sick, take time to recover and see a doctor when necessary.
+ When you're mentally or emotionally unwell, see a mental health professional.

In addition, pursue activities that bring you joy. Get together with loved ones, engage in hobbies, or volunteer for a cause that is important to you. Include time in your week that has nothing scheduled. Give yourself the freedom to do whatever strikes your fancy or to do nothing at all. Praying, meditating, or reflecting regularly on life can also be an important part of self-care (see Resources for meditation app suggestions). And, of course, organize and try to control your work time. Take regular breaks throughout the workday, and give yourself time off during the week. Evenings and weekends are common, but if you're a night owl, make sure you have downtime during the day at some point.

By not relying on just one thing to de-stress or care for yourself, when life throws you a plot twist, you'll have more than one outlet. Small practices are especially helpful because you can move them to different times of day or increase the repetition during an especially stressful time. If you meditate every morning, add another meditation session during stressful periods. I know, I know: when you're stressed and super busy, how will you fit in another ten minutes of meditation? Maybe there's a chore you can temporarily let slide, leaving dirty dishes in the sink a little longer or balancing your checkbook a week later. The payoff will be worth it.

IN DEFENSE OF VACATIONS

The last corporate job I had gave me four weeks of vacation a year, plus holidays and sick time. After years of having much less time off, I suddenly felt like I could live a life outside of work, exploring new interests and spending time with my young children. It was wonderful. Then I moved to freelancing full-time and didn't take a vacation for two years. I worked long hours and was exhausted all the time. I was regularly pushing out of my comfort zone to grow my business, but I wasn't replenishing my energy. I had less time for my family and just didn't enjoy life anymore. My dad saw what was going on and invited us to go camping with him and my mom, helping us get set up with a camper. That was the start of several years' adventures with my parents, giving Bill and me much needed downtime and the boys special time with family. I returned from those trips feeling more positive and relaxed and often with new ideas for my business.

Science backs me up on the importance of vacations. Degges-White warns, "If a woman allows six or more years to pass between vacations, she is 8 times more likely to develop heart disease. Men who forgo their annual vacation times have a 32 percent greater risk of dying of a heart attack."[12] Degges-White also lists some of the health benefits of a vacation, such as improved productivity, reduced aches and pains due to reduced stress, and improved reaction times. Traveling, even short distances, can be beneficial as well. Richard Davidson, founder of the Center for Healthy

Minds, says, "When we travel we are usually breaking our normal routine.... That decreased familiarity is an opportunity for most people to be more fully present, to really wake up."[13]

"Worry ages a person and vacations—whether around the globe or around the backyard fire pit—allow you to turn off the worry and allow your mind to shift into neutral," writes Degges-White. "Think about it, we're advised to let the batteries run low on our electronic devices so that we can then give them a full charge to keep them working more effectively than keeping them 'fully charged, 24/7.' ... Our bodies and brains need that full charge and shut down just like electronic devices do."[14] When we don't take time off, our bodies have a way of forcing us to rest. Particularly with intense tasks like editing, we may find our minds wandering while we work. It's easy to burn out when you don't take regular vacations or work extra hours. How can you do your best work if you're worn out?

Find a way to afford vacation time. Trim your budget and take on an extra project beforehand, if necessary. If you take a staycation, avoid your office space and try to spend time outdoors. Go places, if you can. Even if you can manage only a short time, make it sacred. You need to completely disconnect from your work, so no answering client messages. Abandon all electronic devices, if you can. I promise, the working world will still be there when you get back. How much time should you take? One study shows even a four-night vacation can help you recharge.[15] Whether participants traveled or stayed at home, researchers found that recovery could still be detected thirty days after the vacation and well-being forty-five days after.

How far in advance you need to plan time off depends on how far in advance you schedule client work and other responsibilities. If you're booking work two or three months in advance, you'll want to block off vacation time that far in advance, too. It also depends on mindset. I find it difficult to take a day off without at least a week's notice. It seems like it's more work to schedule time off than to just work the day. At the beginning of the year, I schedule my vacations, blocking them off on my calendar, even if I'm not going anywhere. That helps me mentally prepare to take time off. It's easy to fill that time with work if my plans change.

Help your regular clients plan better by letting them know in advance that you'll be away from your business. This is also a good way to get work ahead of time off. A quick upcoming vacation message can spur a client to send you their project now or plan to send it after your vacation. I find that a month's notice is usually sufficient.

When your vacation or holiday time arrives, put up an out-of-office message on your email, letting people know when you'll respond and what to do in the meantime. If people contact you using a different medium, such as Slack, let people know there, too, that you'll be out of touch for a while. Then let those messages do their job, and stay unplugged from your business.

Avoiding Burnout

The WHO defines burnout as "a syndrome conceptualized as resulting from chronic workplace stress that has not been successfully managed."[16] In addition to a regular self-care routine, there are a few other things you can do to help prevent burnout.

CELEBRATE THE VICTORIES: CREATING A WIN JAR

Researchers have found that it takes five positive statements to outweigh one negative statement.[17] No wonder we often feel like impostors! You can fight impostor syndrome and stay realistically positive by celebrating your victories, big and small. The Quad tackled this in 2016 by creating "win jars": We wrote down our wins on slips of paper and added them to jars we'd selected. Writing down our victories was a way to notice them in the moment and gave us something to review later. At our next business retreat, we shared some of our victories from the year. We also sometimes share our victories on social media, using the hashtag #winjar. We didn't invent these ideas, of course, but they work wonders

FIGURE 7. My win jar. Credit: Erin Brenner

for us all and give us something to remind each other about when someone is feeling low.

Your win jar can be any container that pleases you. Use plain paper or find something special. I've even just printed out emails to put in my jar. Write down the little wins and the big ones. At first, it might be difficult to recognize wins. Try setting a daily or weekly goal to help you start noticing them. Once you start seeing them, you'll more easily recognize them in the future. That sentence you finally wrangled into grammatical beauty? Write down the original and edited versions and put them in your win jar. You rejected a rush job that would have had you working for peanuts? Put it in your win jar. You took a #stetwalk three days this week? Put it in the jar—and don't forget to post pictures on social media to encourage other editors! Sharing your victories online, particularly in supportive communities like an editors' forum, lets others cheer you on, too, which can further boost your self-confidence. Plus you'll be encouraging other people to share their wins.

Editor Kristine Hunt practices another powerful way to reflect on the positive in life. Every day, she creates a "good things today" post on Facebook, listing three or four positives from her day. Hunt's dedication to this practice and her ability to see the good in some of life's hardships are inspiring. Even identifying one good thing can help. Good news has a way of picking us up, whether it's our own news or someone else's. Why not give it a try?

SCOPE CREEP AND BEING OVERLY HELPFUL

Editors are helpers; it's part of the job. But be wary of being too helpful. Avoid taking on responsibilities that should be the author's or that the client should rightfully hire someone else to do. Yes, we want to win client loyalty by doing something a little extra or helping them out of a bind. Just be sure to weigh the costs carefully. You can't work for free if you want to make a living. And when you're always bailing someone out of a bind, they will come to expect it, which has you no longer being helpful but instead increasing your workload for the same money.

Let's say you're proofreading a client project and you discover that the copyeditor didn't do as good a job as they could have. You already know that you can't just copyedit the project without clearing it with the client first, but you want to help the client and earn a little loyalty. So you offer to do a heavier proofread to improve the manuscript. Great! Just be sure to raise the fee enough to compensate for the extra work. Maybe, though, you don't have the time or energy to do a deeper proofread. That's OK. You still need to tell the client the state of things, but ultimately, it's not your responsibility to fix the issue. You could suggest they go back to the original copyeditor to have them fix the issue or suggest another solution that doesn't involve you doing the work.

Be wary of **scope creep** as well. Clients sometimes try to add more to a project than you originally agreed to for the same price and sometimes even in the same time frame. They don't always do this intentionally, but the result is the same. You might decide that a little extra work will win client loyalty and you can afford the small dilution of your fee, but *you* decide what's reasonable, not the client, and be sure to clarify that this is extra work.

As long as you're working with a contract, you have every right to say no to requests that go beyond the original agreement or to charge extra for extra work. Don't let a demanding client derail your other clients' schedules and have you working for less. You'll resent it, you won't make your budget goals, and you could lose other clients if you can't control your schedule. Stand your ground. It's better to lose one client who is abusing your agreement than to lose other clients and harm yourself in the process just to appease one client.

RECOGNIZE THE NEED TO MAKE CHOICES

You can do anything, but you can't do everything.

I really struggle with this one. I've improved over the years, recognizing sooner and more frequently that I'm overfilling my schedule and if I don't adjust something, I'll end up exhausted and stressed out. Where once overworking was a way of life, now it's periods of weeks, and occasionally months, of overworking. Trying to estimate how long something will take is difficult. That's one reason there are so many methods for time management. Another obstacle, though, is our tendency to think time is only scarce now but will be plentiful in the future. Yet time is always limited, as is our energy.

To avoid overcommitting, think about your schedule like an art exhibit, in which you're placing each work of art intentionally and giving it space to be observed, says Sendhil Mullainathan, Roman Family University Professor of Computation and Behavioral Science at Chicago Booth.[18] In other words, strategize how to use your time and energy to your best advantage.

I like the metaphor of filling a jar with rocks, pebbles, and sand: if you put the rocks in first, then the pebbles, and then the sand, everything fits. But if you start with the sand, you won't be able to fit all the rocks and pebbles. The rocks are your priorities, whether work or personal, or the tasks that take the most time. In a daily schedule, a rock might be finishing the edit due that day or shopping for groceries. Pebbles are less important or don't take very long to do. A common pebble might be sending invoices or folding a load of laundry. Sand is the filler tasks, like checking email or loading dishes into the dishwasher. These tasks don't take very long and can fit between bigger tasks.

Do you spend a lot of time on email? You're not alone. Most people do. When we let email take up big chunks of time, we feel busy but we don't accomplish as much, often finding that we didn't get to that rock that was on our schedule. Relegating sand tasks to a period of a few minutes helps us better use our time. Mullainathan recommends setting timers for those tasks that lead to busyness rather than productivity.

By assigning a priority to our tasks and remembering that time and energy are always limited, we can start to make better choices about the obligations we take on and create a more realistic schedule. It will always be a challenge. There's more in the world to do each day than any of us can possibly do, and time estimates will always be just that—estimates. The more you practice making choices based on your limits, the better you'll get at it. (And if you find a way of creating more time or energy, please let me know!)

RECOGNIZE WHEN YOU'RE REACHING YOUR LIMITS

How do you know when you've reached your limit of energy or

focus? It will vary from person to person, but in general when your mind starts to wander, your pace slows, you start making small mistakes, or you resist doing the next task, it's time for a break. Constant tiredness, unsettled emotions, or feeling uncentered are also signs that you've reached your limits and need to recharge. According to career and life coach Caroline Castrillon, being uncentered can mean a number of things:

+ Being consumed by negative thoughts
+ Feeling nervous, stuck, and overwhelmed
+ Being easily distracted and unable to focus
+ Checking your phone compulsively throughout the day[19]

When you spot these signs, it's time for some self-care. Doing so when you first see the signs will help you avoid more serious consequences.

BE KIND TO YOURSELF

The world will constantly push you to do more. The need may be never-ending, but we are not. You must be your own best protector. Be kind to yourself. Practice positive self-talk rather than always berating yourself for your "failures." Castrillon notes that being too critical of yourself can lead you to do worse rather than improve. "Treating yourself with more kindness could be the best way to train your mind for success," she says. "Research has linked self-compassion to everything from improved psychological well-being and better body image to enhanced self-worth and increased motivation. So, make it a habit of speaking to yourself in a way that is understanding and compassionate."[20]

Planning for a Crisis

In 2017, my father died unexpectedly. For two months after, I could barely keep RTE and Copyediting running. All of my thoughts were on my father and what we were going through. How could I think about work? I wish I had had a plan in place for taking an extended leave, but I didn't and the bills still needed paying, so I hung on. Freelancers don't have the option of a paid leave that isn't self-funded. To maintain our businesses, we need a strategy for getting through a personal crisis.

Start by making a financial plan. Depending on your country's healthcare system, you may want to purchase disability insurance to replace at least part of your income if you become unable to work. No matter where you are, build an emergency savings fund. Recommendations of how much you should have vary, though three months' income seems to be the minimum. If you can do that, the next step is to set up an investment account that will earn reasonable returns while letting you access the money when you need it. Both of these things can be a challenge, especially for a freelancer. Just remember that any money you can set aside will help.

The next thing to do is plan for someone else to jump into your business. Choose people you trust who are capable of doing the tasks you need done. A family member may be able to alert clients and pay bills if you're suddenly unable to work, but you may need a fellow editor to help finish any projects. When Molly McCowan was suddenly unable to work because of excruciating pain in her hands, she relied on fellow editors to be her hands for her. Editors contacted clients and took on some of her work. When my dad was rushed to the hospital days before he died, the Quad helped me out in a similar fashion. Laura Poole even flew up to Boston to teach a workshop I had been scheduled to lead.

Outline the tasks you need someone else to do if you're unable to work and who will do them. Write up detailed instructions and give them access to the necessary passwords. You could even write up a template email to send in an emergency. Anything you do in a calm moment will make the crisis a little easier. Make sure your helpers understand what to do ahead of time and give them a copy of the directions to hold on to. Review your plan every year or so to ensure it stays current.

For all your self-care strategies, you may need an extended break from work at some point, whether because of burnout, health issues, or something else. But you are your business, so what do you do?

If you need a break from work, *take it*. Finish up looming deadlines, negotiate upcoming deadlines, and otherwise clear your calendar. If you're putting your emergency plan into action, let your helpers know. Be as honest with clients as you're comfortable with and as the relationship calls for. Even outside of a pandemic, people can be surprisingly understanding, especially when you have a plan for filling their needs. Once that's done, just as with planned time off, truly walk away from your work. Turn on your out-of-office message, turn off your computer, and stay away from your workspace. Avoid work-related social media. Take your life back to basics: eat healthy, get enough sleep, get outside, exercise, see loved ones. Do things that you enjoy. If you're ill and you're not getting better, see a healthcare professional.

RETURNING TO WORK

Depending on the reason you stepped away from work, don't wait too long to return. The longer you're away, the harder it is to come back. Continue to listen to your needs, and be forgiving of yourself. After my father's death, when I was barely hanging on, I found that I couldn't write and editing was a struggle. On those days, I tried to stick with tasks that didn't need as much focus or energy. Ease back into your routine if you can. And be sure to thank clients and helpers for their understanding and assistance while you were gone.

It's only in the last decade or so that I've managed to wrangle the constant-motion mindset and approached work in a more sustainable way. I feel better for it and my work hasn't suffered, but the old instinct still kicks in sometimes. Be kind to yourself as you try to change habits, and if old habits sneak back in, just do your best to change the current situation and avoid it next time.

Key Takeaways

+ Self-care is crucial to business success. Without you, your business won't exist, so take care of you.
+ Self-care has been clinically proven to reduce stress and anxiety, increase energy, and improve concentration, as well as reduce the risk of certain stress-related diseases.
+ Create a regular routine of self-care to help you stay healthy. If you don't already have a routine, make a list of activities that you enjoy or that renew your energy. Build habits by working on one behavior at a time.
+ Needs change over time. Make sure your self-care routine changes with them.
+ Regular vacations are an important part of self-care. Take time off!
+ In addition to self-care, you can avoid burnout by celebrating your victories, defending the boundaries of your responsibilities, making choices, recognizing when you've reached your limit, and being kind to yourself.
+ Make an emergency plan that allows you to be away from your business for an extended period. Build an emergency cash fund if you can, and ask others to take over some of your duties when you need to be out of work. Include your emergency plan in your business book.
+ Listen to your needs to decide the right time to return to work. Ease back into your routine if you can, and thank everyone who helped you out during this time.

Build a Business That Uniquely Fits You

Freelancing has been an excellent choice for me. I've had my struggles, as every business owner does. Some risks have not worked out. I've made mistakes and lost clients for it. I've stressed about late payments and had times when I couldn't pay myself. There's something to struggle against almost every day. Sometimes I just want to give up and have an employer take over my work life again. But then I take a break, and sooner than I'd expect I recommit to my business. I remember how far I've come and how much I've benefited from the freelancing life. My business gives back far more than I put in—and I put in a lot.

When my parents closed their driving school after decades of running it, they had no regrets. The business had been an intimate part of our family life, providing us with a living as well as life lessons. "The school has given us so much over the years," my dad said when he announced they were closing it, "it owes us nothing." My hope for you is that you build a business that, at the end, has given you so much that it owes you nothing, having paid back many times over all the work you've put in.

Remember that your freelance editing business is you. It thrives on your purpose and the effort you put into it. It's a living thing, and you are its lifeblood. Take care of it by taking care of you and realigning your business to your needs whenever they change. Keep your compass close as you make your own map.

Good luck!

Acknowledgments

As an editor, I know that while the author writes the book, they do so with a lot of help. What I didn't know was how enthusiastically that help can be given. There are so many people to thank for their help on this journey. These are just a few of them. Thanks to the following people:

Executive editor Mary Laur at the University of Chicago Press. For all my years of editing, I have never edited for a press. You not only championed this book, but you taught me the process of working with a press and how to do it well.

The Quad (in no particular order)—Amy J. Schneider, Laura Poole, Lori Paximadis, Katharine O'Moore-Klopf, Adrienne Montgomerie, and Sarah Grey. My sister-friends, you encourage me to do ever-bigger things. You don't let me beat myself up when something goes wrong. You teach me every day how to be a better business owner and a better person. A special shoutout to Katharine, who was my first business mentor. Your kindness and expertise helped me launch my business; your "fee" of mentoring someone else started me on this path of sharing what I know with other editors.

The behind-the-scenes people who helped me prep this manuscript, including my favorite editorial assistant, Sean Brenner; beta readers Kristin Cole, Ann Kennedy, and Rachel Pouliot; peer reviewers Karen Conlin, Alicia Chantal, and Cynthia Williams; subheadings reviser Wendy Scavuzzo; copyeditor Erin DeWitt; indexer Alexandra Peace; and proofreader Karen Wise. I appreciate your professional skills and your excitement for this project.

My blog readers, session attendees, business mentees, and students: Your desire to learn encouraged me to share the information that seemed to live only in my head. Your questions kept me learning and improving.

And of course to my guys, Bill, Sean (again), and Duncan. You've always encouraged me in my business, giving me space to do the work, sometimes jumped in to help, and listened to me talk endlessly about both my work and this book. Your belief in me planted the seeds of my own belief in me. Thank you.

Appendix A: Glossary of Terms

about page—A web page that tells the reader briefly about the owners of the website.

AIDA—Attention, interest, desire, and action, which are the steps a prospect goes through before purchasing a service.

audience—The people you are trying to reach with your marketing.

backup services—Services for storing your data on someone else's server to prevent data loss.

board of directors—People elected by company owners (with private companies) or by shareholders (with public companies) to set company strategy and oversee company management.

book packagers—Companies that produce print books for publishers, handling editing, designing, approvals, and other book production tasks.

Boston Box—Originally a model for measuring the value of assets; now adapted into a model for measuring priority that plots time spent against value added on a grid. Also called *growth share matrix*.

bounce rate (email)—The number of email addresses from an email list that could not successfully receive an email you sent.

bounce rate (website)—A percentage that measures how many visitors left a web page after landing on one page and not interacting with it.

brand identity—An identifying aesthetic for a brand, as depicted in items such as a logo, tagline, colors, fonts, and writing voice.

brochure website—The digital equivalent of a print brochure. A brochure website has only a few pages that don't change often, such as a home page, an about page, a services page, and a contact page.

business book—A collection of documents, either print or digital, containing all the necessary information about your business.

business expenses—Purchases necessary for the operation of
a business. Such purchases are generally tax deductible. Also
called *deductions*.

calls to action (CTA)—Short statements that tell the audience
what to do next, often used in marketing and sales copy.

campaigns—Coordinated marketing programs, such as a series of
emails sent to an email list with a closely defined goal.

click map—A graphic depiction of how many times hyperlinks on a
web page or in an email have been clicked on.

click-through rate (CTR)—The percentage of readers who clicked
on a link or a collection of links.

clients—People or organizations that hire freelancers to perform
a task.

code of practice—A set of rules to guide interactions between
clients and freelancers.

cold-calling—Making an unprompted call to a potential client,
usually to inquire about business opportunities.

cold read—A review of the latest version of a manuscript for errors. See also *editorial proofreading*.

comparison proofreading—Comparing live copy to dead copy,
and ensuring all requested changes have been made. Compare
to *editorial proofreading*.

confirmed opt-in email—An email list that recipients opt into on
an initial sign-up page and in a confirmation email. Also called
double opt-in email.

contact page—A web page detailing how to contact someone connected to the website.

context switching—Time spent adjusting to a new environment,
such as when switching apps. Context switching lowers productivity.

copyediting—The revision of a manuscript to improve readability,
grammar, and other sentence-level considerations, as well as
to ensure accuracy. See also *heavy copyedit*, *light copyedit*, and
medium copyedit.

cover letter (with a résumé)—An introductory letter sent to a prospective client, along with a résumé, to give a brief synopsis of one's related work experience when applying for a job.

cover letters (about projects)—Extensive notes written by an editor containing advice for how to revise the manuscript or how the editing was performed. Also called *transmittal notes*.

customer relationship management (CRM) services—Services that help businesses establish and maintain a working relationship with a prospect or client by tracking activities, storing data, and completing tasks, such as sending emails.

dead copy—The last approved version of a manuscript, along with any changes to be added. Compare to *live copy*.

deductions—Purchases necessary for the operation of a business. Such purchases are generally tax deductible. Also called *business expenses*.

developmental editing—Editing a manuscript to help develop its ideas and improve the structure and organization.

discovery call—An introductory call with a prospect to discuss the prospect's needs and how the freelancer can meet those needs.

disk cloning—Creating a copy of a hard drive on a separate, external hard drive.

disk mirroring—Creating a copy of a hard drive on the original computer.

document version control—Keeping track of the different versions of a document, and ensuring that only a select group of contributors is working on it at any given time.

double opt-in email—An email list that recipients opt into on an initial sign-up page and in a confirmation email. Also called *confirmed opt-in email*.

editorial proofreading—Proofreading a document without a previous version to compare it against. Compare to *comparison proofreading*.

employer identification number (EIN)—A number supplied by the US government used to identify a business entity.

engagement—All forms of interaction with a social media post, including shares, comments, and likes.

errors and omissions (E&O) insurance—Insurance against accusations of negligence from a client. Also called *professional liability insurance.*

exit rate—The percentage of website visits that end on the page being measured. For example, if an about page has a 10 percent exit rate, then 10 percent of website visits end on the about page, meaning the visitor leaves the site from that page.

federal income tax—In the United States, a percentage of earned income paid to the federal government.

fees—The costs of particular tasks or services.

file-syncing services—Services that host copies of files that can be accessed online.

filing status—In the United States, the status under which you file your taxes, such as filing as an individual or filing jointly with a spouse.

Flowtime technique—A time-management technique in which you choose a task, work on it until you become tired, take a break, and then repeat the process until the task is finished.

general liability insurance—Insurance for general losses a business might face, such as physical injury, property damage, and medical bills.

gross earnings—The total income a business earns after deducting the cost of goods sold.

gross income—The total amount of money an individual earns from all sources.

gross profit—The total amount of money a business earns from all sources.

gross receipts—The total amount of money a business takes in, including money not generated by sales, such as dividend income, interest, and tax refunds.

growth share matrix—Originally a model for measuring the value of assets; now adapted into a model for measuring priority that plots time spent against value added on a grid. Also called *Boston Box.*

hard bounce—An email that permanently cannot be delivered to the intended recipient's email inbox, such as when the email address is defunct. Compare to *soft bounce.*

heavy copyedit—A copyedit in which concerns like sensitive language, wordiness, and ambiguity are corrected instead of queried and in which a more forceful approach is taken to manuscript organization. Compare to *light copyedit* and *medium copyedit*.

home page—The main page of a website, which provides an overview of the site and links to its various pages.

hub-and-spoke model—A two-part marketing model that connects various methods of outreach (the spokes), such as your social media accounts, with a central source of information (a hub), like your website.

impostor syndrome—A feeling of being a fraud and doubting one's abilities.

income taxes—Taxes paid on earned income.

invoice—A list of services rendered and a request for payment.

key performance indicators (KPIs)—Indicators of progress toward a specific goal.

light copyedit—The correction of errors in language mechanics, grammar, and usage. Often also involves checking cross-references and list organization, as well as querying unclear terms and facts. Compare to *medium copyedit* and *heavy copyedit*.

likes—One-click, wordless interactions with a social media post, the minimum engagement a post can have.

limited liability company (LLC)—A business structure in which the company itself is responsible for its debts and liabilities instead of the company's owners being personally responsible.

limited liability partnership (LLP)—A business partnership in which each partner is responsible for only what they put into the business.

line editing—A form of editing that focuses on paragraph structure, paragraph flow, sentence structure, meaning and logic, readability, and writing style. Also called *content editing, stylistic editing,* or *substantive editing*.

live copy—The latest in-progress version of a manuscript, showing the most recent requests for changes. Compare to *dead copy*.

main message—A marketing statement that contains all the
details the audience needs. Shorter messages should be built
from the main message to ensure consistency across marketing
messages.

manuscript—An author's unpublished written work.

marketing—The process of advertising yourself, your business, or
your clients to potential clients or partners.

marketing plan—An overall strategy for marketing a brand.

marketing vehicles—The tools used to deliver a marketing campaign, such as email.

medium copyedit—A light copyedit with additional attention
paid to stylistic concerns, factuality, sensitive language, and
paragraph-level organization. Compare to *light copyedit* and
heavy copyedit.

net income—Revenue minus production costs and business expenses.

net income after taxes—Net income minus taxes.

net profit—A business's gross receipts minus its expenses, including any salaries.

niche—A specialty within a given field.

noncompete agreement (NCA)—A legally binding agreement in
which one party agrees not to compete with the other party in a
specified way for a defined period.

nondisclosure agreement (NDA)—A legally binding agreement
in which one party agrees to refrain from discussing information from the other party that is denoted as confidential with
unauthorized individuals.

offboarding—The process of ending a work relationship with a
client.

offer—Something of value given in order to entice someone to take
a desired action.

onboarding—The process of beginning a work relationship with a
client.

open rate—The percentage of email recipients who opened an
email.

opt-in email—A series of emails that subscribers requested to receive.

opt-out email—A series of emails that subscribers were signed up to receive by the email sender.

page views—The number of times a web page has been visited during the period measured (*session*). *Unique page views* is the number of people who visit a web page, counting each person once, no matter how many times they visit the page during a session.

persuasion—Use of facts, data, and emotional appeals to encourage a prospect to become a client or take a desired action.

Pomodoro technique—A time-management technique in which the workday is broken into 25-minute chunks separated by 5-minute breaks, with a longer 15- to 20-minute break every two hours.

production costs—Expenses incurred in the creation of a product or service, such as raw materials, labor, and marketing costs.

professional liability insurance—Insurance against accusations of negligence from a client. Also called *errors and omissions (E&O) insurance.*

professionals who write—Clients who have written but don't write exclusively for a living and therefore require more extensive developmental editing and guidance about writing and the publishing process.

project contract—A contract that clearly defines the scope of a project and the responsibilities of both parties.

proofreading—Review or revision of a manuscript to ensure that no errors were missed in prior edits and any final corrections were made. See also *editorial proofreading* and *comparison proofreading.*

prospects—Potential clients.

relationship marketing—A type of marketing that focuses on one-to-one interactions with prospects and clients with the goal of client loyalty.

revenue—The total amount of money received from clients.

sales funnel—A model of the steps a prospect goes through, following *AIDA*, before taking the desired action.

scope creep—Expansion of the scope of a project beyond what was originally agreed upon without a change to the fee and time frame.

S corporations (S corps)—Corporations for which income, losses, deductions, and credits are passed through to shareholders for tax purposes.

segments—Subsets of an audience.

self-employment tax—In the United States, an additional tax on income for the self-employed, which is applied to Social Security and Medicare benefits.

services page—A web page detailing the services offered.

shareholders—People who own a percentage (a *share*) in a company.

shares—Reposting of your posts to other people's social media accounts.

SMART goals—Goals that are **s**pecific, **m**easurable, **a**chievable, **r**elevant, and **t**ime bound.

soft bounce—An email that temporarily cannot be delivered to the intended recipient's email inbox, such as when their inbox is full. Compare to *hard bounce.*

sole proprietorships—Unincorporated business entities that are owned by one person who pays personal income tax on all income minus deductions.

#stetwalk—A hashtag editors use with pictures taken on a short walk, posted on social media, to encourage themselves and other editors to be more physically active.

stylistic editing—A form of editing that focuses on paragraph structure, paragraph flow, sentence structure, meaning and logic, readability, and writing style. Also called *line editing, content editing*, or *substantive editing.*

tactics—Marketing actions intended to produce a specific result.

tagline—A short sentence or phrase associated with a business meant to convey a key idea about it.

text expanders—Apps that produce commonly typed words or phrases through the use of quick keyboard shortcuts.

transmittal notes—Extensive notes written by an editor containing advice for how to revise a manuscript or how the editing was performed. Also called *cover letters (about projects)*.

unique selling proposition (USP)—An identifying trait of a business that makes its products or services unique.

unsubscribe rate—The percentage of email recipients who unsubscribed from an email list.

use cases—Content that explains a situation in which a product or service can be used or a method for using it.

visitors—The number of people who go to a web page during the period being measured. A *unique visitor* is counted only once, even when they visit the web page multiple times during the period. Also called *users*.

visits—The number of times someone views one or more pages on a website during the period being measured.

vision board—A collage of images that represent one's goals.

word of mouth (WOM)—A form of marketing in which people discuss a brand or product with their friends without being asked to do so or without gaining anything from doing so.

Appendix B: Resources and Tools by Topic

You'll find a version of this section on my website in the Editor Resources section (https://www.righttouchediting.com/editor -resources/), which will be kept updated and include clickable links.

All Things Editing

Copyeditors' Knowledge Base, http://www.kokedit.com/ckb.php. Katharine O'Moore-Klopf provides links to associations, tools, and other helpful items and entities.

Business Platforms

Bigin, http://www.zoho.com/bigin/. A simple CRM solution for managing prospective client information and automating business leads.

Christensen, Clayton M., Taddy Hall, Karen Dillon, and David S. Duncan. "Know Your Customers' 'Jobs to Be Done.'" *Harvard Business Review* (September 2016): 54–62, https://hbr.org/2016/09/know-your -customers-jobs-to-be-done?referral=00060. See also the accompanying video, found at https://hbr.org/video/5852531897001/know-your -customers-jobs-to-be-done.

Deliberate Freelancer, https://meledits.com/category/podcast/. Weekly podcasts hosted by magazine editor and writer Melanie Padgett Powers, featuring guests and covering business and health-related subjects for freelancers.

Dubsado, http://www.dubsado.com/. An all-in-one business platform that includes workflow and automation functions.

HoneyBook, http://www.honeybook.com/. An all-in-one business management platform that includes workflow and automation functions.

"The New Freelancer's Business Pack." Right Touch Editing, http://www .righttouchediting.com/resources/business-tools/. Free downloadable resources, tracking sheets, and templates for growing and managing your business.

PandaDoc, http://www.pandadoc.com/. An online document automation solution for creating, managing, and e-signing documents such as proposals, quotes, and contracts.

Resources for Editors from Beacon Point Services, https://beaconpointservices.org/editors-resources/. Editor-created tracking resources, courses, and webinars, plus free downloadable checklists.

17hats, http://www.17hats.com/. A business management platform for small business owners providing many online tools, including scheduling, payments, and lead responses.

Zoho CRM, http://www.zoho.com/crm/. Customizable CRM software for automating business tasks and building and tracking customer relationships.

Editor Training and Coaching

ACES Certificate in Editing—Poynter, https://www.poynter.org/shop/reporting-editing/aces-editing-certificate/.

Archer Editorial Training, https://archer-editorial-training.teachable.com/.

Borel, Brooke. *The Chicago Guide to Fact-Checking*. 2nd ed. Chicago: University of Chicago Press, 2023.

Certificate in Publishing—Toronto Metropolitan University, https://continuing.torontomu.ca/public/category/courseCategoryCertificateProfile.do?method=load&certificateId=198771.

Copyediting Certificate—Emerson College, https://professional.emerson.edu/public/category/courseCategoryCertificateProfile.do?method=load&certificateId=1022704.

Copyediting Certificate—University of California, San Diego, https://extension.ucsd.edu/courses-and-programs/copyediting.

Copyediting Certificate Program—Writer's Digest University, http://www.writersonlineworkshops.com/courses/copyediting-certification-course.

Database of Training for Editors, by Editors. Right Touch Editing, https://bit.ly/TrainingByEditors. A list of training for editors offered independently by editors.

Eby, Kate. "The Essential Guide to Writing SMART Goals." Smartsheet, January 9, 2019, https://www.smartsheet.com/blog/essential-guide-writing-smart-goals.

Editing and Proofreading Training—Publishing Training Centre, http://
www.publishingtrainingcentre.co.uk/courses.

Editing Certificate—Simon Fraser University, https://www.sfu.ca
/continuing-studies/programs/editing-certificate.html.

Editing Certificate—University of Chicago, https://professional.uchicago
.edu/find-your-fit/certificates/editing/apply.

Einsohn, Amy, and Marilyn Schwartz. *The Copyeditor's Handbook: A
Guide for Book Publishing and Corporate Communications*. 4th ed.
Oakland: University of California Press, 2019.

Grätzer, George. *More Math into LaTeX*. Toronto: Springer International
Publishing AG, 2016. Available at http://www.latexstudio.net/wp
-content/uploads/2016/09/More_Math_Into_LaTeX-Springer2016.pdf.

Hart, Geoff. *Effective Onscreen Editing: New Tools for an Old Profession*.
4th ed. Point-Clare, QC: Diaskeuasis, 2019.

Horler, Karin. *Google Docs for Editors*. New York: Editorial Freelancers
Association Publications, 2018.

"Learn LaTeX in 30 Minutes." Overleaf, https://www.overleaf.com/learn
/latex/Learn_LaTeX_in_30_minutes.

Lyon, Jack. *Wildcard Cookbook for Microsoft Word*. Salt Lake City: The
Editorium, 2015.

Montgomerie, Adrienne. *Editing in Word 365*, 2022, https://www.lulu
.com/en/us/shop/adrienne-montgomerie/editing-in-word-365/ebook
/product-p855r4.html?page=1&pageSize=4.

Montgomerie, Adrienne. "PDF Markup Basics for Proofreaders &
Copyeditors." *Right Angels and Polo Bears: Adventures in Editing*
(blog), 2019, https://scieditor.ca/2019/02/pdf-markup-basics-for
-proofreaders-copyeditors/.

Norton, Scott. *Developmental Editing: A Handbook for Freelancers, Authors, and Publishers*. 2nd ed. Chicago: University of Chicago Press,
2023.

Professional Editing Standards Certificate—Queen's University, https://
pros.educ.queensu.ca/certificates/EDIT.

"Professional Editorial Standards 2016." Editors Canada, https://www
.editors.ca/node/11696.

Proofreading and Copyediting Certificate—College of Media and Publishing, https://collegeofmediaandpublishing.co.uk/product/proofreading
-and-editing-course/.

Saller, Carol Fisher. *The Subversive Copy Editor: Advice from Chicago (or,
How to Negotiate Good Relationships with Your Writers, Your Colleagues,
and Yourself)*. 2nd ed. Chicago: University of Chicago Press, 2016.

Schneider, Amy J. *The Chicago Guide to Copyediting Fiction.* Chicago: University of Chicago Press, 2023.

Servais, Erin. AI for Editors, https://www.aiforeditors.com/.

"A Simple Guide to LaTeX." LaTeX-Tutorial, https://latex-tutorial .com/tutorials/.

University of California. "SMART Goals: A How to Guide," http:// www.ucop.edu/local-human-resources/_files/performance -appraisal/How%20to%20write%20SMART%20Goals%20v2.pdf.

Wilkins, Ebonye Gussine. *Respectful Querying with NUANCE.* New York: Editorial Freelancers Association Publications, 2020.

Women's Business Centers, http://www.sba.gov/local-assistance /resource-partners/womens-business-centers. These centers offer free business coaching for women (US residents only).

File Storage and Security

Acronis Cyber Protect Home Office, http://www.acronis.com/en-us /products/true-image/.

Backblaze: B2 Cloud Storage, http://www.backblaze.com/.

Carbonite, http://www.carbonite.com/. Cloud backup and storage.

Dropbox, http://www.dropbox.com/. Online file storage and sharing.

Google Drive, https://www.google.com/drive/. Online file storage, sharing, and collaboration platform.

iCloud, https://www.icloud.com/. Apple's online storage solution.

IDrive, https://www.idrive.com/. Cloud storage and backup.

Microsoft OneDrive, http://www.microsoft.com/en-us/microsoft-365 /onedrive/online-cloud-storage. Cloud storage.

Financial Management and Rate Setting

Chartered Institute of Editing and Proofreading. "Suggested Minimum Rates," http://www.ciep.uk/resources/suggested-minimum-rates.

Cushion, https://cushion.ai/. A bill management program.

Editorial Freelancers Association. "Editorial Rates," http://www.the -efa.org/rates/.

The Editor's Affairs, https://www.whatimeantosay.com/tea. Business management program that includes workflow and automation functions.

Editors' Tracking Programs, https://beaconpointservices.org/editors -tracking-programs/. Business management trackers designed particularly for freelance editors.

FreshBooks, https://www.freshbooks.com/. Accounting software.

Investopedia, http://www.investopedia.com/. The latest news and information on stocks and investing.

Lake, Rebecca. "Budgets: Everything You Need to Know." The Balance,
updated October 19, 2022, http://www.thebalance.com/how-to-make-a
-budget-1289587.

Lewis, Laurie. *What to Charge: Pricing Strategies for Freelancers and Con-
sultants.* Parker, CO: Outskirts Press, 2011.

PayPal, https://www.paypal.com/us/home.

Poinier, Jake. *The Science, Art and Voodoo of Freelance Pricing and Getting Paid.* Phoenix: More Cowbell Books, 2013.

QuickBooks, https://quickbooks.intuit.com/.

Wave Invoicing, https://www.waveapps.com/.

Wise, https://wise.com/. Platform for sending, receiving, exchanging, and
managing money.

YNAB, https://www.ynab.com/. Budgeting, saving, and money management platform.

Zoho Invoice, www.zoho.com/invoice.

Finding Work and Résumé Help

Accidental Boston, https://www.accidentalboston.com/.

Diverse Databases, https://editorsofcolor.com/diverse-databases/.

Editors of Color Database, https://editorsofcolor.com/.

Fiverr, http://www.fiverr.com/.

"Freelance Copy Editor Resume Examples." LiveCareer, http://www
.livecareer.com/resume/examples/copywriting/freelance-copy-editor.

"Freelance Editor Resume Examples." Jobhero, http://www.jobhero.com
/resume/examples/copywriting/freelance-editor.

Freelancer, http://www.freelancer.com/.

Glassdoor, http://www.glassdoor.com/.

Indeed, https://www.indeed.com/.

Luckwaldt, Jen Hubley. "Freelance Resume and Cover Letter Examples
and Tips." The Balance, updated December 16, 2022, http://www
.thebalancecareers.com/resume-tips-for-freelancers-2060763.

Publishers Lunch Job Board, http://www.publishersmarketplace.com
/jobs/.

Reedsy, https://reedsy.com.

Upwork, http://www.upwork.com/.

ZipRecruiter, http://www.ziprecruiter.com/.

Graphic Design

Canva, http://www.canva.com/. Graphic design software to use for free or to purchase.

99designs, https://99designs.com/. Full-service graphic design.

Legal Assistance

Cather, Karin, and Dick Margulis. *The Paper It's Written On: Defining Your Relationship with an Editing Client.* CreateSpace Independent Publishing Platform, 2018.

LegalZoom, http://www.legalzoom.com/.

Rocket Lawyer, http://www.rocketlawyer.com/.

Marketing and Email Platforms

"Are You Adding Links to Your Bios?" Right Touch Editing, January 14, 2021, https://www.righttouchediting.com/2021/01/14/are-you-adding-links-to-your-bios/.

AWeber, http://www.aweber.com/.

Brevo, www.brevo.com. Digital and email marketing platform.

Campaign Monitor, http://www.campaignmonitor.com/.

Constant Contact, http://www.constantcontact.com/.

"Digital Marketing Strategy Worksheet." Right Touch Editing, http://www.righttouchediting.com/wp-content/uploads/2020/10/Digital-Marketing-Strategy-Worksheet.pdf.

"50 Magic Marketing Words That Make Your Offer Irresistible." *Frog Blog*, June 5, 2019, http://www.gcfrog.com/2019/06/05/50-magic-marketing-words-that-make-your-offer-irresistible/.

"46 Proven Call-to-Action Words to Maximize Conversions." Wishpond, https://blog.wishpond.com/post/103290853633/the-25-best-words-to-use-in-your-call-to-action.HubSpot. http://www.hubspot.com/products/marketing/analytics.

"Increase Clicks with These 12 Call-to-Action Phrases." The Daily Egg, April 8, 2020, https://www.crazyegg.com/blog/call-to-action-phrases/.

MailChimp, https://mailchimp.com/.

MailerLite, http://www.mailerlite.com/.

MOO, https://www.moo.com/. Printing and design services.

"100 Call to Action Keywords for Marketing Campaigns." Beacon Technologies, http://www.beacontechnologies.com/blog/2009/12/100-call-to-action-keywords-for-marketing-campaigns.aspx.

Patel, Neil. "16 Call-to-Action Formulas That Make People Want to Click." HubSpot, updated August 25, 2017, https://blog.hubspot.com /marketing/call-to-action-formulas.

Quadros, Mark. "17 Call to Action Examples (+ How to Write the Perfect Social CTA)." AdEspresso, October 21, 2022, https://adespresso.com /blog/call-to-action-examples/.

"The 30 Magic Marketing Words You Should Be Using: Email Marketing Words." VerticalResponse, December 13, 2021, http://www .verticalresponse.com/blog/the-30-magic-marketing-words/.

"The Top 20 Magic Marketing Words That Compel or Repel." ZenBusiness, http://www.zenbusiness.com/blog/top-20-magic-marketing-words -compel-repel/.

Vistaprint, http://www.vistaprint.com/.

Zoho Campaigns, http://www.zoho.com/campaigns/.

Networking Groups

ACES chats on X, https://aceseditors.org/resources/aceschat.

Ask a Book Editor, http://www.facebook.com/groups/askabookeditor/.

Binder Full of Editors, https://www.facebook.com/groups /589911937847496/.

Conscious Language + Design, http://www.facebook.com/groups /consciouslanguage/.

Copyediting-L (CE-L), http://www.copyediting-l.info/.

Editors' Association of Earth (EAE), http://www.facebook.com/groups /EditorsofEarth/.

Editors' Association of Earth (EAE), http://www.facebook.com/groups /EAEAdSpace/.

Editors' Backroom, https://www.facebook.com/groups/editorsbackroom/.

Editors Tea Club. To join, contact EditorsTeaClub@gmail.com.

Editors Who Talk Tech, http://www.facebook.com/groups /769534149785406/.

LGBTQ+ Editors Association, https://www.facebook.com/LGBTQEditors.

Neurodivergent Editors' Lounge, https://www.facebook.com/groups /ndeditorslounge.

Productivity Tips and Tools

Asana, https://asana.com/. Teamwork and workflow organizer.

Borucka, Kate. "15+ Most Effective and Proven Time Management Tech-

niques." TimeCamp, December 1, 2021, http://www.timecamp.com
/blog/2018/07/15-effective-proven-time-management-techniques
-2020/.

Bullet Journal, https://bulletjournal.com/. Mindfulness combined with a
productivity system.

Calendly, https://calendly.com/. Scheduling automation platform.

Circa Notebook System, https://www.levenger.com/circa-326.aspx.

Clockify, https://clockify.me/. Free time tracker for teams.

cloudHQ, https://www.cloudhq.net/g_suite. Gmail productivity tools.

Coda, https://coda.io/about. Document-building platform.

Ducker, Chris. *Virtual Freedom: How to Work with Virtual Staff to Buy
More Time, Become More Productive, and Build Your Dream Business.*
Dallas: BenBella Books, 2014.

"The Flowtime Technique: Abandoning Pomodoro Part 2." Medium.com,
August 16, 2016, https://medium.com/@UrgentPigeon/the-flowtime
-technique-7685101bd191#.ag0za2e33.

HourStack, https://hourstack.com/. Task and time-management platform.

If This Then That (IFTTT), https://ifttt.com/. Business management automation platform.

monday.com, https://monday.com/. Business management and workflow
platform.

"9 Proven Time Management Techniques and Tools." University of
St. Augustine for Health Sciences, http://www.usa.edu/blog/time
-management-techniques/.

Notion, https://www.notion.so/product. Connected online workspace
platform.

Office Time, https://officetime.net/dev/. Time tracker.

"The Pomodoro Technique." Francesco Cirillo, https://francescocirillo
.com/pages/pomodoro-technique.

Quip, https://quip.com/. Platform for standardizing, automating, and
embedding real-time collaborative documents.

RescueTime, https://rescuetime.com/. Time management, tracking, and
coaching platform.

"Scription Chronodex Weekly Planner 2012." Scription, https://scription
.typepad.com/blog/2011/11/scription-chronodex-weekly-planner-2012
-free-download-with-the-cost-of-a-prayer.html.

Timeular, https://timeular.com/. Time-tracking application.

Todoist, https://todoist.com/home. Task management and to-do list application.

Toggl, https://toggl.com/. Time-tracking application.

Trello, https://trello.com/en-US. Business management and workflow
platform.

Professional Member Organizations

ACES: The Society for Editing, https://aceseditors.org/. Offers training, an
annual conference, networking, and exclusive editing resources.

Alliance of Independent Authors (ALLi), http://www
.allianceindependentauthors.org/. Offers advice, education, and support to self-publishing authors. Editors and other publishing professionals can join as Partner Members.

American Medical Writers Association (AMWA), https://www.amwa.org/.
Offers education, conferences, networking, and resources for medical
writers and editors.

Bay Area Editors' Forum (BAEF), http://www.editorsforum.org/. Based
in the San Francisco Bay Area, BAEF provides support via educational
forums and job listings for member editors.

Board of Editors in the Life Sciences (BELS), http://www.bels.org/. Provides training, conferences, and certification for editors working in
the life sciences.

Chartered Institute of Editing and Proofreading (CIEP), http://www.ciep
.uk/. Formerly the Society for Editors and Proofreaders, CIEP offers
training, a conference, publications, legal counsel, and other support for editors worldwide. It also has several chapters, including two
virtual-only chapters for non-UK members, and offers tiered membership based on professional experience.

Editorial Freelancers Association (EFA), http://www.the-efa.org/. Offers
an extensive training program, a conference, and publications, as well
as an email discussion list and a job list and directory, with several
chapters throughout the United States.

Editors Canada, http://www.editors.ca/. Offers online training, conferences, publications, and proficiency certification in editing, with several
branches and twigs, or sub-branches, to join.

European Association of Science Editors (EASE), https://ease.org.uk/.
Promotes standards in the field of science editing and holds conferences and other networking opportunities.

Institute of Professional Editors Limited (IPEd), http://www.iped-editors
.org/. For editors in New Zealand and Australia, IPEd runs regular
conferences, sponsors awards for editors, maintains Australian editing
standards, and helps members with accreditation and professional
development.

Institute of Scientific and Technical Communicators (ISTC), https://istc
.org.uk/. UK-based ISTC offers networking opportunities, conferences,
and research resources for professionals in the field of information
development.

Northwest Editors Guild, http://www.edsguild.org/. Offers conferences
and other networking opportunities to members, as well as mentoring,
a job board, and an email list.

Self-Care

Calm, https://www.calm.com/. Applications and programs to help improve
mental and physical well-being.

"Creating a Healthier Life: A Step-by-Step Guide to Wellness." Substance
Abuse and Mental Health Services Administration (SAMHSA), https://
store.samhsa.gov/sites/default/files/d7/priv/sma16-4958.pdf.

Sattva, https://www.sattva.life/. Guided meditation, chants, and mantras.

Ten Percent Happier, https://www.tenpercent.com/. Podcasts, courses,
mindfulness, and meditations.

Social Media Management and Training

Google Analytics, https://analytics.google.com/.

Hootsuite, http://www.hootsuite.com/.

How to Dominate Social Media Marketing: A Complete Strategy Guide.
Search Engine Journal ebook, https://www.searchenginejournal.com
/social-media-ebook/.

inlytics, https://www.inlytics.io/pricing. LinkedIn Analytics platform.

LinkedIn Lounge, https://espirian.co.uk/linkedin/. LinkedIn training and
best practices from John Esperian.

Listen, https://www.brandwatch.com/products/listen/. Social listening
technology for understanding consumer trends and habits.

Lua, Alfred. "It's Time to Reconsider 'Best Time to Post on Social Media'
Studies. Here's What to Do Instead." Buffer, March 19, 2023, https://
buffer.com/library/best-time-to-post-on-social-media/.

Matomo, https://matomo.org/. Web analytics platform.

MavSocial, https://mavsocial.com/. Social media management platform
for business.

Meta (formerly Facebook) Business Suite, https://business.facebook.com/.

Shield, https://www.shieldapp.ai/. Social media post performance and
growth trackers.

Social Media Examiner, http://www.socialmediaexaminer.com/. Guide to
    using social media.
Tailwind, https://www.tailwindapp.com/. Marketing tools.
Twitter Analytics, https://analytics.twitter.com/.
Zoho Social, http://www.zoho.com/social/. Social media management and
    tracking platform.

Style Manuals and Language Usage

The AP Stylebook Online, https://www.apstylebook.com/.
The Chicago Manual of Style Online, http://www.chicagomanualofstyle
    .org/home.html.
Conscious Style Guide, http://www.consciousstyleguide.com/. Articles,
    guides, and newsletters about using conscious language.
"Efficient Editing: Strategies and Tactics." Chartered Institute of Edi-
    tors and Proofreaders, https://www.ciep.uk/training/choose-a-course
    /efficient-editing-strategies-and-tactics/.
Garner, Bryan A. *Garner's Modern English Usage*. 5th ed. New York: Ox-
    ford University Press, 2022.
Ginna, Peter, ed. *What Editors Do: The Art, Craft, and Business of Book
    Editing.* Chicago: University of Chicago Press, 2017.
Media Literacy Now, https://medialiteracynow.org/.
Merriam-Webster's Dictionary of English Usage. Springfield, MA:
    Merriam-Webster, 1994.
Radical Copyeditor, https://radicalcopyeditor.com/. Articles and resources
    about using inclusive language.

Tools and Technology

Consistency Checker from PerfectIt, https://intelligentediting.com/apps
    /consistency-checker/.
CyberText Newsletter, https://cybertext.wordpress.com/. Computer-
    related subjects, including software, hardware, editing, grammar,
    punctuation, social media, and browsers.
Doc Tools for Google Docs. Ablebits.com, http://www.ablebits.com/google
    -docs-add-ons/doc-tools/index.php.
"Editorial Markup Stamp Library for Acrobat," Ripplewater Publish-
    ing. Adobe Exchange, https://exchange.adobe.com/apps/cc/100535
    /editorial-markup-stamp-library-for-acrobat.
"Efficiency Tools for Editing." *Rabbit with a Red Pen* (blog), November 4,

2021, http://www.rabbitwitharedpen.com/blog/efficiency-tools-for
-editing.

"Google Docs Add-ons." Digital Thoughts, https://sites.google.com/view
/digitalthoughts/docs?authuser=0.

Gordon, Whitson. "How to Clone a Hard Drive." *PC Magazine*, updated
May 18, 2020, http://www.pcmag.com/how-to/how-to-clone-a-hard
-drive.

Harnby, Louise. "Free Downloadable PDF Proofreading Stamps," https://
www.louiseharnbyproofreader.com/blog/free-downloadable-pdf
-proofreading-stamps.

Huculak, Mauro. "How to Set Up a Mirrored Volume for File Redundancy
on Windows 10." Windows Central, September 23, 2016, https://www
.windowscentral.com/how-set-mirrored-volume-file-redundancy
-windows-10.

LibreOffice Draw, http://www.libreoffice.org/discover/draw/. Free tools for
creating and manipulating graphics.

Lyon, Jack. "Add-Ins from Microsoft." Editorium Update. June 15, 2023,
https://editorium.com/archive/. Hundreds of articles on the business
of editing, including tools, finances, ethics, wildcards, and macros.

"Macros and Information Menu." Archive Publications, http://www
.archivepub.co.uk/menu.html. Tips, videos, and instructions from Paul
Beverley for how to create and work with macros, plus many downloadable macros.

Microsoft 365, http://www.office.com/.

"Microsoft Word Tips, Tricks, and Ideas." Tips.net, https://word.tips.net
/index.html.

Montgomerie, Adrienne. "PDF Markup Basics for Proofreaders & Copyeditors." *Right Angels and Polo Bears: Adventures in Editing* (blog),
https://scieditor.ca/2019/02/pdf-markup-basics-for-proofreaders
-copyeditors/.

pdfFiller, http://www.pdffiller.com/. Cloud-based platform for creating
and editing fillable PDFs, and sharing, managing, and collaborating on
documents.

PDF stamps from Diana Stirling. red: http://www.copyediting-l.info
/resources/Red.zip; black: http://www.copyediting-l.info/resources
/Black.zip.

PerfectIt, https://intelligentediting.com. Intelligent and customizable
proofreading software.

Phrase Expander, http://www.phraseexpander.com/. Universal template
building and autocompletion platform that can be used to create shortcuts to automate processes.

Scrivener, https://www.literatureandlatte.com/scrivener/overview. Manuscript creation and writing platform.
Zapier, https://zapier.com/. Business automation platform.

US Government Resources

Better Business Bureau, http://www.bbb.org/.
IRS Forms and Publications, http://www.irs.gov/forms-instructions.
"The Purpose of Form W-9." Investopedia, http://www.investopedia.com
/articles/personal-finance/082714/purpose-w9-form.asp.
SCORE, http://www.score.org/. Mentoring and education platform for
small businesses (US residents only).
Small Business and Self-Employed Tax Center, http://www.irs.gov
/businesses/small-businesses-self-employed/.
US Small Business Administration, http://www.sba.gov/.

Website Hosting and Analytics

Bluehost, http://www.bluehost.com/.
GoDaddy, https://www.godaddy.com/.
Joomla!, https://www.joomla.org/. Content management system with web-
site and online application building tools and training.
Kaushik, Avinash. "Kill Useless Web Metrics: Apply the 'Three Layers of
So What' Test." *Occam's Razor*, http://www.kaushik.net/avinash/kill
-useless-web-metrics-apply-so-what-test/.
Kaushik, Avinash. "Web Analytics 101: Definitions: Goals, Metrics, KPIs,
Dimensions, Targets." *Occam's Razor*, http://www.kaushik.net/avinash
/web-analytics-101-definitions-goals-metrics-kpis-dimensions
-targets/.
Memphis McKay, https://memphismckay.com/. Design firm that creates
custom websites.
Network Solutions, https://www.networksolutions.com/. Domain and
website hosting services.
"Scale Your Business with Web Analytics & Conversion in 2022." Udemy,
https://www.udemy.com/course/web-analytics-conversion-strategy/.
Webflow, https://experts.webflow.com/. Design, development, and marketing experts.
"Why Your Website Needs Great Copy." Right Touch Editing, May 13, 2021,
https://www.righttouchediting.com/2021/05/13/why-your-website
-needs-great-copy/.

Wix, https://www.wix.com/. Website building platform.

WordPress, https://wordpress.com.

Workspace Ergonomics and Organization

"Computer Workstations eTool." Occupational Safety and Health Administration (OSHA), http://www.osha.gov/etools/computer-workstations.

"Elements of Ergonomics Programs." National Institute for Occupational Safety and Health (NIOSH), https://www.cdc.gov/niosh/topics
/ergonomics/ergoprimer/.

Folder Marker, https://foldermarker.com/en/. Program for customizing
folder colors.

Tidy Tova, http://www.tidytova.com/. Virtual or in-person help for reorga-
nizing and decluttering.

Notes

CHAPTER FOUR

1   Neil Patel, "What to Do If Your Domain Name Isn't Available: 13 Strategies," *Neil Patel* (blog), NP Digital, n.d., https://neilpatel.com/blog/domain-name-unavailable/.

CHAPTER FIVE

1   Don't let my experience put you off EFA. It has grown into a national organization in the last couple of decades and offers a lot more benefits these days.
2   As of this writing, private groups on Facebook are visible to anyone searching for them, but only members can see what's been posted.

CHAPTER SIX

1   Michael D. Harris, "When to Sell with Facts and Figures, and When to Appeal to Emotions," *Harvard Business Review*, January 26, 2015, https://hbr.org/2015/01/when-to-sell-with-facts-and-figures-and-when-to-appeal-to-emotions.
2   N. Cowan, "The Magical Number 4 in Short-Term Memory: A Reconsideration of Mental Storage Capacity," *Behavioral and Brain Sciences* 24, no. 1 (2001): 87–114, doi:10.1017/s0140525x01003922.
3   John F. Kihlstrom, "How Students Learn—and How We Can Help Them," University of California, Berkeley, January 17, 2017, https://www.ocf.berkeley.edu/~jfkihlstrom/GSI_2011.htm.
4   Adrienne Montgomerie, "Instant Estimate," *Right Angels and Polo Bears: Adventures in Editing* (blog), n.d., https://scieditor.ca/instant-estimate-2/.
5   Erin Brenner, "Black and White: When Should We Capitalize?" Right Touch Editing, updated October 26, 2021, https://www.righttouchediting.com/wp-content/uploads/2021/10/Style-Guide-and-Publication-Capitalization-Style-for-Black-and-White-as-Race-Terms-10.26.2021.pdf.
6   Copyediting was a publication and training program that Laura and I purchased from McMurry/TMG in 2015. We published a premium

newsletter and a blog and offered webinars, courses, and workshops. We sold Copyediting to ACES in 2018.

7 You can download a marketing strategy worksheet from my website to help you get started: https://www.righttouchediting.com/wp-content /uploads/2020/10/Digital-Marketing-Strategy-Worksheet.pdf.

CHAPTER SEVEN

1 Avinash Kaushik, "Web Analytics 101: Definitions: Goals, Metrics, KPIs, Dimensions, Targets," *Occam's Razor*, April 19, 2010, https:// www.kaushik.net/avinash/web-analytics-101-definitions-goals-metrics -kpis-dimensions-targets/; and Avinash Kaushik, "Kill Useless Web Metrics: Apply the 'Three Layers of So What' Test," *Occam's Razor*, March 10, 2010, https://www.kaushik.net/avinash/kill-useless-web -metrics-apply-so-what-test/.

2 At the time of this writing Scale Your Business with Web Analytics & Conversion in 2022, found at https://www.udemy.com/course/web -analytics-conversion-strategy/, was the latest version of this course.

3 Ann Wylie, "How Long Should Your E-Newsletter Be?" *PR Say*, June 27, 2019, https://prsay.prsa.org/2019/06/27/how-long-should-your-e -newsletter-be/.

4 S. Robin Larin, "Ask an Award Winner: An Interview with James Har-beck," *The Editors' Weekly* (blog), August 17, 2021, https://blog.editors .ca/?p=9558.

5 Adrienne Montgomerie, "The Art of the Cold Call," *Right Angels and Polo Bears: Adventures in Editing* (blog), February 2014, https:// scieditor.ca/2014/02/cold-call-tips/.

6 Jake Poinier, August 27, 2010, comment on Jake Poinier, "Cold Call-ing Tips for Freelancers," *Dr. Freelance*, August 25, 2010, https:// doctorfreelance.com/cold-calling-tips-for-freelancers/.

CHAPTER EIGHT

1 Elyse Tager, "Do You Hate Sales? Then Don't Sell," elysetager.com, June 12, 2018, https://www.elysetager.com/mindset/do-you-hate-sales -then-dont-sell.

2 Ayesha Chari, "Editing Tests, Clients and the Editor," *CIEP Blog*, March 10, 2021, https://blog.ciep.uk/editing-tests-1/.

3 Jacquelyn Smith, "How the Best Salespeople Make the Sale," *Forbes*, December 9, 2011, https://www.forbes.com/sites/jacquelynsmith/2011 /12/09/how-the-best-salespeople-make-the-sale/?sh=9cd39c1581dc.

CHAPTER NINE

1 See, for example, "Why Multitasking Doesn't Work," Cleveland Clinic, March 10, 2021, https://health.clevelandclinic.org/science-clear -multitasking-doesnt-work/; and "Multitasking: Switching Costs," American Psychological Association, March 2006, https://www.apa .org/research/action/multitask.

2 Gloria Mark, Daniela Gudith, and Ulrich Klocke, "The Cost of Inter- rupted Work: More Speed and Stress," Conference on Human Factors in Computing Systems—Proceedings, January 2008, 107–10, https:// www.ics.uci.edu/~gmark/chi08-mark.pdf. See also Talks at Google, "Sensing Attention: Focus, Stress, and Affect at Work | Gloria Mark | Talks at Google" (52:38 min.), YouTube, June 12, 2018, https://www .youtube.com/watch?v=YGqInNFXkvE.

3 Sabina Nawaz, "Your To-Do List Isn't Working: Here's How to Fix It in 1 Step," *Inc.*, November 6, 2017, https://www.inc.com/sabina-nawaz /transform-your-to-do-list-with-this-1-quick-productivity-hack.html.

4 Samantha Enslen, "Creating a Style Guide in Five Easy Steps" (audio conference), Copyediting, December 10, 2014.

5 Using programmed style sheets, PerfectIt checks Word document for issues of style, punctuation, word choice, and more.

6 See Review Geek Team, "How Many Monitors Do You Need?" *Review- Geek*, January 25, 2021, https://www.reviewgeek.com/68254/how-many -monitors-do-you-need/; and Don Reisinger, "Why I Use 3 Monitors to Boost Productivity (and You Should, Too)," *Inc.*, May 9, 2019, https:// www.inc.com/jason-aten/apples-iphone-13-event-a15-processor -details-missing.html.

CHAPTER TEN

1 We helped save the client time and money by comparing the two un- edited files they sent. That allowed us to copy the edits for the text that hadn't changed into the latest version of the file and edit only the new copy.

2 "Best Practices for Naming Electronic Records," Wisconsin Histori- cal Society, October 2017, 4, https://www.wisconsinhistory.org/pdfs/la /FileNaming-Final.pdf.

3 "Record Keeping for a Small Business," Small Business Administra- tion, 9, https://www.sba.gov/sites/default/files/files/PARTICIPANT _GUIDE_RECORD_KEEPING.pdf.

CHAPTER ELEVEN

1 Download this list at https://www.righttouchediting.com/resources
   /business-tools/.

2 Matthew Stibbe, "How to Do a Time and Motion Study to Make Real
   Change," *I Done This Blog*, December 18, 2018, http://blog.idonethis
   .com/how-to-do-a-time-and-motion-study-to-make-real-change/.
   For more on the Boston Box, see Dagmar Recklies, "The Boston Box,
   also Known as Growth-Share-Matrix," themanager.org, May 5, 2015,
   https://www.themanager.org/2015/05/the-boston-box-also-known-as
   -growth-share-matrix/.

3 Chris Ducker, *Virtual Freedom: How to Work with Virtual Staff to Buy
   More Time, Become More Productive, and Build Your Dream Business*
   (Dallas: BenBella Books, 2014), 23.

4 Melanie Padgett Powers, "#26: Delegate, Automate and Terminate to
   Improve Your Business," *Deliberate Freelancer*, https://meledits.com
   /26-delegate-automate-and-terminate-to-improve-your-business/.

5 Melanie Padgett Powers, "#2 Discover Your Unique Brilliance," *Deliberate Freelancer*, 6:30–8:43, https://meledits.com/2-discover-your
   -unique-brilliance/.

6 Tova Weinstock, "The Ultimate Organizing Checklist: Get Your
   Desk in Order," Tidy Tova, https://static1.squarespace.com/static
   /56b3635c45bf21a91ce09e9e/t/59824ob96b8f5b46344e1baa
   /1501708473781/The+Ultimate+Organizing+Checklist+-+Desk.pdf/.
   For more from Weinstock, see her website at https://www.tidytova
   .com/.

7 Asana, *Anatomy of Work Index 2021: Overcoming Disruption in a Dis-
   tributed World* (2021), 9, https://resources.asana.com/rs/784-XZD-582
   /images/PDF-FY21-Global-EN-Anatomy%20of%20Work%20Report
   .pdf.

CHAPTER TWELVE

1 "Locke's Goal-Setting Theory: Setting Meaningful, Challenging Goals,"
   MindTools.com, n.d., https://www.mindtools.com/pages/article
   /newHTE_87.htm.

2 Sagan Morrow, "Performance Reviews for Maximizing Productivity
   and Improving Client Relationships" (conference session, Editors
   Canada: Editors Transform, virtual, June 13, 2021).

CHAPTER THIRTEEN

1 Lisa Cordaro, "How to Be a Savvy Freelancer," *The Serialist* (blog), Au-

gust 24, 2016, https://theserialistblog.wordpress.com/2016/08/24/how
-to-be-a-savvy-freelancer/.

2   For more questions to ask about leads, read Lisa Cordaro, "How to
    Stay Safe in Freelance Business," *The Serialist* (blog), April 16, 2018,
    https://theserialistblog.wordpress.com/2018/04/16/how-to-stay-safe
    -in-freelance-business/.

3   In particular, see Cordaro, "How to Stay Safe in Freelance Business," as
    well as Cordaro, "How to Be a Savvy Freelancer"; and Vanessa Plaister,
    "Customer Service: A Cautionary Tale of Red Flags and Safety Nets,"
    CIEP Blog, July 10, 2019, https://blog.ciep.uk/customer-service-red
    -flags/.

4   Sue Littleford, "Customer Service: It's All about Imagination,"
    CIEP Blog, June 19, 2019, https://blog.ciep.uk/customer-service
    -imagination/.

5   Sue Littleford, email message to the author, December 30, 2021.

CHAPTER FOURTEEN

1   Diana Pavlac Glyer, *Bandersnatch: C. S. Lewis, J. R. R. Tolkien, and the
    Creative Collaboration of the Inklings* (Kent, OH: Kent State University
    Press/Black Squirrel Books, 2015), 166.

2   Karyn Greenstreet, "What Is a Mastermind Group? A Definition and
    Tutorials," The Success Alliance, https://www.thesuccessalliance.com
    /what-is-a-mastermind-group/.

3   For more about how to create your own mastermind group, read my
    article "Band of Editors: The Value of Small Groups," Right Touch
    Editing, May 28, 2020, https://www.righttouchediting.com/2020/05/28
    /band-of-editors-the-value-of-small-groups/.

CHAPTER FIFTEEN

1   Suzanne Degges-White, "You Really Do 'Need' a Vacation," *Psychol-
    ogy Today*, July 15, 2018, https://www.psychologytoday.com/us/blog
    /lifetime-connections/201807/you-really-do-need-vacation.

2   Brigid Schulte, "How Busyness Leads to Bad Decisions," BBC, Decem-
    ber 2, 2019, https://www.bbc.com/worklife/article/20191202-how-time
    -scarcity-makes-us-focus-on-low-value-tasks.

3   Matthew Glowiak, "What Is Self-Care and Why Is It Important for
    You?" Southern New Hampshire University, April 14, 2020, https://
    www.snhu.edu/about-us/newsroom/health/what-is-self-care.

4   "Long Working Hours Increasing Deaths from Heart Disease and
    Stroke: WHO, ILO" (press release), World Health Organization, May

17, 2021, https://www.who.int/news/item/17-05-2021-long-working
-hours-increasing-deaths-from-heart-disease-and-stroke-who-ilo.

5   Glowiak, "What Is Self-Care and Why Is It Important for You?"

6   Glowiak.

7   Moira Lawler, "What Is Self-Care and Why Is It So Important for Your
Health?" *Everyday Health*, May 19, 2021, https://www.everydayhealth
.com/self-care/.

8   Lawler.

9   Work with your doctor or a registered dietician to determine what
healthy eating and healthy weight goals are for you. Much of diet culture pushes the idea that a person must be thin to be healthy, shaming
fatness without cause.

10 Kate Lucey, "How to Recognize When a Self-Care Practice Is No
Longer Self-Care," *Everyday Health*, August 12, 2021, https://www
.everydayhealth.com/self-care/how-to-recognize-when-a-self-care
-practice-is-no-longer-self-care/.

11 Lucey.

12 Degges-White, "You Really Do 'Need' a Vacation."

13 Caroline Castrillon, "Why Taking Vacation Time Could Save
Your Life," *Forbes*, May 23, 2021, https://www.forbes.com/sites
/carolinecastrillon/2021/05/23/why-taking-vacation-time-could-save
-your-life/?sh=6c389a3924de.

14 Degges-White, "You Really Do 'Need' a Vacation."

15 Cornelia Blank, Katharina Gatterer, Veronika Leichtfried, Doris Poll-
hammer, Maria Mair-Raggautz, Stefan Duschek, Egon Humpeler, and
Wolfgang Schobersberger, "Short Vacation Improves Stress-Level and
Well-Being in German-Speaking Middle-Managers—A Randomized
Controlled Trial," *International Journal of Environmental Research
and Public Health* 15, no. 1 (January 13, 2018): 130, https://pubmed
.ncbi.nlm.nih.gov/29342844/.

16 "Burn-Out an 'Occupational Phenomenon': International Classifica-
tion of Diseases," World Health Organization, May 28, 2019, https://
www.who.int/news/item/28-05-2019-burn-out-an-occupational
-phenomenon-international-classification-of-diseases.

17 Marcial Losada and Emily Heaphy, "The Role of Positivity and
Connectivity in the Performance of Business Teams: A Nonlinear
Dynamics Model," *American Behavioral Scientist* 47, no. 6 (February 1, 2004): 740–65, https://journals.sagepub.com/doi/pdf/10.1177
/0002764203260208.

18 Brigid Schulte, "How Busyness Leads to Bad Decisions," BBC, Decem-

ber 2, 2019, https://www.bbc.com/worklife/article/20191202-how-time
-scarcity-makes-us-focus-on-low-value-tasks.

19 Caroline Castrillon, "How to Train Your Mind for Success,"
The Corporate Escape Artist with Caroline Castrillon, https://
corporateescapeartist.com/how-to-train-your-mind-for-success/.

20 Castrillon.

Index

PAGE NUMBERS WITH AN *F* FOLLOWING INDICATE FIGURES.

professional liability insurance, 72–74, 300, 303
professional organizations, 264–66, 314. *See also individual associations and organizations*
professional standards, 65, 308
profits, 31, 56, 300
Project Data Tracker (Chambers), 207
projects: goals for, 226; issues with, 240; management of, 261; red flag identification, 244–45; request forms, 152–53; saying no, 245–46; templates, 152–53, 160, 164, 272. *See also* administrative tasks; business services; contracts; rates; tracking
proofreading, 17–18, 45, 143, 298, 299, 303
proposals, 158–61. *See also* business services, selling
Publishing Training Centre, UK, 28, 308

QR codes, 91
Quad, 269–70, 284, 290. *See also* Grey, Sarah; Montgomerie, Adrienne; O'Moore-Klopf, Katharine; Paximadis, Lori; Poole, Laura; Schneider, Amy J.
Queen's University, Kingston, ON, 27, 308
Quick Start Guide, 178
QuickBooks (accounting software), 67, 68, 310
Quills and Queries Editing, 84
Quip, 184, 198, 313

racism, 16
rates, 30–52; administration fees, 47; agencies, 22–23; budgets, 30–34, 310; determining factors, 34–40; and fast-food drive-thrus, 245; high fee in hopes of rejection, 246; hourly rates, 40–41; negotiations, 47–51, 287; package rates, 45–46; premium fees, 39–40; project rates, 43–45; rate charts, 38, 40, 309; royalties, 107; rush fees/jobs, 47, 143; stylistic

edit example, 44–45; unit rates, 41–43; on website, 126; working for exposure, 107, 166
record keeping, 189–201; archiving data, 198–200; backups, 195–98; filing system, 190–95; version control, 189–90. *See also* administrative tasks; tracking
red flags, 157, 163–64, 241–48
Reedsy, 21, 22, 311
referrals, 141, 271
refunds, 245
rejections, 162–64
relationship marketing, 110–11, 148, 303
Respectful Querying with NUANCE (Wilkins), 239
résumés, 98–99, 144, 310–11
Right Angels and Polo Bears (Montgomerie), 186, 317–18
Right Touch Editing (RTE): as agency, 2–3, 21–22, 57–58; branding story, 78; Database of Training for Editors, 28, 307; defined for branding, 79–80; developing name, 84–85; marketing, 311; "The New Freelancer's Business Pack," 306–7; USP, 82–83. *See also* Brenner, Erin
Rocket Lawyer, 56, 61, 160, 311
Romance Refined, 85
routines, 277–84
royalties, 107
RSS feeds, 103
rush fees/jobs, 47, 143

S corporations (S corps), 56, 304
sales, 152–58, 225, 304
Saller, Carol Fisher, 239
samples: sample edits (for yourself), 43, 44, 153, 163, 165, 239, 244; samples, free (for the client), 119, 143, 157–58, 161, 163
Saunders, Heather (Just the Write Type), 80
scams, 153–54
Schneider, Amy J. (Featherschneider), 115–16, 127